Psychological Science in Action

APPLYING PSYCHOLOGY TO EVERYDAY ISSUES

REVISED EDITION

EDITED BY
MELİKŞAH DEMİR
MELISSA BIRKETT
K. LAURIE DICKSON
AND MICHELLE MILLER

Northern Arizona University

cognella
academic publishing

Bassim Hamadeh, CEO and Publisher
Christopher Foster, General Vice President
Michael Simpson, Vice President of Acquisitions
Jessica Knott, Managing Editor
Kevin Fahey, Marketing Manager
Jess Busch, Senior Graphic Designer
Marissa Applegate, Acquisitions Editor
Luiz Ferreira, Licensing Associate

First published in the United States of America in 2013 by Cognella, Inc.

Trademark Notice: Product or corporate names may be trademarks or registered trademarks, and are used only for identification and explanation without intent to infringe.

Printed in the United States of America

ISBN: 978-1-62131-424-0

www.cognella.com   800-200-3908

Contents

Note to Instructors

Teaching an introduction to psychology course is a diverse and rewarding teaching experience, accompanied by unique triumphs and challenges. One universal challenge involves student questions about the role of psychology in their own lives or the "real world" and the common misperception that psychology in not a "real" science. If you have had challenges like these in your classrooms, you are not alone. Instructors teaching this course to 1.5 million students in the United States annually, regularly address these difficult questions. We came to this project with more than a decade of teaching experience in introduction-to-psychology courses. In our courses, we strive to provide current examples from empirical literature to address student questions and demonstrate the achievements of psychological science. We think that this approach not only demonstrates the applications of psychology to everyday challenges, but also reinforces the perspective that psychological science *really* is a science. Collaboratively, we began the process of compiling the very best examples of contemporary empirical research. We wanted to guide students in the reading of and writing about empirical research articles to enhance their understanding of how to apply the result of psychological science to everyday situations, such as vocabulary-enhancing programs for infants or an older adult who believes that memory loss is unavoidable with age. We believe that this anthology will complement your textbook by providing specific examples about the application of psychological science and by guiding students as they learn to read primary sources.

In an attempt to ensure that your students get the most out of the articles presented in this anthology, we have provided a brief introduction with tips for reading empirical or review articles (e.g., how to analyze differences between the two selections in terms of their content and structure. In addition, unlike other anthologies, we have provided an introduction to each article (that explains why the research in that selection is important). We have also added several practical application assignments at the end of each chapter for students to practice applying psychological science to everyday issues. These two unique features help facilitate the achievement of the student-learning outcomes outlined in the American Psychological Association's Guidelines for the Undergraduate Psychology Major. For instance, students reading this anthology will be able to distinguish between statistical significance and practical significance, engage in critical and creative thinking, and understand and apply psychological principles to personal, social, and organizational issues.

We hope that you find this anthology useful for facilitating student understanding of the real-world applications of psychological science.

Chapter 1

Psychological Science

An Introduction to Empirical Research Articles in Psychology

When you think about psychology, what comes to mind? What do psychologists do? Most people think that psychologists help people deal with emotional problems through therapy. It is true that some psychologists are therapists, but there is much more to psychology than therapy. Just think … psychology focuses on understanding humans, including behavioral, physical, cognitive, emotional, and social aspects. Any aspect of being human is fair game for psychologists to explore! Psychologists study how people learn, think, feel, develop, and adapt so that they can navigate through a complex and challenging world. Individuals do not exist in a vacuum; rather, we are embedded in social relationships, societies, local communities, and global cultures, so psychologists need to understand humans within these contexts. Understanding human behavior and mental processes opens up exciting and novel ways to help people.

Most of you who are reading this book may not become psychologists or major in psychology. Even so, you either chose or were required to take this course because the understanding of psychological knowledge plays an important role in many other academic disciplines and professions, and it can be applied to almost all issues that humans face.

Through our many years of teaching this course, we have heard quite a few students remark that they are interested in psychology because they want to help people. We want you to understand that you can help people with your newfound psychological knowledge in a wide range of ways. The world is rife with problems that psychology can address, including social, occupational, and health challenges.

Two important challenges, health and environmental problems, currently receive a great deal of attention in our society. Given that "50–80% of the quality of our health and health care is rooted in behavioral, social and cultural factors" (National Institutes of Health Fact Sheet, 2006, p. 7), it is clear that psychological knowledge can be used to enhance individuals' health and our health care system. Regarding environmental problems, psychologists can facilitate a more sustainable future for both people and the natural environment by studying the fundamental connections between human behavior and the environmental crisis. We can use our understanding of humans to develop strategies to alter human behavior in positive ways. None of these issues have simple solutions, but psychological science can help address these problems.

The discipline of psychology has two major components—scientific research and application. Modern research psychology is a science because it uses of scientific methods in the pursuit of accumulated knowledge. Not surprisingly, it uses similar scientific methodologies that have led to our knowledge base in biology, physics, chemistry, medical science, and other natural and physical sciences. On the surface, the only difference across these disciplines is the phenomenon under study. As you learn more about each of these disciplines, you will come to realize that there is tremendous overlap, not just in the methods used but also in the focus of the study. For example, biologists, physicians, and psychologists study various aspects of health, including the factors that influence the development of an illness, coping with an illness, and recovery from an illness.

The American Psychological Association (APA), the largest professional organization for psychologists in the world, provides guidelines for undergraduate education that emphasize the importance of understanding that psychology is a science (Halpern, 2009). Research has shown that many first-year students have misconceptions about psychology and that many hold unsubstantiated beliefs about human behavior (Amsel et al., 2009). Similarly, the general public is often misinformed about the scientific foundation of psychology.

Despite the scientific progress made by the discipline of psychology, some people still question the scientific nature of psychology. Why do you think this is? We think that some of this misunderstanding arises from the fact that when most people think about psychology or psychologists, they only imagine a therapist seeing patients or confuse psychologists with psychiatrists (physicians who typically use medication in their treatment of patients). The general public rarely imagines a research scientist studying human behavior using scientific methods—and realistic depictions of research psychologists almost never appear in mass media. (*The Sopranos, What About Bob?, K-Pax, Two and a Half Men,* and *Good Will Hunting* are just a few examples from movies and TV). Rarely do they imagine a research scientist who studies human behavior using scientific methods—and realistic depictions of research psychologists almost never show up in mass media. Alan Kazdin, a former president of the APA, further speculated that the unscientific stigma placed on psychology is most likely due to misrepresentation of psychological research in the media and the plethora of self-help books, talk shows, and child-rearing books by individuals without psychological training (Kazdin, 2009). Additionally, many famous historical psychologists, including Freud, Jung, and other psychoanalytic psychologists, were not scientists, though they made significant contributions to the development of scientific psychology.

Students and the general public need to understand that there are two very different professions (practitioners and research psychologists) that happen to share the same name—psychology. Most professionals in psychology work in academia, research, or applied settings. Our discipline brings together science and application in a broad range of venues, including the use of evidence-based practices in clinical and practitioner-related endeavors, education,

health behaviors, and marketing, to name just a few. In writing this book, our goal was to highlight how psychological knowledge (derived from the scientific study of humans and their environments) can address a variety of real-life issues.

This book contains a set of carefully selected research articles that will complement and expand on the information that you are learning from reading your main psychology textbook; all of the articles are geared toward improving our everyday lives as well as our collective human future. We think you will be surprised at the range of questions you can address with psychology research:

- What is the best way to get results from the time you spend studying?
- Can "mindfulness" really improve someone's well-being?
- Do babies actually learn anything from those DVDs advertised to parents?
- Is there any way to get people to enjoy their jobs more?
- How can we persuade people to be more environmentally responsible?
- Does playing violent video games affect how people treat one another in real life?
- What can we do about bullying in schools?

These are just some of the important questions that you will be able to answer after you finish reading this book.

Although the research articles we picked are reasonably nontechnical, they still require some special effort on your part because the style they follow is probably unfamiliar to you. For this reason, the rest of this chapter will guide you through the special quirks of organization, presentation, and terminology associated with research writing in psychology. It will also alert you to several critical issues having to do with how research studies are set up, carried out, and interpreted–i.e., what we call *methodological* concerns. These methodological concerns will be the focus of many of the assignments listed in this book, so be sure to pay special attention to them.

INTRODUCTION TO EMPIRICAL RESEARCH ARTICLES IN PSYCHOLOGY

The articles in this book are empirical research articles, sometimes also called empirical studies, empirical papers, research studies, research papers, or a similar term. Empirical research articles report on the outcome of one or more scientific research projects or "studies,"1 presented according to a set format that stays fairly consistent across different papers. We'll cover the details of that format in a bit, but in general, the format involves:

1. giving an overview of prior research in the research topic and explaining the purpose of the present study. This is the Introduction section of the paper.
2. describing exactly how the study was conducted. This is the Method section of the paper.
3. describing the results and what they mean, explaining why the results are important or describing ideas for future research. These are the Results and Discussion sections of the paper.

For example, let's say that a researcher wants to find out if the quality of a person's social network (meaning relationships they have with friends, associates, coworkers, and so forth) could have any impact on that person's physical health. She recruits a group of people to participate in her study, then administers a detailed set of survey questions designed to measure the quality of social networks and a second set of questions designed to measure physical health levels. She finds that people with many strong, positive social relationships tend to be in better health, and that this connection between social networks and health is substantial enough that it is unlikely to be a fluke of random chance.

In her empirical research article, she will explain what is already known about social networks and health as well as what researchers don't yet know about this topic. Then, she will describe how her study will help address these remaining questions. She will go on to explain exactly how her survey was written and distributed, including how she recruited her study participants and any relevant personal characteristics about the participants as a group (e.g., the

gender breakdown and average age). She will explain how she analyzed the results, point out the significant correlation between social networks and health, and then wrap up by commenting on why her findings are important. (See the last chapter in this book for more information about the connections between social relationships and health.)

Another common format for reporting research results is called the review article. Review articles pull together the results of a variety of studies on a topic, rather than reporting on just one or a few in detail. They may or may not show the actual results associated with different studies, and they often summarize the results in a very shortened form. Oftentimes, review articles strongly reflect the author's point of view about a particular controversy or question within psychology—in other words, the author may "editorialize" more than what is typical for empirical research articles. This book contains a combination of empirical research articles and review articles. When you start reading each one, be sure you know which kind it is—this will save you time and effort as you work through it.

One thing that both of these article types have in common is that they are almost always written in a standard style called *APA format* or *APA style*. "APA" stands for the American Psychological Association, which we mentioned a few paragraphs back. Later in your psychology coursework, you will probably learn to write in APA style yourself and master its many intricacies. In this book, we will briefly look at APA style from the reader's perspective, with the purpose of helping you glean information from APA articles as easily as possible.

First, it helps to understand the purpose of having a standard style. One thing it does is streamline the process of understanding the article's main points. Psychology research projects can be fiendishly complex, full of different variables, procedures, theories, and terms. Having the information presented in a standardized order at least cuts down on the need to hunt around for exactly what the study authors did and why. It also makes it easier to compare across different articles on the same topic, allowing the reader to look past differences in presentation style in order to concentrate on substantive differences. Finally, APA style makes it reasonably easy to track down the sources that the author(s) used—which you might need to do if, say, you are writing a paper on that topic and want to find additional relevant research. That said, one thing that APA style does *not* do is create graceful, entertaining, or even particularly smooth prose. Aesthetically speaking, APA style is a boxy pickup truck, not a sleek sports car—it's a dependable way to get from point A to B, made for function, not beauty.

This fact is most apparent in how APA style credits different authors for ideas cited in an article. You may have already noticed in this chapter that the text is broken up with parentheses containing names and dates. These are the *in-text citations*, which are used in APA style instead of footnotes or end notes. In-text citations can be placed at the end of a sentence or in the middle, but they always indicate that an idea, finding, or statement came from a specific written work. The authors of that work are listed along with the date of publication. When an idea is derived from multiple works, all of the different works are listed in the same citation, in alphabetical order. The down side of in-text citations is that they function as a sort of "speed bump" (D. Daniel, February 27, 2009), breaking up the flow of the text. On the plus side, they allow you to quickly see the source of an idea without having to jump between the text and footnotes.

This focus on proper citation of other authors' work might seem picky, but in fact, it directly relates to one of the most important issues you will be learning about in your academic career: plagiarism. Your college or university has its own definition and policy regarding plagiarism, which you should read over carefully, but plagiarism is generally defined as presenting the work of somebody else as your own, without properly crediting that person. In its most extreme form, plagiarism could mean purchasing an entire paper and turning it in as your own work, but it also includes things like using a quote from a book you read without properly identifying and citing that book (note that just putting quotation marks around something does NOT qualify as "proper citation"). Before attempting the assignments in this book (or any other written coursework), consult the plagiarism policies of your school and your instructor, and be sure to *ask questions* about anything you don't understand. Most schools have serious penalties for

plagiarism, so when it comes to citing other people's work, its better to be safe than sorry!

Besides understanding the quirks of APA style, it is also important to know what authors go through to get their articles published, and how this differs from other kinds of psychology writing, such as web sites, magazine articles, and popular books. Psychology research articles almost always have to go through a process called *peer review* before a journal will agree to publish them. Here is how peer review works: Upon completing a research project, the authors[2] write a paper, called a "manuscript," about the work and submit the manuscript to a scholarly journal for review.

In the first step of peer review, the editor identifies other researchers (usually two to four) who are experts on the topic and who will volunteer to read and comment on the manuscript. It can take anywhere from six weeks to a year or more for all the reviewers to finish putting together detailed comments. The journal editor then uses these comments to make a decision about whether the manuscript should *definitely* be published with no changes (this is very rare), *definitely* be published with minor changes, *maybe* be published with major changes, or *not be published* at all.

If the authors get a "maybe," they have to decide whether to submit the manuscript to a completely different journal or instead to "revise and resubmit" the article to the same journal. The revise-and-resubmit option is commonly what authors choose to do, even though it is quite arduous: Authors have to go back and address *all* of the issues raised in all of the reviewers' comments—and in the end, the journal is under no obligation to accept the manuscript even with the changes.

Publishing in peer-reviewed journals is considered to be part of academics' scholarly responsibilities, and it improves their chance of gaining promotions, tenure[3], and even grant money. Peer review ensures that work is meticulously checked for quality, and it is a necessary process for the cumulative nature of our knowledge base in science and our understanding of human behavior in psychology. Whenever you read about psychology research, keep in mind whether it went through peer review or not—it makes an enormous difference in the quality and significance of the work.

HOW RESEARCH ARTICLES ARE STRUCTURED AND HELPFUL TIPS FOR READING THEM

Empirical articles. APA-style empirical research articles almost always have a standard set of sections, which are presented in a standard order. Knowing about this standardized format will make it much easier to figure out what the researchers did and what their results mean. Here are the sections that you will see in almost any empirical article:

Abstract. The abstract is a brief (usually around 250 words) summary of what the article. It gives an overview of what the purpose of the research is, how the research question was addressed, what the results were, and what the results mean.

a. What to look for in the abstract: Pay particular attention to any jargon or unfamiliar terms. If these are in the abstract, they are sure to show up multiple times in the rest of the article. So make sure you understand these terms right from the start.

b. Don't move on until you are sure you can answer these questions in your own words: What is the study about? Who participated in the study (children, adults, people with a particular disorder, etc.)? What was the main research method used (survey, laboratory procedure, etc.)?

Introduction. This is the first substantive part of the article; in a quirk of APA style, it does *not* actually say "Introduction" at the top. In the Introduction, the authors expand on the reasons why they conducted the research, and they also review prior research that forms the background for what they did. Many times, authors will take the approach of summarizing, first what we do know about a topic, and then what we still *don't* know. They will then preview the specific ways in which they chose to research the topic (e.g.,

by conducting a survey), and usually they will state the hypothesis or hypotheses they tested.

a. What to look for in the *Introduction*: Pay particular attention to the part where the authors discuss prior research. (Sometimes, this is called the "literature review".) Are there any controversies or disagreements? If so, these are probably going to be an important reason why the present research was conducted. Also important are any theories or other technical explanations. Lastly, pay attention to any stated hypotheses.

b. Don't move on until you are sure you can answer these questions in your own words: Why was the research done in the first place? What are the main theories that relate to this research? Are there any major differences of opinion about the topic of research, and if so, what are they? What do we already know about this topic? What do we *not* know about this topic? What is the authors research question or hypothesis?

Method section. This part contains the detailed description of exactly how the research was carried out. It is often broken down into subsections addressing who the study participants were, what materials were used (e.g., survey questions), what procedures were followed to gather the data, if special equipment or apparatus was used, and if any other special techniques were used to gather and analyze the data.

a. What to look for in the *Method section*: As you read over the Method section, stay focused on how the setup of the study connects back to the original research question. Also, as you read, try to form a mental picture of exactly what happened in the study from start to finish. It may be helpful to sketch out an informal diagram that shows what happened at different points along the way. Lastly, if there are different groups (such as a control group and a treatment group), be sure you understand how those groups were formed and how they differ from one another.

b. Don't move on until you are sure you can answer these questions in your own words: What did participants do from the time they started the study to when they finished? What was the major technique or techniques used—e.g., questionnaire, brain scanning, observation, laboratory procedure? Why did the researchers set up the study in this particular way? In other words, how did the methods used allow the researchers to test the hypothesis they laid out in the Introduction section?

Results section. This part contains the technical information about how the data were analyzed—that is, how the researchers tallied up the information they got from each participant and whether the information supports or contradicts the study hypotheses.

a. What to look for in the *Results section*: For beginning psychology students, the Results section is usually the hardest to understand. In fact, it can be so densely packed with numbers that it hardly resembles normal writing at all. Realistically, you may not yet be able to decode every statistical test presented in this section. With that in mind, try focusing on a few important parts that will convey whether the hypothesis was supported or not. First, look for the *descriptive statistics* that summarize the overall breakdown of the data gathered: mean scores on different tests, tallies of responses, and so forth. Then, pay special attention to any *tables* or *figures* (charts, graphs, etc.): These will show you the major differences among different groups, different tests, and so forth. Lastly, look for the summary part of this section, where the authors will usually explain whether their hypotheses were supported or not.

b. Don't move on until you are sure you can answer these questions in your own words:

How did the researchers quantify the responses they got—averages, counting up different responses, or by some other means? Did the different groups or treatment conditions produce different patterns of results? What were the patterns of differences—e.g., which group produced higher scores? Can you summarize the pattern of results in your own words, especially any patterns shown in tables or figures? Did the results support the authors' hypotheses? Were you surprised by the results?

Discussion section. This is where the authors focus on the "big picture" aspects of their findings—what was surprising about them, how their results should be interpreted and applied, how theories should be changed in light of what they found, and in the case of controversies, which side is supported more. Oftentimes, researchers will discuss any limitations of the study, such as questions that can't be addressed or other shortcomings. Similarly, they may address any potential criticisms of their study. Lastly, they often discuss future research projects that should be done to build on and extend the present study.

a. What to look for in the *Discussion section*: It's tempting to skim over this section after spending so much effort on the prior ones. Don't do it! This is actually the *most* substantive part of the entire article: The the authors talk about the meaning of what they did. This is also the place where authors have the most latitude to offer opinions. Be sure to pay attention to any points where the authors are presenting their own interpretation of the results, and make a note of whether you agree or disagree with their interpretation. Also be sure to note whether or not the authors return to any controversies or disagreements they talked about in the Introduction. Lastly, note any practical applications and suggestions for future research.

b. Don't move on until you are sure you can answer these questions in your own words:

Can you summarize the study's findings and why they are important? Can you explain why the results came out the way they did? Did the Discussion section answer the questions raised earlier in the Introduction? What are the practical applications of the study findings? Do current theories need to change based on this study? Do you agree with the authors' interpretation of the results? What is the single most important thing that this study tells us about behavior and/or the mind?

References section. This last part is like a traditional bibliography, except that it lists only sources that were specifically referenced in the article. Anything else that may have inspired the authors or served as background will *not* be cited. Unlike the other sections of the paper, this is one where it is OK to skim rather than read for detail. If you are writing a research paper on the study topic or you just want to read more about it, the References section is a great place to get ideas for additional source materials.

Review articles. Unlike empirical articles, review articles are somewhat "free-form." They usually have an abstract, but otherwise, the authors are free to break the material into sections as they see fit. Often, the authors will structure the sections around reviewing prior findings, highlighting controversies, and pointing out unanswered questions. They will also often have a substantive section at the end—titled "conclusions," "discussion," "directions for future research," or something similar—where they summarize what we know and don't know about a topic and offer their own interpretation of the various research findings. As you read a review article, be sure you understand any specialized terminology the author uses. If you can't figure a term out, try looking it up in the glossary of your main textbook.

After you read the article, be sure you can answer the following questions in your own words: What is the topic of the article? What are the major findings and theories we now have about this topic? What are the main unanswered questions or controversies? What is the author's opinion about those questions? Do you agree with the author's opinion? What is

the single most important conclusion we should draw about the topic, based on this article? What are the practical applications of the information in the article?

How research articles are presented in this book. In some of the articles you'll read here, we have edited out a few details that are not essential for the purposes of this anthology. Others are presented in their entirety. Regardless of the editing, most share the basic structural elements discussed above.

Before each selection, we included a short overview to introduce you to the topic and explain why that particular article is important. In this overview, we also highlight the most important points we want you to take away from reading the article. Then after the article, there are a series of *practical application tasks.* These tasks are brief assignments that ask you to apply what you learned in a real-world situation.

METHODOLOGICAL ISSUES TO WATCH FOR

Because psychology is a science, it is very important for researchers to properly design their studies and analyze the results. Researchers debate a great deal about the best ways to do this. Likewise, it's important for you, the reader, to understand the methods used to execute and analyze a study, and also the limitations of the study's methods.

Your main textbook discusses the scientific method and common research techniques in detail, so we won't recap those here. However, here are some major concepts that are critical for understanding the studies in this book. Psychology research studies gather *data* (survey responses, for example) that are used to test hypotheses. *Hypotheses* are statements that can be tested: Examples include "people with high-quality social networks are healthier" or "playing violent video games increases indifference to other people's suffering." To test hypotheses, studies are set up with variables. Some variables—called *independent variables*—are under the control of researchers, who look at whether or not those variables lead to changes in other variables, called dependent variables. *Dependent variables* are outcomes, such as scores on a test of sensitivity to other people.

In some research projects, researchers control the independent variable. For example, they may choose which participants will play a violent video game and which participants will play a nonviolent video game. Ideally, the researchers will do so through the process of *random assignment*.[4] This means that the researchers use some method of randomly determining which participant ends up in which group, such as a coin flip or by using the random number generator in an Excel spreadsheet. Random assignment ensures that the groups will be similar overall before the study is carried out, and that there isn't any secondary factor that causes the two groups to respond differently to the independent variable. This in turn enables the researchers to conclude, with reasonable certainty, that the independent variable *caused* changes in the dependent variable.

In the video game example, the researchers might flip a coin to determine who plays the violent game and who plays the nonviolent game. By random chance, participants in both groups will be similar overall on any factors that might affect the outcome of the study, such as personality differences, prior gaming experience, gender, aggressive tendencies, and so forth. If, at the end of the study, the group who played the violent game is more indifferent to suffering than the group who played the nonviolent game, the researchers can reasonably conclude that the game *caused* a change in sensitivity to other people's suffering.

In other cases, the researchers don't control any of the variables, but rather allow them to happen naturally. For example, they may simply assess how many close friendships their participants have and how physically healthy they are. This type of study can show that two variables are linked, or *correlated*, but they cannot conclusively show that one variable caused the other variable to change. In the social networks example, it is possible that people who have lots of good friends and people who are in good physical health share some other factor in common, so it's not possible to state conclusively that having lots of close friends causes physical health to improve. This distinction is so important that researchers reserve the term *experiment* to refer only to studies where researchers control the independent variable. As you read each study in this book, ask yourself whether the

design allowed the researchers to make conclusions about causation or merely correlation.

Causation versus correlation is a topic that is discussed in nearly every introductory psychology and research methods textbook. However, researchers continue to explore other methodological issues that tend not to be discussed in textbooks. One such issue is effect size versus statistical significance. As your textbook probably describes, *statistical significance* refers to the likelihood that an effect—e.g., a difference between two groups' scores on a test—was due to chance. When an effect is statistically significant, that means there is only a small likelihood that the difference resulted from a mere fluke of whom the researchers happened to sample.

Statistical tests are designed to give estimates of this likelihood, and there are agreed-upon thresholds that researchers use to determine cutoffs for saying when a finding is significant. What these tests do NOT tell you is how big the differences were or if those differences would be meaningful in practical terms. If sample sizes are very large, it is possible for an effect to be statistically significant even though its size is so small as to be of little real-world importance. For example, you may have heard that girls tend to have lower self-esteem than boys, particularly as they enter adolescence. It is true that some studies have found statistically significant differences between girls' and boys' self-esteem, and that the size of the difference tends to increase during adolescence (Kling, Hyde, Showers, & Buswell, 1999). However, the size of the disparity is so small that you would probably never notice it in a realistic situation (Hyde, 2005). Think of it this way: On average, ten-year-olds are taller than nine-year-olds. The height difference is real, yet if you were in a room full of nine- and ten-year-olds, would you be confident that you could distinguish them based on height alone (example adapted from Cohen, 1988)? Similarly, many of the gender differences you read about—such as self-esteem—are simply too small to make a practical difference (Hyde, 2005). Misinterpreting these small differences can lead to real negative consequences: In the self-esteem example, there is a risk that teachers and parents could ignore self-esteem issues in boys based on the erroneous assumption that such problems only affect girls (Hyde, 2005). Mindful of these risks, contemporary researchers often complement their significant findings by providing effect sizes as well. Be aware of the distinction whenever you are reading psychology research, and always ask yourself whether the differences observed were *statistically significant*, large with respect to *effect size*, or both.

Another distinction that your textbook may not discuss in detail is the difference between *field research* and *lab research*. As the name implies, lab research takes place in a special setting created just for purposes of the study, such as a researcher's laboratory. Lab research tends to be highly controlled, meaning that the researcher can hold constant many factors that could affect the outcome of the study, such as time of day, number of people present at the time, instructions given to participants, and many more. By contrast, field research takes place in real-world environments, sometimes termed "naturalistic" settings. Rather than bring participants to a special, controlled research environment, field researchers go out and make observations about behavior as it takes place in the real world. Field research can take a number of specific forms, including *naturalistic observation* (observing behavior as it occurs in a natural setting, without interfering) and *program evaluation* (evaluating the effectiveness of a psychological intervention in a natural setting) (Graziano & Raulin, 2000). It can also take the form of a *field experiment*, in which researchers control the independent variable in a real-world situation. Field research and lab research are both useful and valid ways to conduct psychology research, but there are advantages and disadvantages to both. Field research tends to be more *generalizable*, in the sense that the findings will more easily map onto behavior in the real world. However, in the field it is more difficult to control all the different factors that could affect the results. Researchers balance these concerns—control versus generalizability—as they design their studies. The articles in this book include both field and laboratory research; be sure that you can correctly categorize each one, and think through how the design affects the interpretation of the results.

Clearly, conducting good psychological research is a complex task, and learning to read and interpret this research is a major undertaking. But if you want to use psychology in everyday life, it is one of the best skills you can possibly acquire. Let's get started!

REFERENCES

Amsel, E., Johnston, A., Alvarado, E., Kettering, J., Rankin, R., & Ward, M. (2009). The effect of perspective on misconceptions in psychology: A test of conceptual change theory. *The Journal of Instructional Psychology, 36* (4), 289–295.

Cohen, J. (1988), *Statistical Power Analysis for the Behavioral Sciences* (2nd ed.). New York, NY: Routledge.

Graziano, A. M., & Raulin, M. L. (2000). *Research Methods: A process of inquiry* (4th ed.). Boston: Allyn and Bacon.

Halpern, D. F. (2009). National conference on undergraduate education in psychology: An introduction. *PTN: Psychology Teacher Network, 19(1),* 1–16.

Hyde, J. S. (2005). The gender similarities hypothesis. *American Psychologist, 60* (6), 581–592.

Kazdin, A. E. (2009). Psychological science's contributions to a sustainable environment: Extending our reach to a grand challenge of society. *American Psychologist, 64* (5), 339–356.

Kling, K. C., Hyde, J. S., Showers, C. J., & Buswell B. N. (1999). Gender differences in self-esteem: A meta-analysis. *Psychological Bulletin, 125* (4), 470–500.

National Institutes of Health. (2006). *National Institutes of Health fact sheet: Better living through behavioral and social sciences.* Retrieved from http://report.nih.gov/NIHfactsheets/ViewFactSheet.aspx?csid=32

ENDNOTES

1. In this book, we will use the term *"study"* to refer to a scientific research project within psychology. Sometimes people use the term "experiment" interchangeably with "study," but we have chosen not to do this. The reason is that, technically, a study is only a true experiment if it is set up in a very specific way, as we will discuss later in this chapter.

2. Most research projects in psychology are carried out by teams rather than a researcher working alone. Therefore, there will usually be multiple authors listed for any one article. The order in which they are listed tells you approximately how big a role each person played in the project: The first, or "lead," author listed usually did most of the conceptual work of planning and setting up the project and usually did the bulk of the writing as well. Subsequent authors may have contributed in a variety of ways, such as analyzing

data, writing certain parts of the article, and reviewing relevant research articles. Many times, all authors collaborate on the conceptualization of the project, coming to a consensus about the research hypothesis and other important ideas.

3. At colleges and universities, "tenure" refers to the process by which a professor's colleagues decide that he or she should be a permanent member of the faculty. In order to achieve tenure, professors have to show that they have achieved excellence and high productivity in the arenas that are most important to their institutions, typically, research and teaching. Contrary to popular belief, tenure does not assure a professor a "job for life"—tenured professors have to continue showing that they are top performers in teaching and research, and if they are seriously deficient in those areas, they can be dismissed. Even so, tenure is the most important milestone in an academic career.

4. It's important not to confuse *random assignment* with random sampling. Random assignment refers to how participants are placed in different groups within the study, while random sampling refers to the process of randomly selecting who will be asked to participate in the study. Random assignment is commonly used in psychology research, while random sampling is quite rare.

PRACTICAL APPLICATION ASSIGNMENTS

1. A friend from your psychology class is considering a career in psychological research and is looking forward to the day she gets to see her name in print on a research article in psychology. Based on the information presented in Chapter 1, write an email to your friend exploring the process of writing an article for publication in a peer-reviewed journal in psychology. What steps can your friend expect to follow and how will her research be reviewed?

2. Your best friend Chelsea comes to you for advice, knowing that you are taking a psychology course. In one of her classes, her instructor asked the students to find a peer-reviewed article about happiness. Chelsea found a two-page article on happiness in *O: The Oprah Magazine* and asked you if it is a peer-review article. First answer her question, and then explain what counts as a peer-review article and briefly summarize the process involved.

3. Let's apply what you've learned so far to an important challenge in psychology— reading a research article. Look ahead to Chapter 9 where you will find an article about the effects of exposure to violent media on helping behavior. Before you read this article closely, review the structure of this article to see if it is a good example of the types of articles described in Chapter 1. Is this an *empirical research* article or a *review* article? Does this article contain all of the typical sections of an article? Is this article written in APA format? What clues help you to know this?

Once you have looked over the structure of this article, you should begin to read with the goal of addressing the questions organized in the checklist of important information for each section. An example of this checklist is below. Follow the example and fill in the sections that are missing.

Section	Important Questions	My Answers
Abstract	Are there any unfamiliar or jargon terms used in the abstract? If so, what do they mean? What is the study about? Who participated in the study? What was the main research method used in this study?	
Introduction	Why was this research conducted? What are the main theories that are important in this research? Are there any major differences of opinion about this research area, and if so, what are they? What do we already know about this topic? What do we not know about this topic? What is the author's research question or hypothesis?	
Methods (*Study 1 only*)	What did participants do from the time they started the study and completed it? What was the main technique used in this study? Why did the researchers set the study up this way?	
Results (*Study 1 only*)	How did the researchers quantify the responses they got?	In the first study, the researchers collected ratings of violence and severity of violence on a scale, counted the percent of participants who helped a victim of violence, and timed how long it took for a participant to respond to a victim in need. They also counted how many people reported hearing a violent fight.
	Did the groups or treatment conditions produce different patterns of results? If so, what were the patterns?	Participants who liked fighting video games were less likely to help a victim of violence. Participants who played a violent video game took longer to help a person in need, were less likely to recognize a violent situation, and were less likely to believe that a situation was violent.
	Did the results support the researchers' hypotheses or predictions? Were you surprised by the results?	The results supported the researchers' hypotheses. I was surprised by the results! I did not expect playing a violent video game to be related to being slower to help someone in need!
Discussion	Can you summarize the study's findings and why they are important? Can you explain why the results came out the way they did? Did the Discussion section answer questions raised in the Introduction? What are the practical applications of this study's results? Do current theories need to change based on the results of this study? Do you agree with the authors' interpretation of the results? What is the single most important thing this study tells us about behavior and/or the mind?	
References	Are references included?	

Chapter 2

Cognitive Psychology: Do College Students Know How to Study Effectively?

Metacognitive Strategies in Student Learning

Do Students Practise Retrieval When They Study on Their Own?

By Jeffrey D. Karpicke, Andrew C. Butler,
and Henry L. Roediger III

EDITORS' INTRODUCTION

Think back to one of your favorite movies. Can you remember one or more lines word for word? Most movie fans can. Now think back to the first few sentences the teacher of your Introduction to Psychology course said at the beginning of your last class meeting. Can you remember that statement word for word? Almost certainly, the answer is no. Why is that? Memory is a complex and sometimes baffling aspect of the human mind, but it is something we have begun to understand through the research of cognitive psychologists.

When you think of the word "psychology," do you think of counseling, emotions, psychological problems, personal relationships, and development? What about topics like memory, reasoning, language, attention, and perception? Cognitive psychologists study and evaluate exactly these kinds of mental processes. One important application of research in cognitive psychology is in education. Through thousands of empirical studies, cognitive psychologists have developed a solid understanding of human memory. This understanding has allowed them to develop empirically tested study strategies that will result in the best retention of class material in the least amount of time. Here is a list of suggestions, all based on memory research, that you can put into practice in your own academic life:

1. First, keep in mind that human memory is an evolutionary *adaptation*—in other words, a characteristic that helps us survive in our environment—whose main purpose is to retain information that is relevant to our survival (Nairne, Thompson, & Pandeirada, 2007). It follows that if we want to remember something, we need to see the connection between the information and the pressing concerns in our life. The mind simply does not "soak up" irrelevant information very well, so your attitude (e.g., whether or not you think the material is important, your intention to use the material in the future, whether or not you see the material as relevant to your life) will likely affect your memory. Another important part of your learning attitude is whether you see memory ability as something that can be improved with practice and good strategy, as opposed to an inborn ability that can't be changed. When psychologists study memory experts (like the ones in this article about the National Memory Championships, http://www.slate.com/id/2114925/), they usually find that their great performances result from practicing good strategies, particularly strategies that organize and give meaning to material (Chase & Simon, 1973). By contrast, extraordinary inborn abilities, such as a "photographic" memory, just don't explain differences between great performers and poor performers, particularly because such abilities are exceedingly rare (Solso, 2000). In sum, if you are frustrated with your ability to retain class material, don't give up—try a better strategy and stick with it!

2. The *spacing effect* is another quirk of memory that can have a major impact on the payoff you get for your study time. According to this effect, shorter, spaced study sessions give better results than the same amount of time spent in longer sessions (see, e.g., Challis, 1993; Hintzman, 1969; Tsao, 1948). For example, if you have eight hours to spend on studying for a test, you would be better off with four two-hour sessions (or eight one-hour sessions, if you can manage it) than you would with one eight-hour cram session.

3. When we take in, or "encode" information, we tie it together with all kinds of other information that happens to be present at the time. All of these interrelated pieces of information can then become *retrieval cues* for triggering memories. Long-term memory is particularly dependent on retrieval cues: Memories do not simply jump into mind because we want them to; rather, they are triggered by some associated information. Take the following example: In your Introduction to Psychology class, you probably learned that Sigmund Freud invented psychoanalysis. When you encoded that fact, you also—without realizing it—connected it to other information in the environment, such as the color of the classroom walls, the time of day, even your emotional state. These retrieval cues can, when present, help you retrieve the fact about Freud. However, unless you know that fact very well, you might *fail* to retrieve it when those cues are missing. What might happen if you went to the final exam at a different time of day, in a different classroom? Could this make it harder for you to remember information you learned in your class during the semester? This tendency to remember better when you are in the same setting can be a real liability for students when they have to recall information in a completely different setting than where they study. Fortunately, cognitive psychologists have discovered an antidote to this problem: Ignore the common advice to study in the same time and place every day, and instead vary your study settings as much as possible (Smith, Glenberg, & Bjork, 1978). By doing so, you avoid becoming dependent on a single set of retrieval cues, and you have a better chance of remembering crucial information no matter where you happen to be.

4. The *testing effect* refers to the fact that answering test questions produces better retention than virtually any other study method. This critically important fact about memory is the subject of the following empirical research article titled *Metacognitive strategies in student learning: Do students practise retrieval when they study on their own?* (Karpicke, Butler, & Roediger, 2009). The term "metacognitive" refers to people's understanding of how their own memories work. In this article, the authors question whether university students understand that testing themselves on studied material is a very powerful study strategy, and whether students actually use this strategy instead of less-effective approaches. To address these questions, they surveyed students at Washington University using both open-ended and multiple-choice questions regarding the study techniques students use and why they use them. They then contrasted these student beliefs and behaviors with the large body of research on which techniques are actually effective (be sure to pay attention to what the authors have to say about this research in the Introduction and Discussion sections).

As you read the article, consider two methodological issues in particular: First, do you think that using only students from a selective university (Washington University) limits the *generalizability* of their findings? Also, consider the choice of research methods—would the results have been different if the research had been done as a laboratory study or naturalistic observation instead of as a survey? Afterward, think about whether the authors' characterization of college students applies to you and the students you know. Do you agree that students are unaware of the testing effect? Do you think they would study differently if they *were* aware of it?

REFERENCES

Challis, B. H. (1993). Spacing effects on cued-memory tests depend on level of processing. *Journal of Experimental Psychology: Learning, Memory, and Cognition, 19* (2), 389–396.

Chase, W. G., & Simon, H. A. (1973). The mind's eye in chess. In W. G. Chase (Ed.), *Visual Information Processing*, (pp. 215–281). New York: Academic Press.

Hintzman, D. L. (1969). Recognition time: Effects of recency, frequency, and the spacing of repetitions. *Journal of Experimental Psychology, 79* (1), 192–194.

Jeffrey D. Karpicke, Andrew C. Butler, and Henry L. Roediger III, Metacognitive Strategies in Student Learning: Do Students Practise Retrieval When They Study on Their Own? *Memory*, vol. 17, no. 4, pp. 471–479.

Nairne, J. S., Thompson, S. R., & Pandeirada, J. N. S. (2007). Adaptive memory: Survival processing enhances retention. *Journal of Experimental Psychology: Learning, Memory, and Cognition, 33* (2), 263–273.

Smith, S. M., Glenberg, A., & Bjork, R. A. (1978). Environmental context and human memory. *Memory & Cognition, 6* (4), 342–353.

Solso, R. L. (2000). *Cognitive psychology* (6th ed.). Boston: Allyn and Bacon.

Tsao J. (1948). Studies in spaced and massed learning: I time period and amount of practice. *The Quarterly Journal of Experimental Psychology, 1* (1), 29–36.

ABSTRACT

Basic research on human learning and memory has shown that practising retrieval of information (by testing the information) has powerful effects on learning and long-term retention. Repeated testing enhances learning more than repeated reading, which often confers limited benefit beyond that gained from the initial reading of the material. Laboratory research also suggests that students lack metacognitive awareness of the mnemonic benefits of testing. The implication is that in real-world educational settings students may not engage in retrieval practise to enhance learning. To investigate students' real-world study behaviours, we surveyed 177 college students and asked them (1) to list strategies they used when studying (an open-ended, free report question) and (2) to choose whether they would reread or practise recall after studying a textbook chapter (a forced report question). The results of both questions point to the same conclusion: A majority of students repeatedly read their notes or textbook (despite the limited benefits of this strategy), but relatively few engage in self-testing or retrieval practise while studying. We propose that many students experience illusions of competence while studying and that these illusions have significant consequences for the strategies students select when they monitor and regulate their own learning.

A powerful way to enhance student learning is by testing information. When students have been tested on material they remember more in the long term than if they had repeatedly studied it. This phenomenon is known as the *testing effect* and shows that the act of retrieving information from memory has a potent effect on learning, enhancing long-term retention of the tested information (for review, see Roediger & Karpicke, 2006a). The testing effect is especially striking in light of current findings showing limited benefits of repeated reading for student learning (see Callender & McDaniel, 2009; McDaniel & Callender, 2008). Our recent research has generalised the testing effect to educational materials (Butler & Roediger, 2007; Karpicke & Roediger, 2007,

2008; Roediger & Karpicke, 2006b) and real-world classroom environments (see McDaniel, Roediger, & McDermott, 2007). Testing enhances learning not only if instructors give tests and quizzes in the classroom, but also if students practise recall while they study on their own. If students were to practise retrieval of information while studying, this strategy would have the potential to greatly improve academic performance. However, we do not know the extent to which students practise recall while they study in real-world educational settings (relative to other less-effective strategies like repeated reading) or whether students who practise recall do so because they are aware of the mnemonic benefits. These are important and practically relevant research questions but few studies have been aimed at answering them (see, e.g., Kornell & Bjork, 2007).

The objective of this research was to determine the extent to which students practise recall relative to other study strategies in real-world educational settings. In addition, we wanted to examine whether students who choose to engage in retrieval practice do so because they know that testing promotes long-term retention. Another reason students may use testing during studying is to determine what information is known and what is not known so that future study time can be allocated to the unknown material (see Dunlosky, Hertzog, Kennedy, & Thiede, 2005; Dunlosky, Rawson, & McDonald, 2002). This is a fine justification for testing, but it differs from using testing as a learning device in its own right. To accomplish these goals we created a new study strategies questionnaire and surveyed a large sample of undergraduate students. Although there are a variety of study strategy inventories in the education literature (see Entwistle & McCune, 2004; Pintrich, Smith, Garcia, & McKeachie, 1993; Weinstein, Schulte, & Palmer, 1987), these and other inventories do not specifically assess whether students practise retrieval while studying. Our survey included a free report question asking students to list the strategies they use while studying and a forced report question that asked them to choose between repeated reading or repeated testing. The purpose of including both forced and free report question formats was to gain converging evidence aimed at the target issue and to circumvent possible response biases created by using

either format alone (see Schuman & Presser, 1996; Schwarz, 1999). We predicted that relatively few students would report self-testing as a study strategy and that the majority of students would report choosing to reread or engage in some other non-testing activity when forced to choose a study strategy. We also predicted that most students who selected self-testing would be unaware of the mnemonic benefits of testing.

In the first section of this paper, we provide a brief overview of relevant research on repeated reading, repeated testing, and students' metacognitive awareness of the testing effect. Next, we present the results of our survey of study strategies. In the final section, we interpret the survey results in light of current theories of metacognition and self-regulated learning and then discuss the practical and educational implications of our findings.

Motivation for the Survey: Prior Research on Repeated Reading vs Repeated Testing

The testing effect refers to the finding that taking a test enhances long-term retention more than spending an equivalent amount of time repeatedly studying. There are clear and direct implications of the testing effect for student learning. One way for students to enhance their learning would be to practise recalling information while studying. However, research on the testing effect has also shown that when students are asked to assess their own learning they sometimes fail to predict that testing enhances learning more than repeated reading (e.g., Karpicke & Roediger, 2008). In short, there is a rapidly growing body of research (briefly reviewed below) indicating that testing has powerful effects on learning, but students lack metacognitive awareness of the testing effect.

Students often report that they repeatedly read their notes or textbook while studying (Carrier, 2003; Pressley, Van Etten, Yokoi, Freebern, & Van Meter, 1998; Van Etten, Freebern, & Pressley, 1997). Yet there are several reasons to question the effectiveness of repetitive reading beyond reading a single time. Basic research on memory has shown that spending extra time maintaining or holding items in memory does not by itself promote learning (Craik & Watkins, 1973) and students may spend large amounts of additional time studying despite no gain in later memory for the items, a phenomenon called "labour-in-vain" during learning (Nelson & Leonesio, 1988). Recent research with educationally relevant materials has shown that repeatedly reading prose passages produces limited benefits beyond a single reading (Amlund, Kardash, & Kulhavy, 1986; Callender & McDaniel, 2009).

This is especially true when repeated readings are massed together in a single learning session, although spaced rereading tends to produce positive effects (Rawson & Kintsch, 2005). In short, memory research has shown many times that repetitive reading by itself is not an effective strategy for promoting learning and long-term retention (for review, see McDaniel & Callender, 2008).

In contrast, several studies have shown that repeated testing is a potent method for producing robust learning. In one of our studies (Karpicke & Roediger, 2008), we had students learn a set of Swahili vocabulary words across alternating study and test periods. In study periods, students studied a Swahili word and its English translation (*ma-shua—boat*) and in test periods they saw the Swahili words as cues to recall the English words (*mashua—?*). The students learned the words in one of four conditions and students in all conditions took a final test 1 week after initial learning. In two learning conditions, once a word was correctly recalled it was dropped from further test periods. The students who recalled each word only once in these two conditions recalled just 35% of the items on the final test a week later. In the other two conditions, students continued to repeatedly recall words even after they had recalled them once. Students who repeatedly recalled the words during learning recalled about 80% of the items on the final test. Repeated retrieval practice—even after students were able to successfully recall items in the learning phase—produced large positive effects on long-term retention.

Were students aware of the effect of repeated testing on long-term retention? At the end of the initial learning phase we asked students to predict how many pairs they would recall on the final test a week later. There was no difference in average predictions across the four conditions: All groups predicted they would recall about 50% of the items. Despite the large effect of repeated retrieval on retention, students were not aware of the mnemonic benefit of testing. Similar findings have occurred in other experiments examining the testing effect and students' judgements of learning (e.g., Agarwal, Karpicke, Kang, Roediger, & McDermott, 2008; Karpicke, McCabe, & Roediger, 2006; Roediger & Karpicke, 2006b).

In sum, basic laboratory research on human learning and memory has shown that (1) repeated reading by itself is a questionable and often ineffective study strategy, (2) repeated retrieval practice produces robust learning and long-term retention, but (3) students appear to lack metacognitive awareness of the testing effect. The implication of this basic research is that students may not practise retrieval when they study in real-world educational settings. Instead they may spend their time repeatedly reading material when they study. The objective of our survey was to examine the prevalence of retrieval practice, relative to other study strategies, in students' real-world study behaviours and students' metacognitive awareness of the benefits of self-testing.

A Survey of Students' Learning Strategies

One reaction we have encountered when we present our research on the testing effect goes something like this: "This is completely obvious. Of course testing enhances learning. We already knew this. None of this is new or surprising." Perhaps the testing effect is obvious to some instructors—but is it obvious to students? If so, we would expect students to report that they frequently practise recall while studying. But our basic laboratory research has consistently shown that students lack metacognitive awareness of the testing effect. In fact, students sometimes predict that repeated reading will produce better long-term retention than repeated testing (Roediger & Karpicke, 2006b). The intent of our survey was to determine whether students' self-reported study behaviours would converge with our laboratory findings.

METHOD

We surveyed 177 undergraduate students at Washington University in St. Louis about the strategies they use to study for exams. The students were participants in various learning and memory

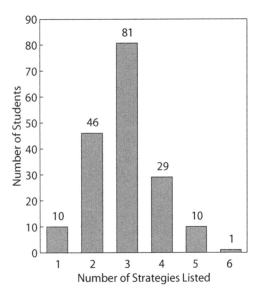

Figure 1. Frequency distribution showing the number of strategies listed by students.

experiments in our laboratory and they completed the survey at the very end of their experimental session. Washington University students are a select group with average SAT scores greater than 1400 (Verbal + Quantitative). Our survey included two questions aimed at identifying how often the students practised recalling information while studying. Question 1 was an open-ended free report question in which students listed the strategies they used when studying and then rank ordered the strategies in terms of how frequently they used them. All 177 students answered Question 1. Question 2 was a forced report question that asked students to imagine they were studying a textbook chapter for an exam and to choose one of three alternatives: (1) repeated reading of the chapter, (2) practising recall of material from the chapter (with or without the opportunity to reread the chapter, in different versions of this question), or (3) engaging in some other study activity. A total of 101 students answered Version 1 of Question 2 (testing without restudy) and the other 76 students answered Version 2 (testing with restudy). Students completed the entire questionnaire in about 5 to 10 minutes. Our goals were to identify students' typical study strategies and to assess how frequently they repeatedly read material or engaged in retrieval practice, and our analysis focused on the frequency with which students reported these particular strategies.

RESULTS

Question 1: Students' free report of study strategies. The first question on the survey asked: "What kind of strategies do you use when you are studying? List as many strategies as you use and rank-order them from strategies you use most often to strategies you use least often." We initially reviewed all responses from all students. Based on our initial assessment, we identified 11 strategies that occurred relatively frequently (more than once across all student responses). Two independent raters then categorised all responses. There was close to 100% agreement between the two raters and the first author resolved any scoring discrepancies.

Figure 1 shows the frequency distribution of the number of strategies listed by students in response to Question 1. The figure shows that most students listed and described three strategies ($M = 2.9$). Table 1 shows the 11 strategies and the percent of students who listed each strategy. The table also shows the percent of students who ranked each strategy as their number one strategy and the mean rank of each strategy. Repeated reading was by far the most frequently listed strategy with 84% of students reporting it. Not only did students indicate that they repeatedly read while studying, but they also indicated that rereading was a favoured strategy—55% of students reported that rereading was the number one strategy they used when studying. Table 1 also shows another key finding: Only 11% of students (19 of 177) reported that they practised retrieval while studying. These students unambiguously indicated in their list of strategies that they practised testing themselves by recalling information while they studied. Only 1% (2 of 177 students) identified practising recall as their number one strategy. The results in Table 1 clearly show that a large majority of students repeatedly read their textbook or notes, but relatively few students engage in self-testing by practicing recall while studying.

Table 1 also shows that students reported other strategies that could be interpreted as forms of self-testing. For example, 43% of students indicated that they answer practice problems while studying and 40% reported using flashcards. Each activity could be interpreted as a type of self-testing, but of course

TABLE 1 Results of Question 1

Strategy	Percent who list strategy		Percent who rank as #1 strategy		Mean rank
1. Rereading notes or textbook	83.6	(148)	54.8	(97)	1.5
2. Do practice problems	42.9	(76)	12.4	(22)	2.1
3. Flashcards	40.1	(71)	6.2	(11)	2.6
4. Rewrite notes	29.9	(53)	12.4	(22)	1.8
5. Study with a group of students	26.5	(47)	0.5	(1)	2.9
6. "Memorise"	18.6	(33)	5.6	(10)	2.0
7. Mnemonics (acronyms, rhymes, etc)	13.5	(24)	2.8	(5)	2.4
8. Make outlines or review sheets	12.9	(23)	3.9	(7)	2.1
9. Practise recall (self-testing)	10.7	(19)	1.1	(2)	2.5
10. Highlight (in notes or book)	6.2	(11)	1.6	(3)	2.3
11. Think of real life examples	4.5	(8)	0.5	(1)	2.8

Percent of students listing different learning strategies, percent who ranked strategies as their #1 strategy, and mean rankings of strategies. Raw numbers of students are in parentheses.

Mean number of strategies listed was 2.9 (SD=0.96). Percentages of students indicating their #1 strategy do not add to 100% because some students merged multiple strategies when reporting their #1 strategy (e.g., indicating that rereading and rewriting notes were their #1 strategy).

there are ways students might use these study methods without engaging in retrieval practice. For example, students may read practice questions and then look up and copy answers from the text. This would qualify as answering practice problems, but students who do this would not be practising or even attempting recall of the answers. Likewise, students may write facts on flashcards and repeatedly read them rather than practising recall. A clear limitation of the free response question is that our procedure did not prompt each student to elaborate on potentially ambiguous answers (cf. the ethnographic interviewing technique of Pressley and colleagues; Pressley et al., 1998; Van Etten et al., 1997). Nevertheless, even if we considered the 40% of students who use flash-cards or the 43% who answer practice problems as students engaging in forms of self-testing, these percentages are dwarfed by the 84% of students who repeatedly read while studying.

The results of Question 1 indicate that repeated reading is the most popular study strategy among college students (see too Carrier, 2003), far more popular than practising retrieval, even though retrieval

practice is a more effective study strategy. Students listed a variety of study strategies, but indicated that they use these alternative study strategies far less frequently than repeated reading. Question 2 asked students to choose repeated reading or self-testing and prompted them to explain the reasoning behind their choice. By including a second question in forced report format we hoped to find converging evidence and to resolve ambiguities inherent in our first open-ended free report question.

Question 2: Forced report questions about repeated studying vs testing. Question 2 was a forced report question about repeated studying versus repeated testing. There were two versions of the question. Version 1 asked students to consider testing without going back and re-studying, and Version 2 involved testing followed by restudying (to get feedback after attempting recall). The first version was given to 101 students and the second version was given to 76 students. Version 1 of Question 2 was as follows:

Imagine you are reading a textbook chapter for an upcoming exam. After you have read the chapter one time, would you rather:

TABLE 2 Version 1 of Question 2

Imagine you are reading a textbook chapter for an upcoming exam. After you have read the chapter one time, would you rather:	Overall		Test for feedback		Test to practise recall	
A. Go back and restudy either the entire chapter or certain parts of the chapter	57.4	(58)				
B. Try to recall material from the chapter (without the possibility of restudying the material)	17.8	(18)	9.9	(10)	7.9	(8)
C. Use some other study technique	20.7	(21)				

Percent of students who chose to restudy, self-test (without restudying), or do something else after reading a textbook chapter. Raw numbers of students are in parentheses ($N = 101$).

We were unable to score ambiguous responses given by four students.

a. Go back and restudy either the entire chapter or certain parts of the chapter.

b. Try to recall material from the chapter (without the possibility of restudying the material).

c. Use some other study technique.

The students were asked to select one alternative and write a brief explanation for their choice. The scenario described in the question was based directly on our research showing that taking a recall test, even without feedback, enhances long-term retention more than spending the same amount of time restudying (Roediger & Karpicke, 2006b).

Table 2 shows the percentage of students who chose to restudy, self-test, or do something else after reading a textbook chapter. Most students unambiguously selected an alternative and explained their choice, but four students gave ambiguous responses that could not be scored. The table shows that 57% of students chose to restudy (option A) and 21% indicated that they would use some other study technique (option C). Thus 78% of students indicated they would *not* want to test themselves after reading a textbook chapter. Only 18% of the students indicated that they would self-test after studying (option B). To examine students' metacognitive awareness of the mnemonic benefits of testing, we separated students' responses based on their explanation for why they

chose self-testing. This analysis showed that 10% of all students (or more than half of those who chose self-testing) reported they would self-test to generate feedback and guide their future studying (even though Version 1 of this question stated that students could not restudy after testing). Only 8% of all students indicated that they would test themselves because practising retrieval would help them do well on the upcoming exam. This pattern of responding suggests that most students were unaware of the mnemonic benefits of self-testing. The results of Version 1 of this forced report question provide converging evidence with our first free report question. Relatively few students reported that they would test themselves after studying a textbook chapter and even fewer indicated they would test themselves because they knew the act of practising recall was valuable for learning.

In Version 2 of Question 2 the scenario and alternatives were identical to Version 1 except that option B read "Try to recall material from the chapter (with the possibility of restudying afterward)." We imagined this would increase the number of students choosing testing perhaps to levels near ceiling if students recognised that testing followed by rereading would produce far superior learning to rereading without testing. Table 3 shows the percent of students who chose each option. The percentage of students choosing self-testing increased when students could reread after the test (42% in Question 2 vs 18% in Question 1) and the percentage was about equal to the percentage of students choosing repeated reading (42% vs 41%). Students' explanations of their choices indicated that the increased likelihood of choosing testing was due to the possibility of re-studying after the test. Of the 32 students who chose self-testing, 25 provided unambiguous explanations that we categorised as testing for feedback or testing to practise recall. A total of 23 students (30%) indicated that they would test themselves to generate feedback they could use when restudying whereas only two students (3%) chose testing because they believed the act of practising recall would help them remember in the future. The results of Version 2 of Question 2 expand on the results of Version 1 by showing that students were more likely to select self-testing when they could restudy after testing, but that very few students are aware that the act of practising recall itself enhances learning. What is perhaps most striking about the data in Table 3 is that even when students had the option of rereading after self-testing, the majority of students (58%) continued to indicate that they would *not* test themselves.

DISCUSSION

The objective of this research was to collect bench-mark data on college students' real-world study behaviours to assess how often students use retrieval practice relative to other strategies and whether they know about the mnemonic benefits of self-testing. Our basic laboratory studies suggested that students are not aware of the testing effect, leading us to predict

that they may not practise retrieval while studying in real-world settings. The results of our survey support this prediction. The majority of students indicated that they repeatedly read their notes or textbook while studying. Relatively few reported that they tested themselves, and of those who engaged in self-testing, only a handful reported doing so because they believed the act of practising retrieval would improve their learning. Our survey results point to the conclusion that many students do not view retrieval practice as a strategy that promotes learning. If students do practise recall or test themselves while studying they do it to generate feedback or knowledge about the status of their own learning, not because they believe practising recall itself enhances learning.

Our results agree with laboratory experiments showing that students lack metacognitive awareness of the testing effect when they monitor their own learning. A growing body of research has shown that students sometimes predict that practising retrieval will produce no effect on retention (Karpicke & Roediger, 2008) or that they will remember more in the long term if they repeatedly study material rather than test it (Agarwal et al., 2008; Karpicke et al, 2006; Roediger & Karpicke, 2006b). If we assume that metacognitive monitoring processes guide students' decisions to choose different learning strategies—an assumption at the core of the influential monitoring-and-control framework of metacognition (Nelson & Narens, 1990)—then the implication of these labo-ratory results is that students may not choose to test themselves when they regulate their own learning

TABLE 3 Version 2 of Question 2

Imagine you are reading a textbook chapter for an upcoming exam. After you have read the chapter one time, would you rather:	*Overall*		*Test for feedback*		*Test to practise recall*	
A. Go back and restudy either the entire chapter or certain parts of the chapter	40.8	(31)				
B. Try to recall material from the chapter (with the possibility of restudying afterward)	42.1	(32)	30.3	(23)	2.6	(2)
C. Use some other study technique	17.1	(13)				

Percent of students who chose to restudy, self-test followed by restudying, or do something else after reading a textbook chapter. Raw numbers of students are in parentheses (N =76).

in real-world educational settings. Our survey data confirm that this lack of awareness of the testing effect has consequences for students' real-world study behaviours.

In addition to agreeing with basic laboratory findings, our survey results also agree to some extent with a recent survey by Kornell and Bjork (2007). They surveyed college students about their study behaviours and asked the students, "If you quiz yourself while you study ... why do you do so?" The students selected one of four alternatives: 18% selected "I learn more that way than I would through rereading;" 68% selected "To figure out how well I have learned the information I'm studying;" 4% indicated "I find quizzing more enjoyable than rereading;" and 9% said "I usually do not quiz myself." Kornell and Bjork's data indicate that the majority of students (91%) do quiz themselves while studying, but few do so because they view the act of quizzing itself as a method of enhancing learning (Kornell and Bjork reasoned that the 18% of students who selected "I learn more that way than I would through rereading" believed that quizzing produced a direct mnemonic benefit; cf. Roediger & Karpicke, 2006a). Likewise, our survey data indicate that few students view practising recall as an activity that enhances learning. However, far more students indicated that they tested themselves in the Kornell and Bjork survey than in our study, and this may be due to a difference in survey procedures. Whereas we used a combination of free and forced report questions to gauge how often students practise retrieval, Kornell and Bjork used one question focused on why students might quiz themselves and the framing of this question may have influenced students' responses (see Schuman & Presser, 1996; Schwarz, 1999). It is well known that a single question can be framed in different ways and alter the choices and decisions people make (Tversky & Kahneman, 1981). Nevertheless, our results generally agree with those of Kornell and Bjork in showing that few students view retrieval practice as a method of enhancing learning. Further, the differences between the two sets of results highlight potentially important differences between free and forced report methods of questioning.

Our results fit with the broad theoretical notion that students experience illusions of competence when monitoring their own learning (Bjork, 1999; Jacoby, Bjork, & Kelley, 1994; Koriat & Bjork, 2005). Koriat and Bjork (2005) argued that illusions of competence tend to occur when students' judgements of learning are biased by information available during study, but not available during testing (see also Jacoby et al., 1994). Several experimental findings are consistent with this view. For example, students' judgements of learning are less accurate when made in study trials than in test trials (Dunlosky & Nelson, 1992). Students are less accurate at judging the difficulty of anagrams when the solution is present than when it is not (Kelley & Jacoby, 1996). We believe repeated reading produces a similar illusion of competence. Specifically, repeatedly reading material like text passages increases the fluency or ease with which students process the text. Students may base their assessments of their learning and comprehension on fluency even though their current processing fluency with the text right in front of them, is not diagnostic of their future retention. Our survey results show that the illusions students experience during learning may have important consequences and implications for the decisions they make and the strategies they choose when studying on their own.

Students generally exhibit little awareness of the fact that practising retrieval enhances learning. A clear practical implication is that instructors should inform students about the benefits of self-testing and explain why testing enhances learning. When students rely purely on their subjective experience while they study (e.g., their fluency of processing during rereading) they may fall prey to illusions of competence and believe they know the material better than they actually do. A challenge for instructional practice is to encourage students to base their study strategies on theories about why a particular strategy—like practising repeated retrieval—promotes learning and long-term retention.

REFERENCES

Agarwal, P.K., Karpicke, J.D., Kang, S.H.K., Roediger, H.L., & McDermott, K.B. (2008). Examining the testing effect with open- and closed-book tests. *Applied Cognitive Psychology, 22,* 861–876.

Amlund, J.T., Kardash, C.A.M., & Kulhavy, R.W. (1986). Repetitive reading and recall of expository text. *Reading Research Quarterly, 21*, 49–58.

Bjork, R.A. (1999). Assessing our own competence: Heuristics and illusions. In D. Gopher & A. Koriat (Eds.), *Attention and peformance XVII. Cognitive regulation of performance: Interaction of theory and application* (pp. 435–459). Cambridge, MA: MIT Press.

Butler, A.C, & Roediger, H.L. (2007). Testing improves long-term retention in a simulated classroom setting. *European Journal of Cognitive Psychology, 19*, 514–527.

Callender, A.A., & McDaniel, M.A. (2009). The limited benefits of rereading educational texts. *Contemporary Educational Psychology, 34*, 30–41.

Carrier, L.M. (2003). College students' choices of study strategies. *Perceptual and Motor Skills, 96*, 54–56.

Craik, F.I.M., & Watkins, M.J. (1973). The role of rehearsal in short-term memory. *Journal of Verbal Learning and Verbal Behavior, 12*, 599–607.

Dunlosky, J., Hertzog, C, Kennedy, M.R.F., & Thiede, K.W. (2005). The self-monitoring approach for effective learning. *Cognitive Technology, 10*, 4–11.

Dunlosky, J., & Nelson, T.O. (1992). Importance of the kind of cue for judgments of learning (JOL) and the delayed-JOL effect. *Memory & Cognition, 20*, 374–380.

Dunlosky, J., Rawson, K.A., & McDonald, S.L. (2002). Influence of practice test on the accuracy of predicting memory performance for paired associates, sentences, and text material. In T.J. Perfect & B.L. Schwartz (Eds.), *Applied metacognition* (pp. 68–92). Cambridge, UK: Cambridge University Press.

Entwistle, N., & McCune, V. (2004). The conceptual bases of study strategy inventories. *Educational Psychology Review, 16*, 325–345.

Jacoby, L.L., Bjork, R.A., & Kelley, C.M. (1994). Illusions of comprehension, competence, and remembering. In D. Druckman & R.A. Bjork (Eds.), *Learning, remembering, believing: Enhancing human performance* (pp. 57–80). Washington, DC: National Academy Press.

Karpicke, J.D., McCabe, D.P., & Roediger, H.L. (2006). *Testing enhances recollection: Process dissociation estimates and metamemory judgments.* Poster presented at the 47th Annual Meeting of the Psychonomic Society, Houston, TX.

Karpicke, J.D., & Roediger, H.L. (2007). Repeated retrieval during learning is the key to long-term retention. *Journal of Memory and Language, 57*, 151–162.

Karpicke, J.D., & Roediger, H.L. (2008). The critical importance of retrieval for learning. *Science, 319*, 966–968.

Kelley, C.M., & Jacoby, L.L. (1996). Adult egocentrism: Subjective experience versus analytic bases for judgment. *Journal of Memory and Language, 35*, 157–175.

Koriat, A., & Bjork, R.A. (2005). Illusions of competence in monitoring one's knowledge during study. *Journal of Experimental Psychology: Learning, Memory, and Cognition, 31*, 187–194.

Kornell, N., & Bjork, R.A. (2007). The promise and perils of self-regulated study. *Psychonomic Bulletin & Review, 14*, 219–224.

McDaniel, M.A., & Callender, A.A. (2008). Cognition, memory, and education. In H.L. Roediger (Ed.), *Cognitive psychology of memory, Vol. 2 of Learning and memory: A comprehensive reference* (pp. 819–843). Oxford, UK: Elsevier.

McDaniel, M.A., Roediger, H.L., & McDermott, K.B. (2007). Generalizing test-enhanced learning from the laboratory to the classroom. *Psychonomic Bulletin & Review, 14*, 200–206.

Nelson, T.O., & Leonesio, R.J. (1988). Allocation of self-paced study time and the "labor-in-vain effect." *Journal of Experimental Psychology: Learning, Memory, and Cognition, 14*, 676–686.

Nelson, T.O., & Narens, L. (1990). Metamemory: A theoretical framework and new findings. In G.H. Bower (Ed.), *The psychology of learning and motivation* (Vol. 26, (pp. 125–141)). New York: Academic Press.

Pintrich, P.R., Smith, D.A.F, Garcia, T., & McKeachie, W.J (1993). Reliability and predictive validity of the Motivated Strategies for Learning Questionnaire (MSLQ). *Educational and Psychological Measurement, 53*, 801–813.

Pressley, M., Van Etten, S., Yokoi, L., Freebern, G, & Van Meter, P. (1998). The metacognition of college studentship: A grounded theory approach. In D.J. Hacker, J. Dunlosky, & A.C. Graesser (Eds.), *Metacognition in educational theory and practice* (pp. 347–366). Mahwah, NJ: Lawrence Erlbaum Associates Inc.

Rawson, K.A., & Kintsch, W. (2005). Rereading effects depend on time of test. *Journal of Educational Psychology, 97*, 70–80.

Roediger, H.L., & Karpicke, J.D. (2006a). The power of testing memory: Basic research and implications for educational practice. *Perspectives on Psychological Science, 1*, 181–210.

Roediger, H.L., & Karpicke, J.D. (2006b). Test enhanced learning: Taking memory tests improves long-term retention. *Psychological Science, 17*, 249–255.

Schuman, H., & Presser, S. (1996). *Questions and answers in attitude surveys.* Thousand Oaks, CA: Sage.

Schwarz, N. (1999). Self-reports: How the questions shape the answers. *American Psychologist, 54*, 93–105.

Tversky, A., & Kahneman, D. (1981), The framing of decisions and the psychology of choice. *Science, 211*, 453–458.

Van Etten, S., Freebern, G., & Pressley, M. (1997). College students' beliefs about exam preparation. *Contemporary Educational Psychology, 22*, 192–212.

Weinstein, C.E., Schulte, A.C., & Palmer, D.R. (1987). *Learning and Study Strategies Inventory (LASSI).* Clearwater, FL: H&H Publishing.

PRACTICAL APPLICATION ASSIGNMENTS

1. Prepare a presentation for your school's tutoring service about psychology and study skills. a) List at least four specific things students should do or NOT do, based on the research you read here as well as in your main textbook. b) In your presentation, explain why students should know about the research. c) Describe the Karpicke et al. research in your own words. d) Explain at least three limitations of their research.

2. Write a pitch to a venture capitalist who you are hoping will fund your new education software company. In your pitch, give an overview of a new "app" you will create to help college students study and learn better. Explain what the application will do; then explain why it will be effective, referring to memory research.

3. You've learned that a good friend from high school is having some difficulty coping with the academic demands of college. Your friend puts in plenty of time studying and is highly motivated, but just seems to "blank out" on exams. Write an email to your friend giving advice on how to study better, based on applied memory research. Be sure to include the following concepts AND explain them in your own words: testing effect, illusions of competence, and rereading. Also, include at least one other memory-related concept of your choosing.

Chapter 3
Clinical Psychology: Is Psychotherapy Effective?

Mindfulness-Based Cognitive Therapy for Individuals Whose Lives Have Been Affected by Cancer

A Randomized Controlled Trial

By Elizabeth Foley, Andrew Baillie, Malcolm Huxter,
Melanie Price, and Emma Sinclair

EDITORS' INTRODUCTION

Robert is devastated by the news that his mother, Jennifer, was recently diagnosed with breast cancer. In addition to his worries about her physical health, he is also concerned that she might be depressed and not functioning well because she hasn't returned his phone calls and is not planning to host the upcoming Thanksgiving family dinner. While her chances of recovery are good, Robert is worried about her psychological health. He wants to help her reduce her depression and improve her quality of life.

Can psychological science provide effective ways to help with Jennifer's depression? Can psychological therapies help improve her well-being and overall psychosocial functioning? Clinical psychologists have developed several techniques that alleviate the symptoms of a variety of psychological problems. Clinical psychology is concerned with the study and treatment of abnormal behavior, such as severe depression and anxiety, or disorders such as schizophrenia and attention deficit disorder (visit http://www.div12.org for more information). Specifically, clinical psychology aims to understand, predict, and prevent psychological disorders as well as to assuage psychological maladjustment and improve individuals' well-being and development. Clinical psychologists achieve these goals by integrating psychological science and therapy, for example by developing instruments to assess psychological problems (e.g., severe anxiety) and conducting psychotherapy (e.g., cognitive behavioral therapy). Clinical psychologists also conduct empirical research to examine the effectiveness of different therapies and techniques aimed to improve the lives and well-being of their clients. The article in this chapter provides an excellent example of how psychological knowledge is applied in therapy to improve the well-being of individuals diagnosed with cancer by decreasing their depression symptoms while at the same time testing the effectiveness of the therapy.

What happens to the psychological well-being of individuals diagnosed with serious health problems such as cancer and epilepsy? Decades of empirical research have shown that the psychosocial well-being and functioning of those with a serious health problem worsens following the diagnosis, a finding reported in different age groups (e.g., adolescents, adults) and cultures. Specifically, a considerable number of individuals diagnosed with cancer experience severe emotional distress, depression, anxiety, and problems in their social relationships (Bultz & Carlson, 2006; Dalton, Laursen, Ross, Mortensen, & Johansen, 2009; Namiki et al., 2007). For instance, both males and females diagnosed with cancer experience clinical levels of psychological distress such as depression (Goldzweig et al., 2009; Hegel et al. 2006). Accordingly, it is critical to consider the psychological well-being of individuals diagnosed with cancer regardless of their chances for recovery and available medical treatment.

Thanks to advances in psychological science, new forms of psychotherapy have been introduced, including positive psychotherapy (Seligman, Rashid, & Parks, 2006) and mindfulness-based cognitive therapy (MBCT; Segal, Williams, & Teasdale, 2002).These new empirical approaches to therapy are often modified to address the needs of special groups/populations, such as those diagnosed with cancer. The important question, though, is whether the new forms of psychotherapy are effective in alleviating symptoms of psychological disorders and improving the overall well-being of individuals diagnosed with serious health problems. The article you are going to read by Foley, Baillie, Huxter, Price and Sinclair (2010) addresses this question.

Foley and her colleagues (2010) investigated the effectiveness of mindfulness-based cognitive therapy (MBCT) for individuals diagnosed with cancer. They randomly assigned their participants to a treatment or wait-list condition. Foley and her colleagues first examined whether MBCT alleviated psychological distress and improved the overall functioning of individuals diagnosed with cancer in the treatment group following their participation in MBCT when compared to those in the wait-list condition. They also assessed the well-being of individuals in this group a few months later to test whether or not the effects of the treatment were maintained over time. In an attempt to further test the effectiveness of MBCT, they then provided the same treatment to those in the wait-list condition and assessed the same outcomes at the end of the intervention/therapy. We highlight this aspect of the study because sometimes psychologists compare individuals who received the treatment (called the experimental group) to individuals who do not receive the treatment (called the control group). This common practice raises ethical issues when researchers are working with vulnerable populations and/or deny the control group an intervention they believe will improve the lives and well-being of the participants. To avoid any ethical concerns, Foley and her colleagues (2010) provided the intervention to the individuals in the wait-list control group after they found that the intervention was effective.

Thinking back to Chapter 1, can you correctly identify the dependent and independent variables in the study? How many participants were assigned to the treatment and wait-list conditions? Were there any differences between the groups before the intervention started? Why is it essential to show that the two groups are similar to each other in terms of dependent variables before the intervention? What happened to the well-being of individuals in the wait-list group after their participation in MBCT? By looking at Table 2, can you identify two variables with the two strongest intervention effects in the treatment group? What do these effects suggest? Finally, can you identify two limitations of the current study?

REFERENCES

Bultz, B. D., & Carlson, L. E. (2006). Emotional distress: The sixth vital sign—future directions in cancer care. *Psycho-Oncology, 15* (2)*, 93–95.

Dalton S. O., Laursen, T. M., Ross, L., Mortensen, P. B., & Johansen, C. (2009). Risk of hospitalization with depression after a cancer diagnosis: A nationwide, population-based study of cancer patients in Denmark from 1973 to 2003. *Journal of Clinical Oncology, 27* (9), 1440–1445.

Elizabeth Foley, Andrew Baillie, Malcolm Huxter, Melanie Price, and Emma Sinclair, Mindfulness-Based Cognitive Therapy for Individuals Whose Lives Have Been Affected by Cancer: A Randomized Controlled Trial, *Journal of Consulting and Clinical Psychology*, vol. 78, no. 1, pp. 72–79.

Goldzweig G., Andritsch E., Hubert A., Brenner B., Walach N., Perry S., & Baider L. (2009). Psychological distress among male patients and male spouses: What do oncologists need to know? *Annals of Oncology, 21* (4), 877–883.

Hegel, M.T., Moore, C. P., Collins, E. D., Kearing, S., Gillock, K. L. et al. (2006). Distress, psychiatric syndromes, and impairment of function in women with newly diagnosed breast cancer. *Cancer, 107* (12), 2924–2931.

Namiki, S., Saito, S., Tochigi, T., Numata, I., Ioritani, N., & Arai, Y. (2007). Psychological distress in Japanese men with localized prostate cancer. *International Journal of Urology, 14* (10), 924–929.

Segal, Z. V., Williams, J. M. G., & Teasdale, J. D. (2002). *Mindfulness based cognitive therapy for depression: A new approach to preventing relapse.* New York, NY: Guilford Press.

Seligman, M. E. P., Rashid, T., & Parks, A. C. (2006). Positive psychotherapy. *American Psychologist, 61* (8), 774–788.

ABSTRACT

This study evaluated the effectiveness of mindfulness-based cognitive therapy (MBCT) for individuals with a diagnosis of cancer. *Method:* Participants ($N = 115$) diagnosed with cancer, across site and stage, were randomly allocated to either the treatment or the wait-list condition. Treatment was conducted at 1 site, by a single therapist, and involved participation in 8 weekly 2-hr sessions that focused on mindfulness. Participants meditated for up to 1 hr daily and attended an additional full-day session during the course. Participants were assessed before treatment and 10 weeks later; this second assessment occurred immediately after completion of the program for the treatment condition. The treatment condition was also assessed at 3 months postintervention. All postinitial assessments were completed by assessors who were blind to treatment allocation. *Results:* There were large and significant improvements in mindfulness (effect size [ES] = 0.55), depression (ES = 0.83), anxiety (ES = 0.59), and distress (ES = 0.53) as well as a trend for quality of life (ES = 0.30) for MBCT participants compared to those who had not received the training. The wait-list group was assessed before and after receiving the intervention and demonstrated similar change. *Conclusions:* These improvements represent clinically meaningful change and provide evidence for the provision of MBCT within oncology settings.

Anxiety and depression commonly occur following cancer diagnosis and during or after cancer treatment. This distress may be a reaction to the unique challenges of cancer or may be influenced by underlying vulnerability to anxiety and depressive disorders. Meditative practices employing mindfulness techniques have been proposed to reduce distress and improve quality of life in the face of similar challenges. Mindfulness is often defined as remembering to pay attention in a certain way: On purpose, in the present moment, and nonjudgmentally (Kabat-Zinn,

1990). Indeed, clinical trials have supported the use of one form of mindfulness-based training, Kabat-Zinn's mindfulness-based stress reduction (MBSR; Kabat-Zinn, 1990), in cancer patients (Carlson & Garland, 2005; Carlson, Speca, Patel, & Goodey, 2003, 2004; Shapiro, Bootzin, Figueredo, Lopez, & Schwartz, 2003; Speca, Carlson, & Goodey, 2000). Mindfulness-based cognitive therapy (MBCT; Segal, Williams, & Teasdale, 2002) is a recent refinement of MBSR for major depression that focuses more specifically on the ruminative processes that may maintain recurrent depressive episodes. Rumination is the process of repetitive, passive thinking or brooding about aspects of negative experience without action to relieve the situation (Nolen-Hoeksema, 1991). It is possible that such ruminative processes may impact the changes in distress and quality of life resulting from cancer diagnosis and treatment. It was hypothesized that MBCT might improve distress and quality of life among cancer patients.

The psychological journey associated with a diagnosis of cancer is characterized by a series of challenges (Brennan, 2001). Adjustment to the diagnosis and treatment, the disruption of one's current life situation, the reevaluation of life directions, and tolerance of ongoing uncertainty are some aspects of this journey. Many cancer patients experience emotional distress, and for many this may be considered a normal response to the existential threat that cancer represents rather than the result of a psychopathological process (Anand, Srivastava, & Dalai, 2001; Dalai & Misra, 2006). For others, this distress is longer lasting and more severe.

The prevalence of clinical levels of distress in cancer patients has been estimated in the 35%-45% range (Carlson, Angen, et al, 2004; Carlson & Bultz, 2003; Zaboraa, Brintzenhofeszoc, Curbow, Hooker, & Piantadosi, 2001). Depression and anxiety disorders have been consistently noted as the most common presentations across site and stage of illness (Bultz & Carlson, 2006; Carlson, Angen, et al., 2004; Derogatis, Morrow, & Fetting, 1983; Kangas, Henry, & Bryant, 2005; Mehnert, 2004). Thus, for some individuals, these may not be temporary emotions that remit with time, but may represent serious challenges to quality of life that require treatment in their own right.

Mindfulness meditation promotes the management of distress for individuals with a range of health-related challenges including cancer (Grossman, Niemann, Schmidt, & Walach, 2004; Matchim & Armer, 2007; Smith, Richardson, Hoffman, & Pilkington, 2005). MBSR (Kabat-Zinn, 1990), the most widely used mindfulness program, incorporates aspects of mindfulness meditation and behavior therapy in 7–8 weekly sessions. A randomized waitlist controlled trial of MBSR for cancer patients demonstrated significant improvements in symptoms of stress and mood disturbance in individuals with a variety of cancer diagnoses, stages of illness, and ages (Speca et al., 2000). The benefits of MBSR have also been demonstrated with respect to sleep, mental adjustment, and physical well-being in several smaller studies for cancer patients (e.g., Carlson & Garland, 2005; Carlson, Speca, et al., 2003, 2004; Shapiro et al., 2003).

MBCT is a refinement of MBSR that more specifically targets the cognitive processes associated with relapse to depression (Segal et al., 2002). This program encourages participants to disengage from reactive and ruminative states of mind, which are proposed to reactivate depressive patterns (Lau, Segal, & Williams, 2004; Sheppard & Teasdale, 2004). Two randomized controlled trials have provided support for MBCT in preventing relapse in individuals with three or more previous episodes of depression who are currently well (Ma & Teasdale, 2004; Teasdale et al., 2000). Evidence is emerging for the broader applicability of MBCT, as pilot studies have demonstrated effectiveness for current depression (Kenny & Williams, 2007) and residual depressive symptoms (Kingston, Dooley, Bates, Lawlor, & Malone, 2007). Two uncontrolled studies in health settings have provided support for MBCT with cardiac patients (Griffiths & Hutton, 2007) and for individuals with diabetes (Fearson & Chadwick, 2007).

There has been little discussion in the literature regarding the similarities and differences between MBSR and MBCT. Both are facilitated through about eight weekly sessions of around two hours duration; daily mindfulness meditation practice is an important component, and a full-day session of meditation practice is now routinely offered across MBSR and MBCT programs (Kabat-Zinn, 1990; Segal et al., 2002). The most significant difference between these programs is the explicit focus on cognition within MBCT (Segal et al., 2002). Psychoeducation on the relationship between thinking and mood is introduced within the second session of MBCT, and a specific focus on the role of cognitive patterns on current functioning is maintained throughout the program. MBCT tends to be offered within smaller groups (8–12 participants); in comparison, MBSR is often offered to large groups of participants (Segal et al., 2002). The MBCT program also includes instruction in a short meditation practice (the 3-min breathing space), options for skillful action (e.g., nourishing activities), and relapse prevention (identifying relapse signatures and action planning; Segal et al., 2002). MBCT integrates cognitive therapy with MBSR.

MBCT was designed to target unhelpful relationships to thoughts (e.g., rumination) that may lead to an episode of depression in those with a history of this disorder. Rumination may exacerbate distress in response to a range of stressors, and so MBCT may be more widely applicable (Harvey, Watkins, Mansell, & Shafran, 2004). Rumination has been attributed to the development and maintenance of various forms of psychological distress (Thomsen, 2006). Moreover, in general, reactions to stressful life events that are characterized by rumination about the causes, meaning, and consequences of those events have been associated with the development of psychological distress (Alloy, Abramson, & Francis, 1999). Because anxiety and depression are commonly experienced by cancer patients and given that ruminative processes have been identified as important etiological factors for these presentations, it is useful to assess the effectiveness of MBCT for cancer patients.

This paper represents the first randomized controlled trial of MBCT in oncology. It was hypothesized that, compared to a wait-list control group, MBCT participants would demonstrate significant improvements in depression, anxiety, distress, and quality of life.

METHOD

Design

Individuals with a cancer diagnosis completed an assessment at baseline and then were randomized to the treatment or the wait-list condition. Participants were assessed, immediately following the treatment or wait-list phase, by a clinician who was blind to treatment allocation. These assessments involved structured interviews and self-report psychometric measures. Participants in the treatment condition additionally completed psychometric measures at 12 weeks postcompletion of intervention. The wait-list participants received the MBCT training following their second assessment and completed psychometric measures immediately after the course. All assessments and intervention groups were conducted at the Sydney Cancer Centre, Sydney, Australia.

This project was approved by the institutional ethics review boards at Macquarie University and Sydney South West Area Health Services—Eastern Sector. Participants provided written informed consent prior to research activity.

Participants

A priori power analysis showed that 51 participants in each group would give 80% power to detect a medium-sized difference (effect size = 0.5) with α = .05. Recruitment was more successful than anticipated, and 115 participants were included. Participation was open to cancer patients 18 years of age and older with adequate English-language competency. Individuals were invited to contact Elizabeth Foley directly after being informed of the study by local media articles and clinical staff at the Sydney Cancer Centre. The duration of the recruitment period was 2 weeks. Data were collected for this study from October 2006 until November 2007.

On the basis of a computer-generated allocation sequence, sealed, opaque envelopes detailing treatment allocation were prepared by an individual who was not involved in the study. These envelopes were opened, in order, by Elizabeth Foley, after the baseline assessment. Participants were informed of the condition that they had been allocated to at the closing of the initial assessment.

Table 1 Demographic Characteristics for Treatment and Wait-List Samples

Characteristic	Treatment ($n = 55$)	Wait-list group ($n = 60$)
Mean age in years (SD)	54.82 (9.08)	55.52 (11.89)
Women	42 (76.4%)	47 (78.3%)
Employed	25 (45.5%)	26 (43.3%)
Time since initial diagnosis in years (SD)	2.2 (2.56)	2 (4.08)
Cancer site		
Breast	26 (47.3%)	22 (36.7%)
Gynecological	6 (10.9%)	1 (1.7%)
Lymphoma	6 (10.9%)	2 (3.3%)
Prostate	4 (7.3%)	4 (6.7%)
Bowel and colon	3 (5.5%)	6 (10.0%)
Lung	2 (3.6%)	2 (3.3%)
Head and neck	2 (3.6%)	3 (5.0%)
Melanoma	1 (1.8%)	5 (8.3%)
Myeloma	1 (1.8%)	5 (8.3%)
Leukemia	0 (0%)	3 (5.0%)
Other	4 (7.3%)	7 (11.7%)
Cancer stage		
I	6 (11%)	10 (17%)
II	20 (36%)	17 (28%)
III	16 (30%)	18 (30%)
IV	13 (24%)	15 (25%)

Note. Other = specific cancer diagnoses nominated by fewer than 3 participants.

We assessed 116 individuals for eligibility for the study. One individual was excluded due to significant cognitive impairment, associated with the site of the cancer. One hundred and fifteen participants were recruited into the study. Mean participant age was 55.18 years ($SD = 10.60$), with a range of 24–78 years. Most were female (77%) and many were currently employed (44%). There were no significant differences between groups on these demographic characteristics: age, $t(113) = -0.352$, $p = .726$; gender, $x^2(1) = 0.0008$, $p = .98$; employment status, $x^2(1) = 0.0020$, $p = .967$. Table 1 displays the mix of cancer site and stage among participants. The most common diagnosis was breast cancer (42%). Over half of the participants were diagnosed with late stage disease (Stage III or IV). The percentage of participants with early versus late stage disease was similar across groups, $x^2(1) = 1.2888$, $p = .7320$. The groups were not significantly different in the reported time since diagnosis, $t(113) = 1.805$, $p = .074$. Participants within the treatment group entered the trial just over 2 years, on average, after their initial diagnosis and most commonly reported an 18-month duration since initial diagnosis ($SD = 2.56$ years, range = 1 month to 11 years). Those in the wait-list condition reported an average of 2 years since initial diagnosis, with 2 years most commonly reported ($SD = 4.08$ years, range = 1 month to 13 years).

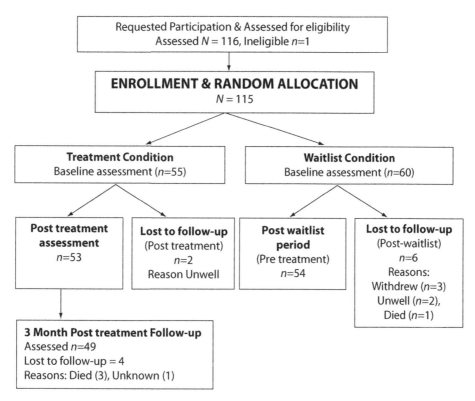

Figure 1. Flowchart of study participants.

Attrition

Figure 1 displays the flow of participants across the study. Participants needed to attend at least six of the eight weekly sessions to be considered as having received treatment.

Treatment

Treatment sessions involved intensive training in mindfulness meditation, the provision of theoretical material, and group discussion, as directed by the original MBCT manual (Segal et al., 2002). The program was delivered in eight weekly 2-hr sessions with a group of 8–12 individuals. Participants were provided with handouts containing information pertinent to each session, including suggested reading from Jon Kabat-Zinn's *Full Catastrophe Living* (1990). All participants received a copy of this text, which discusses the main themes of the MBCT/ MBSR programs: The various forms of mindfulness meditation, the mind-body connection, stress, and reactivity. Daily home practice of mindfulness meditation of up to one hour was recommended, and 40-min recordings of three classic meditations were given to support this practice: The body scan, a moving meditation, and a general mindfulness meditation

(recorded by Elizabeth Foley; refer to Segal et al., 2002, for scripts of these meditations). A daylong session of meditation was facilitated for participants between Sessions 6 and 7 of the course. This involved 5 hr of silent meditation, during which participants were guided in the continuous practice of mindfulness by Elizabeth Foley, and concluded with a period of group discussion.

The original MBCT program was modified for delivery with cancer patients. Didactic information became specific to the common challenges associated with cancer, including the experience of anxiety, depression, and pain. The body scan meditation was particularly difficult for many participants, as psychological avoidance of the site of the cancer and other sensations in the body was common. Facilitation of this meditation was sensitive to this difficulty; there was an option for "graded practice" (e.g., beginning with just awareness of the touch of clothing in that area) and for attending to a different aspect of the present moment (e.g., to the breath or to sounds before returning to the body when ready). Many participants could not hold a particular posture for long, so options for sitting, standing, and lying down were provided. The weekly class was divided into two 1-hr sessions, to allow a break for those who were experiencing fatigue or physical discomfort. Modifications to the suggested length and form of home practice were made if participants were unwell. For instance, individuals undergoing chemotherapy often practiced twice a day for shorter periods. Carers were invited to participate and to provide assistance to those experiencing functional impairment. Thirty-two percent of patients had their carers participate in the course.

All 14 treatment groups were facilitated by Elizabeth Foley, whose experience includes over a decade of personal mindfulness practice; the distance-learning MBCT course (through the Centre for Mindfulness Research and Practice at Bangor University, Wales, United Kingdom); the MBCT Intensive Training Retreat, the MBSR Teacher Training Practicum (endorsed by the Centre for Mindfulness in Medicine, Healthcare and Society at the University of Massachusetts Medical Centre); various workshops with authors of MBCT and MBSR; and the facilitation of more than 15 mindfulness courses prior to the current study. Regular supervision of MBCT group facilitation was provided by Malcolm Huxter, a clinical psychologist with almost 20 years' experience in the practice and clinical application of mindfulness-based approaches.

Measures

Primary outcome measures assessed levels of depression, anxiety, and quality of life. Levels of mindfulness were considered a secondary outcome.

Current levels of depression were assessed with the 17-item structured interview Hamilton Rating Scale for Depression (HAM-D; Williams, 1988). This measure requires clinicians to consider the frequency and intensity of various symptoms over the past week and to assign a rating value for each item. A higher score represents an increase in symptom severity. Benchmarks of clinically meaningful improvement have been published for the HAM-D as equaling 7.74 points (Grundy, Lambert, & Grundy, 1996). This measure is widely used in clinical and research settings and has acceptable psychometric properties (Rabkin & Klein, 1987).

Current levels of anxiety were assessed with the 14-item structured interview version of the Hamilton Anxiety Rating Scale (HAM-A; Shear et al., 2001). This measure requires clinicians to consider the frequency and intensity of various symptoms over the past week and to assign a rating value to each item. A higher score represents higher symptom severity. Shear et al. (2001) have reported high interrater and test-retest reliability.

The Hamilton interviews were conducted by three clinical psychologists. Elizabeth Foley has more than 40 hrs experience using these measures and conducted all initial assessments. Two additional psychologists conducted all other interviews, and these clinicians had at least 5 hr experience using the Hamilton scales. Additional training in the administration of the measures consisted of clinical discussion, written guidelines, and the observation of five actual assessments by Elizabeth Foley. Consistent ratings allowed the clinicians to proceed independently. All initial assessments were conducted face-to-face, and the following assessments were conducted by phone. All assessments were done within a week of their target. The blindness of raters was tested: One rater guessed participant condition with 47.5% accuracy, and the other rater guessed it with 52.5% accuracy. These results were not meaningfully different from the 50% expected by chance.

Distress was measured with the Depression, Anxiety Stress Scale, short form (DASS; Lovibond & Lovibond, 1995), a self-report measure of features of depression, physical arousal, psychological tension, and agitation. Higher scores on this measure indicate higher symptom severity, with a 6.2-point decrease on the DASS-21 considered clinically meaningful change (according to criteria from Jacobson, Follette, & Revenstorf, 1984). The internal consistency and concurrent validity of the DASS-21 are within the acceptable-to-excellent ranges (Antony, Bieling, Cox, Enns, & Swinson, 1998).

The Functional Assessment of Cancer Therapy—General (FACT-G; Cella et al., 1993) is a 28-item self-report measure of quality of life for cancer patients. Items relate to physical, social, emotional, and functional well-being. Higher scores indicate higher well-being, and a 5.4-point change in the total score has been identified as clinically significant (Cella et al., 1993). The reliability and validity of the FACT-G have been well documented in clinical trials and clinical settings (Cella et al., 1993; Lieberman, Golant, & Altman, 2004; Winstead-Fry & Schultz, 1997).

The Frieburg Mindfulness Inventory, short form (FMI; Walach, Buchheld, Buttenmuller, Kleinknecht, & Schmidt, 2006), is a 14-item self-report measure of mindfulness. Items relate to attentive awareness of the present moment, disidentification, diminished emotional reactivity, an accepting attitude, and insightful understanding of personal experience. Higher scores indicate higher levels of mindfulness. Evidence of the stability of the short form was provided by Walach et al. (2006), who reported a reliability coefficient of 0.86 and construct validity.

Strategies of Analyses

Missing data were substituted for those who did not provide follow-up data ($n = 8$; see Figure 1) in order to provide an intention-to-treat analysis. The last available data point was carried forward so that all analyses were on 115 participants.

Differences between the treatment and wait-list conditions were evaluated with SPSS Mixed Models Version 14. Inclusions included a random slope effect to allow for individual variation in the rate of change, a random intercept effect to allow for individual variation in initial severity, and an autoregressive error structure. Random effects for group allocation and stage of diagnosis were entered as covariates and did not account for significant variance. A Bonferroni decision rule was used to correct for multiple comparisons, so the alpha level was set at .01 for the five outcomes.

RESULTS

Adherence to Practice

The adherence to home practice was recorded during the treatment phase of the study, and participants were encouraged to complete a daily home practice form. This form requested details of daily meditation including the frequency and type of practice. These forms were collected at the end of the treatment phase and indicated an average of 30 min for daily meditation practice during the program ($SD = 11.80$, range 0–45 min). At 3 months post-training,

individuals in the treatment condition reported the following continued practice: 62% ($n = 34$) reported daily/regular meditation, 31% ($n = 17$) reported occasional meditation, and 7% ($n = 4$) said that they were not meditating.

Table 2 shows baseline and posttreatment scores on dependent variables; mean scores, standard deviations, and effect sizes are noted for continuous measures. At baseline, there was no significant difference between groups on dependent variables: HAM-D, $t(113) = 1.133$, $p = .26$; HAM-A, $t(113) = 0.692$, $p = .49$; DASS, $t(113) = 0.423$, $p = .67$; FACT-G, $t(113) = 0.085$, $p = .93$; FMI, $t(113) = 0.242$, $p = .81$.

The average baseline levels on the HAM-D for both conditions fell within the moderately depressed range according to guidelines by Williams (1988). The average baseline levels on the HAM-A were within the mild anxiety range for both conditions (Shear et al., 2001). The average baseline levels of quality of life (FACT-G) for both conditions were below the average level of 80.1 points expected for the general population and below the level of 80.9 points expected for cancer patients (Cella et al., 1993).

The Effectiveness of MBCT

Change in severity of symptoms. There was a significant interaction between time and treatment condition for the HAM-D, with individuals receiving MBCT demonstrating significantly greater improvement on clinician-rated depression than did individuals in the wait-list condition, $F(1, 166) = 18.78$, $p < 001$. The average improvement on the HAM-D was 9.76 points for the treatment condition and 4.11 points for wait-list group. The magnitude of change in the treatment group is reliable and clinically meaningful, exceeding the 7.4-point cutoff proposed by Grundy et al. (1996).

There was a significant interaction between time and treatment condition on the HAM-A, with the treatment condition demonstrating significantly greater improvement in clinician-rated anxiety than did the wait-list group, $F(1, 115) = 10.25$, $p = .002$. There was an average improvement of 10 points for the treatment group versus 5.7 points for the wait-list group.

There was a significant interaction between time and treatment condition on the DASS, $F(1, 115) =$

Measure/group	Time 1 M (SD)	Time 2 M (SD)	Pre-post effect size	Time 3 M (SD)	Pre-post effect size
HAM-D					
Treatment	16.02 (7.28)	6.26 (5.43)	1.34	5.76 (5.30)	1.41
Wait list	14.38 (8.12)	10.27 (6.93)	0.51		
Difference in pre-post effect sizes			0.83		
HAM-A					
Treatment	15.58 (8.79)	5.58 (5.13)	1.14	5.16 (5.06)	1.19
Wait list	14.37 (9.93)	8.90 (8.39)	0.55		
Difference in pre-post effect sizes			0.59		
DASS					
Treatment	16.98 (10.57)	10.67 (6.98)	0.60	10.99 (7.31)	0.57
Wait list	16.13 (10.88)	15.52 (10.71)	0.07		
Difference in pre-post effect sizes			0.53		
FACT-G					
Treatment	71.62 (14.81)	78.80 (14.87)	0.49	79.15 (14.86)	0.51
Wait list	71.38 (14.67)	74.18 (13.30)	0.19		
Difference in pre-post effect sizes			0.30		
FMI					
Treatment	18.31 (7.65)	23.29 (7.17)	0.65	24.15 (7.65)	0.76
Wait list	17.98 (6.81)	18.65 (6.44)	0.10		
Difference in pre-post effect sizes			0.55		

Note. Treatment, $N = 55$; wait list, $N = 60$. HAM-D = Hamilton Rating Scale for Depression; HAM-A = Hamilton Anxiety Rating Scale; DASS = Depression, Anxiety Stress Scale; FACT-G = Functional Assessment of Cancer Therapy—General; FMI = Frieburg Mindfulness inventory.

13.60, $p < .001$, with the treatment group reporting significantly less distress than did the wait-list group. There was an average improvement on the DASS of 6.31 points for the treatment group versus 0.61 points for the wait-list group. The magnitude of improvement for the treatment group is clinically meaningful and exceeds the 6.2-point cutoff based on the criteria suggested by Jacobson et al. (1984).

Quality of life. The interaction between time and treatment condition was not significant. There was a strong trend for the treatment condition improving more than the wait-list condition, $F(1, 12) = 6.70$, $p = .011$. Average improvement on the FACT-G was

Table 3 Descriptive Statistics for Outcome Measures of the Wait-List Group at Times 2 and 3

Measure/group	Preintervention M (SD)	Postintervention M (SD)	Pre-post effect size
DASS			
Treatment	16.98 (10.57)	10.67 (6.98)	0.60
Wait list	15.52 (10.71)	9.26 (8.08)	0.58
FACT-G			
Treatment	71.62 (14.81)	78.80 (14.87)	0.49
Wait list	74.18 (13.30)	82.16 (14.94)	0.60
FMI			
Treatment	18.31 (7.65)	23.29 (7.17)	0.65
Wait list	18.65 (6.44)	25.56 (5.45)	1.07

Note. Treatment, $N = 55$; wait list, $N = 60$. Effect size calculated as the difference between means divided by the pretreatment standard deviation. DASS = Depression, Anxiety Stress Scale; FACT-G = Functional Assessment of Cancer Therapy—General; FMI = Frieburg Mindfulness Inventory.

7.18 points for the treatment group and 2.80 points for the wait-list group. The magnitude of increase on the FACT-G for the treatment group is above the clinically meaningful cutoff of 5.4 points (Cella et al., 1993).

Mindfulness. There was a significant interaction between time and treatment condition, with the treatment group reporting significantly higher FMI scores following the MBCT course than did the wait-list group, $F(1, 115) = 18.51$, $p < .001$. Average improvement on the FMI was 4.98 points for the treatment group and 0.67 points for the wait-list group.

Were Treatment Gains Maintained?

According to the effect sizes for the 3-month postintervention assessment for the treatment group, the treatment gains were maintained across time (see Table 2). The magnitude of follow-up effect sizes is comparable to that of posttreatment effect sizes across all outcome measures.

Did the Groups Respond in the Same Way?

Table 3 displays the descriptive statistics for self-report measures for the treatment and wait-list groups at pre- and postintervention. These data represent pre- and postintervention assessment for this group.

Comparable medium-to-large effect sizes indicate that the wait-list group demonstrated treatment gains similar to those of the treatment group following participation in MBCT. This result strengthens conclusions about the effectiveness of MBCT for cancer patients.

All participants were asked for written feedback on the intervention after participation, and no negative effects were reported. Feedback was consistently positive.

DISCUSSION

This study provides support for the use of mindfulness training within oncology settings. Results provide novel evidence for MBCT as an effective intervention for cancer patients. This randomized controlled trial demonstrated clinically significant improvements in depression, anxiety, and distress and a trend for improved quality of life in the treatment group compared to a wait-list control group. Three-month posttreatment data indicate that treatment gains were maintained over time. The wait-list group responded in the same way to MBCT as did the treatment group, and this provided additional evidence for the stability of these results.

The magnitude of improvement across outcome measures, after wait-list variance was accounted for, was within the moderate-to-large ranges. Such treatment effects are comparable to those achieved by Teasdale et al. (2000) in the original MBCT chronic depression trial and those achieved by Speca et al. (2000) in the trial of MBSR for mixed-diagnosis cancer patients. The effect sizes in the current study are larger than those reported in a recent randomized controlled trial of an individual intervention for cancer patients with depression (supportive counseling and medication) and are similar to those found in a recent uncontrolled study of individual cognitive behavior therapy for depressed cancer patients (Hopko et al, 2008). Literature on the success of group interventions for anxiety and depression in cancer patients is limited (Newell, Sanson-Fisher, & Savolainen, 2002). The current treatment gains were considerably larger than those reported in an uncontrolled group program for anxiety and depression in women with breast cancer (Wellisch et al., 1999).

The level of psychological distress reported in this sample at baseline was considerable. High levels of anxiety, depression, and distress and lower quality of life were reported by participants. These levels may have been associated with the high proportion of individuals with later stage cancers in this sample (i.e., 45%). Although on average, participants identified 2 years as the time since initial diagnosis, many were coping with secondary cancers and current treatment.

Despite the reported high levels of distress of this sample, self-selection for the groups was very high and attrition was very low. These factors may be associated with the high level of "striving" that was observed in participants. It is likely that contextual factors such as socioeconomic status, gender, or culture might have a notable impact on this propensity. Striving has been reported elsewhere as a common experience of cancer patients, who may concentrate energy on various lifestyle activities that may improve their prognosis and sense of control (Girgif, Adams & Sabbitt, 2005; Miller et al., 1998). Such determined application to the intervention may also help to put the magnitude of effect sizes in context. Future research may

investigate the interaction of participant motivation with MBCT treatment outcomes. It would also be interesting to contrast populations on these variables (e.g., individuals with cancer compared with chronically depressed individuals).

These results challenge the suggestions that MBCT is unlikely to be effective for individuals experiencing distress in response to a major life stressor (Ma & Teasdale, 2004). The current sample is likely to differ significantly from those experiencing recurrent depression. Despite the etiological differences in these populations, the mechanisms of change in MBCT may be similar. Improved awareness of negative thinking and improved ability to disengage from ruminative responses are likely to reduce distress and build resilience across populations.

Future research might address the limitations of the current study. Although participants in this study were recruited from across cancer centers, the training was provided at a single cancer center by one facilitator. Future research may aim to provide the course at multiple treatment sites by several facilitators. Future research would also benefit from the inclusion of a measure of fidelity to the treatment manual and a measure of interrater reliability for clinician-rated measures. The generalizability of results is further limited by the invitation for individuals to self-select for participation in this study. This is likely to have resulted in atypically high motivation to engage with the program. The waitlist controlled design of the current study limits conclusions, as between-groups differences may have been due to a variety of nonspecific factors.

Future research may include an active comparison group, which is considered as equally credible by participants, such as relaxation training. This study did not address the issue of timing of the intervention in relation to diagnosis, and future research may consider the optimal timing for the intervention. Future research may also document a range of demographic details (e.g., income, education), the timing of recurrences, and whether participants are currently undergoing treatment, as these factors may affect outcomes. It would also be interesting to evaluate the effects of MBCT on positive outcomes, such as posttraumatic growth and existential meaning. Longer term follow-up of participants may help to clarify the stability of gains over time, and further investigation of the dose effects of mindfulness practice for cancer patients is required.

In conclusion, this study provides evidence for the effectiveness of MBCT for mixed-diagnosis cancer patients. Statistically and clinically significant changes in depression, anxiety, distress, and quality of life were observed in MBCT participants compared to a wait-list control group.

REFERENCES

Alloy, L.B., Abramson, L.Y., & Francis, E.L. (1999). Do negative cognitive styles confer vulnerability to depression? *Current Directions in Psychological Science, 8,* 128–132.

Anand, J., Srivastava, A., & Dalai, A.K. (2001). Where suffering ends and healing begins. *Psychological Studies, 46,* 114–126.

Antony, M.M., Bieling, P.J., Cox, B. J., Enns, M.W., & Swinson, R.P. (1998). Psychometric properties of the 42-item and 21-item versions of the Depression Anxiety Stress Scales in clinical groups and a community sample. *Psychological Assessment, 10,* 176–181.

Brennan, J. (2001). Adjustment to cancer: Coping or personal transition? *Psycho-Oncology, 10,* 1–18.

Bultz, B.D., & Carlson, L.E. (2006). Emotional distress: The sixth vital sign—future directions in cancer care. *Psycho-Oncology, 15,* 93–95.

Carlson, L.E., Angen, M., Cullum, J., Goodey, E., Koopmans, J., Lamont, L., & Bultz, B.D. (2004). High levels of untreated distress and fatigue in cancer patients. *British Journal of Cancer, 90,* 2297–2304.

Carlson, L.E., & Bultz, B.D. (2003). Cancer distress screening: Needs, models, and methods. *Journal of Psychosomatic Research, 55,* 403–409.

Carlson, L.E., & Garland, S.N. (2005). Impact of mindfulness-based stress reduction (MBSR) on sleep, mood, stress and fatigue symptoms in cancer outpatients. *International Journal of Behavioral Medicine, 12,* 278–285.

Carlson, L.E., Speca, M., Patel, K.D., & Goodey, E. (2003). Mindfulness-based stress reduction in relation to quality of life, mood, symptoms of stress, and immune parameters in breast and prostate cancer outpatients. *Psychosomatic Medicine, 65,* 571–581.

Carlson, L.E., Speca, M., Patel, K.D., & Goodey, E. (2004). Mindfulness-based stress reduction in relation to quality of life, mood, symptoms of stress and levels of Cortisol, dehydro-epiandrosterone sulfate (DHEAS) and melatonin in breast and prostate cancer outpatients. *Psychoneuroendocrinology, 29,* 448–474.

Cella, D.F., Tulsky, D.S., Gray, G., Serafian, B., Lloyd, S., Linn, E., & Harris, J. (1993). The Functional Assessment of Cancer Therapy (FACT) Scale: Development and validation of the general measure. *Journal of Clinical Oncology, 11,* 570–579.

Dalal, A.K., & Misra, G. (2006). Psychology of health and well-being: Some emerging perspectives. *Psychological Studies, 51,* 91–104.

Derogatis, L.R., Morrow, G.R., & Fetting, J. (1983). The prevalence of psychiatric disorders among cancer patients. *JAMA, 249,* 751–757.

Fearson, S., & Chadwick, P.M. (2007, July). Is mindfulness-based cognitive therapy helpful for people with diabetes? Paper presented at the Fifth World Congress of Behavioural and Cognitive Therapies, Barcelona, Spain.

Girgif, A., Adams, J., & Sabbitt, D. (2005). The use of complementary and alternative therapies by patients with cancer. *Oncology Research, 15,* 281–289.

Griffiths, K., & Hutton, J. (2007, July). A mindfulness-based cognitive therapy group for cardiac patients. Paper presented at the Fifth World Congress of Cognitive and Behavioral Therapies, Barcelona, Spain.

Grossman, P., Niemann, L., Schmidt, S., & Walach, H. (2004). Mindfulness-based stress reduction and health benefits: A meta-analysis. *Journal of Psychosomatic Research, 57,* 35–43.

Grundy, C.T., Lambert, M.J., & Grundy, E.M. (1996). Assessing clinical significance: Application to the Hamilton Rating Scale for Depression. *Journal of Mental Health, 5,* 25–33.

Harvey, A.G., Watkins, E., Mansell, W., & Shafran, R. (2004). *Cognitive behavioural processes across psychological disorders: A transdiagnostic approach to research and treatment.* Oxford, England: Oxford University Press.

Hopko, D., Bell, J., Armento, M., Robertson, S., Mullane, C, Wolf, N., & Lejuez, C. (2008). Cognitive-behavior therapy for depressed cancer patients in a medical care setting. *Behavior Therapy, 39,* 126–136.

Jacobson, N.S., Follette, W.C., & Revenstorf, D. (1984). Psychotherapy outcome research: Methods for reporting variability and evaluating clinical significance. *Behavior Therapy, 15,* 336–352.

Kabat-Zinn, J. (1990). *Full catastrophe living: Using the wisdom of your body and mind to face stress, pain, and illness.* New York, NY: Delacorte.

Kangas, M., Henry, J.L., & Bryant, R.A. (2005). The course of psychological disorders in the first year after cancer diagnosis. *Journal of Consulting and Clinical Psychology, 73,* 763–768.

Kenny, M., & Williams, J. (2007). Treatment-resistant depressed patients show a good response to mindfulness-based cognitive therapy. *Behaviour Research and Therapy, 45,* 617–625.

Kingston, T., Dooley, B., Bates, A., Lawlor, E., & Malone, K. (2007). Mindfulness-based cognitive therapy for residual depressive symptoms. *Psychology and Psychotherapy: Theory, Research and Practice, 80,* 193–203.

Lau, M.A., Segal, Z.V., & Williams, J.M. G. (2004). Teasdale's differential activation hypothesis: Implications for mechanisms of depressive relapse and suicidal behaviour. *Behaviour Research and Therapy, 42,* 1001–1017.

Lieberman, M.A., Golant, M., & Altman, T. (2004). Therapeutic norms and patient benefit: Cancer patients in professionally directed support groups. *Group Dynamics: Theory, Research, and Practice, 8,* 265–276.

Lovibond, P.F., & Lovibond, S.H. (1995). The structure of negative emotional states: Comparison of the Depression Anxiety Stress Scales (DASS) with the Beck Depression and Anxiety Inventories. *Behaviour Research and Therapy, 33,* 335–343.

Ma, S., & Teasdale, J.D. (2004). Mindfulness-based cognitive therapy for depression: Replication and exploration of differential relapse prevention effects. *Journal of Consulting and Clinical Psychology, 72,* 31–40.

Matchim, Y., & Armer, J.M. (2007). Measuring the psychological impact of mindfulness meditation on health among patients with cancer: A literature review. *Oncology Nursing Forum, 34*, 1059–1066.

Mehnert, A. (2004). Prevalence of post traumatic stress disorder, anxiety and depression in a representative sample of breast cancer patients. *Psycho-Oncology, 13*(Suppl. 2), 62.

Miller, M., Boyer, M., Butow, P., Gattellari, M., Dunn, S., & Childs, A. (1998). The use of unproven methods of treatment by cancer patients. *Supportive Care in Cancer, 6*, 337–343.

Newell, S., Sanson-Fisher, R., & Savolainen, N. (2002). Systematic review of psychological therapies for cancer patients: Overview and recommendations for future research. *Journal of the National Cancer Institute, 94*, 558–584.

Nolen-Hoeksema, S. (1991). Responses to depression and their effects on the duration of depressive episodes. *Journal of Abnormal Psychology, 100*, 569–582.

Rabkin, J.G., & Klein, D.F. (1987). The clinical measurement of depressive disorders. In M.R. Hirschfeld & M. Katz (Eds.), *The measurement of depression* (pp. 30–83). New York, NY: Guilford Press.

Segal, Z.V., Williams, J.M.G., & Teasdale, J.D. (2002). *Mindfulness-based cognitive therapy for depression: A new approach to preventing relapse.* New York, NY: Guilford Press.

Shapiro, S.L., Bootzin, R.R., Figueredo, A. J., Lopez, A.M., & Schwartz, G.E. (2003). The efficacy of mindfulness-based stress reduction in the treatment of sleep disturbance in women with breast cancer: An exploratory study. *Journal of Psychosomatic Research, 54*, 85–91.

Shear, M.K., Vander Bilt, J., Rucci, P., Endicott, J., Lydiard, B., Otto, M. W., & Frank, D.M. (2001). Reliability and validity of a structured interview guide for the Hamilton Anxiety Rating Scale (SIGH-A). *Depression and Anxiety, 13*, 166–178.

Sheppard, L.C, & Teasdale, J.D. (2004). How does dysfunctional thinking decrease during recovery from major depression? *Journal of Abnormal Psychology, 113*, 64–71.

Smith, J.E., Richardson, J., Hoffman, C, & Pilkington, K. (2005). Mindfulness-based stress reduction as supportive therapy in cancer care; Systematic review. *Journal of Advanced Nursing, 52*, 315–327.

Speca, M., Carlson, L.E., & Goodey, E. (2000). A randomized, wait-list controlled clinical trial: The effect of a mindfulness meditation-based stress reduction program on mood and symptoms of stress in cancer outpatients. *Psychosomatic Medicine, 62*, 613–622.

Teasdale, J.D., Segal, Z.V., Williams, J., Ridgeway, V.A., Soulsby, J.M., & Lau, M. A. (2000). Prevention of relapse/recurrence in major depression by mindfulness-based cognitive therapy. *Journal of Consulting and Clinical Psychology, 68*, 615–623.

Thomsen, D.K. (2006). The association between rumination and negative affect: A review. *Cognition & Emotion, 20*, 1216–1235.

Walach, H., Buchheld, N., Buttenmuller, V., Kleinknecht, N., & Schmidt, S. (2006). Measuring mindfulness: The Freiburg Mindfulness Inventory (FMI). *Personality and Individual Differences, 40*, 1543–1555.

Wellisch, D.K., Hoffman, A., Goldman, S., Hammerstein, J., Klein, K., & Bell, M. (1999). Depression and anxiety symptoms in women at high risk for breast cancer: Pilot study of a group intervention. *American Journal of Psychiatry, 156*, 1644–1645.

Williams, J.B. (1988). A structured interview guide for the Hamilton Depression Rating Scale. *Archives of General Psychiatry, 45*, 742–747.

Winstead-Fry, P., & Schultz, A. (1997). Psychometric analysis of the Functional Assessment of Cancer Therapy—General (FACT-G) scale in a rural sample. *Cancer, 79*, 2246–2252.

Zaboraa, J., Brintzenhofeszoc, K., Curbow, B., Hooker, C., & Piantadosi, S. (2001). The prevalence of psychological distress by cancer site. *Psycho-Oncology, 10*, 19–28.

PRACTICAL APPLICATION ASSIGNMENTS

1. Your uncle is a physician who believes that the only concern one should have when treating cancer patients is to find a medical procedure that would improve their physical condition. Your uncle also does not think that the psychological well-being of cancer patients is important. Write an email to your uncle in which you try to persuade him of the value of considering patients' psychological health as well. In this email, a) provide information about the prevalence of clinical levels of distress in cancer patients, b) explain what psychologists have been doing to improve the well-being of cancer patients, and c) highlight three findings from the Foley et al. (2010) article regarding the effectiveness of psychological therapy in improving the well-being of cancer patients.

2. Imagine the following scenario: Your grandmother was diagnosed with breast cancer one year ago. The family members feel sad and devastated not only because of the diagnosis but also about her recent depression. In a family gathering, she shares with everyone that she received an invitation to the Cancer Center to participate in a study that investigates the effectiveness of Mindfulness-Based Cognitive Therapy (MBCT) in improving the well-being of cancer patients. Convince your grandmother and your family members of the value of her participating in this study by making three points. In doing so, make sure you highlight how she might benefit initially from her participation in the study and the likely benefits three months after.

3. You just joined a research group at a cancer center as a consultant for research strategies. In your second meeting, the group reviews a proposal that aims to improve the well-being of cancer patients by implementing Mindfulness-Based Cognitive Therapy. One of the staff members opposes this proposal by stating that MBCT is similar to Mindfulness-Based Stress Reduction (MBSR), and there is no empirical evidence regarding the short- and long-term effectiveness of MBCT in improving the well-being of cancer patients. After the meeting, Dr. Oz, the director of the center, asks you to prepare an official report about this proposal. In your report, emphasize the differences between MBCT and MBSR and then provide evidence supporting the effectiveness of MBCT in improving the well-being of cancer patients. Make sure you highlight the effect sizes reported in the research for depression and anxiety and how long these effects are maintained. Finally, state your opinion about this proposal. Should it be rejected or accepted? Why or why not?

Chapter 4

Developmental Psychology: Are Infant-directed Media Programs Educational?

Do Babies Learn from Baby Media?

By Judy S. DeLoache, Cynthia Chiong, Kathleen Sherman,
Nadia Islam, Mieke Vanderborght, Georgene L. Troseth,
Gabrielle A. Strouse, and Katherine O'Doherty

EDITORS' INTRODUCTION

For her first birthday, Danika received a "Baby Einstein" video from her grandmother. Grandma Jones thinks that shows like this one stimulate and promote language and cognitive development. Susan, Danika's mother, wonders if the claims are true.

Most likely, you have seen or read something about these videos that claim to make babies smarter. Have you ever wondered whether babies benefit from watching these shows? Have you ever wondered if anyone has ever tested to see if babies "get smarter" from watching videos like this one? Fortunately, developmental psychologists have empirically tested the veracity of the claims that infant-directed media programs are educational.

The American Academy of Pediatrics (1999) recommends that children under the age of two avoid screen media. Yet, by three months of age, about 40 percent of infants regularly watch screen media and 90 percent of children watch infant-directed media programs by their second birthday (Zimmerman, Christakis, & Meltzoff, 2007). Typically, young ones watch screen media 1 to 1.5 hours a day. American families with children under the age of two own, on average, five or six infant-directed videos/DVDs (Barr, Danziger, Hilliard, Andolina, & Ruskis, 2010). Parents report that their children watch infant-directed programs because they think they are educational and enjoyable for the babies. They also confess that they use the videos as a "babysitter" so that they could "get something done" or "have a break from the baby's demands." (Zimmerman et al., 2007).

Garrison and Christakis (2005) found that 76 of the 100 best-selling infant-directed DVDs listed on Amazon.com in 2005 made one or more educational claims, with the majority of the claims related to cognitive, physical, and social-emotional development. The marketing materials for these media products often mention educational research and list awards and professional endorsements to bolster parents' perceptions regarding the appeal and value of these shows as learning tools (Zimmerman et al., 2007). Have you noticed that programs claim to "inspire early language development—from simple gestures to first spoken words" and "teach number recognition and order for numbers 6 to 10"? In addition to the implicit and explicit claims of educational benefits in the marketing messages of these videos, the titles, such as "Brainy Baby" and "Baby Einstein," imply educational benefits as well (Fenstermacher et al., 2010). It is no wonder that parents think that exposing their infants to these videos will have educational benefits!

For this chapter, you will read an empirical research study that tested the extent to which infants learned vocabulary words from a popular video. DeLoache and her colleagues (2010) designed an experiment that was conducted in the babies' homes, but they did not rely on the parents to measure the dependent variable, word learning. Why do you think they conducted the research study in the family home? As you read the article, think about the advantages of using an objective measurement of word learning, instead of relying on parents' reports of word learning. Additionally, think back to the discussion in Chapter 1 of the advantages of random assignment of participants to the experimental conditions and the reasons that the researchers used a "blind" tester.

REFERENCES

American Academy of Pediatrics. (1999). Media education. *Pediatrics, 104* (2), 341–343.

Barr, R., Danzinger, C., Hilliard, M., Andolina, C., & Ruskis, J. (2010). Amount, content, and context of infant media exposure: A parental questionnaire and diary analysis. *International Journal of Early Years Education, 18* (2), 107–122.

DeLoache, J. S., Chiong, C., Sherman, K., Islam, N., Vanderborght, M., Troseth, G. L., Strouse, G. A., & O'Doherty, K. Do Babies Learn from Baby Media? *Psychological Science, 21*(11), 1570–1574.

Fenstermachera, S. K., Barr, R., Salerno, K., Garcia, A., Shwery, C. E., Calvert, S. L., & Linebarger, D. L., (2010). Infant-directed media: An analysis of product information and claims. *Infant and Child Development, 19* (6), 557–576.

Garrison, M. M., & Christakis, D. A. (2005). A teacher in the living room: Educational media for babies, toddlers, and preschoolers. Menlo Park, CA: The Henry J. Kaiser Family Foundation.

Zimmerman, F. J., Christakis, D. A., & Meltzoff, A. N. (2007). Television and DVD/video viewing in children younger than 2 years. *Archives of Pediatrics* & Adolescent Medicine, *161* (5), 473–479.

ABSTRACT

In recent years, parents in the United States and worldwide have purchased enormous numbers of videos and DVDs designed and marketed for infants, many assuming that their children would benefit from watching them. We examined how many new words 12- to 18-month-old children learned from viewing a popular DVD several times a week for 4 weeks at home. The most important result was that children who viewed the DVD did not learn any more words from their month-long exposure to it than did a control group. The highest level of learning occurred in a no-video condition in which parents tried to teach their children the same target words during everyday activities. Another important result was that parents who liked the DVD tended to overestimate how much their children had learned from it We conclude that infants learn relatively little from infant media and that their parents sometimes overestimate what they do learn.

One of the most remarkable marketing phenomena of recent history was ignited by the 1997 release of the first Baby Einstein video (The Baby Einstein Co., Littleton, CO), which was followed by a host of other videos and DVDs designed and marketed specifically for infants and very young children. American parents alone spend hundreds of millions of dollars yearly on these products, with the Baby Einstein series leading in popularity and sales worldwide.

Most companies that market these DVDs feature quotes from parents touting the virtues of the company's products. In these testimonials on Web sites and in advertisements, parents frequently mention the remarkable degree of attention that children pay to the DVDs (as well as the fact that their children's absorption in the DVDs enables them to get household chores done and even take the occasional shower). Prominently featured are parent testimonials that their children learn a great deal from watching infant DVDs. Our own experience with parents of young children has led us to suspect that a substantial proportion believe that infants benefit from commercial media products, and recent research indicates that 40% of mothers of young children believe that their children learn from television (Rideout, 2007).

But how well do infants actually learn from visual media? Because development typically proceeds at a very rapid pace in the first years of life, parents may misattribute ordinary developmental progress to their children's media exposure. For example, on one commercial Web site, a parent reported that her 18-month-old child had very few words until she started watching one of the company's videos, at which point her vocabulary "suddenly blossomed." However, a very well-documented phenomenon in early language development is the "word spurt," a rapid increase in the acquisition of new words during the second year of life (e.g., Benedict, 1979; Goldfield & Reznick. 1990). It would be easy for parents to

misattribute their children's sudden linguistic advances to recent video experience.

Although several empirical studies have examined the relation between early television viewing and a variety of outcome measures, most have been large-scale surveys yielding correlational data (e.g., Rideout, Vandewater, & Wartella, 2003; Schmidt, Rich, Rifas-Shiman, Oken, & Taveras, 2009; Zimmerman, Christakis, & Meltzoff, 2007). Only a relatively small number of laboratory studies have examined specific aspects of young children's interaction with visual media (see Anderson & Pempek, 2005; DeLoache & Chiong, 2009).

Further, only a few of those studies have specifically focused on infants' *learning* from video. In one such study (Kuhl, Tsao, & Liu, 2003), 9-month-olds from English-speaking families watched several presentations, either live or video, of an adult speaking Mandarin. A month later, the researchers tested whether this exposure had prolonged the infants' sensitivity to the Mandarin speech sounds. Only children whose Mandarin exposure had occurred in live interactions showed any impact of that experience.

Laboratory studies of infants' imitation of simple actions presented on video have established that 12- to 30-month-olds are able to reproduce a modest number of observed actions (e.g., Barr & Hayne, 1999; Hayne, Herbert, & Simcock, 2003; McCall, Parke, & Kavanaugh, 1977). Imitation is substantially better, however, when children experience the same demonstrations live.

Young children's word learning from commercial television has also been examined. A large-scale parent survey reported a negative correlation between vocabulary size and television exposure: For every hour of baby media that infants between 8 and 16 months of age watched on their own, they were reported to know 6 to 8 fewer words (Zimmerman et al., 2007). Kremar, Grela, and Lin (2007) obtained similar results in a laboratory study in which children under 22 months of age learned few object names presented on a clip from a Teletubbies television episode.

In a recent experimental investigation of early learning from video, Robb, Richert, and Wartella (2009) assessed word learning from home viewing of a commercial DVD designed to teach words to young children. According to parent reports, the 12- to 15-month-old participants learned relatively few of the words featured on the DVD: Children who had substantial exposure to it performed no better than did those with none. These results are intriguing, but the fact that the primary data were parent reports is of some concern.

Accordingly, we conducted an experiment using objective testing to directly examine the extent to which infants learn from a very popular commercial infant DVD promoted to foster word learning. Six aspects of the study were designed to ensure a highly valid assessment of the potential for early learning from video: (a) The entire experiment was conducted in the children's own homes. (b) The conditions mimicked everyday situations in which young children view videos. (c) A best-selling video was used. (d) The children received extensive exposure to the video. (e) They were tested for their understanding of the specific words featured on the video. (f) The tester was blind to the condition to which each child had been randomly assigned.

METHODS

Participants

Participants were 72 infants between 12 and 18 months of age (M = 14.7 months). They were recruited from a large metropolitan area and a small city. The sample was predominantly White and middle-class. None of the infants had had any exposure to the target DVD. Eighteen children (including approximately equal numbers of girls and boys) were randomly assigned to each of four conditions.

Materials

A best-selling commercial DVD designed and marketed for infants from "12 months of age and up" was used in the research. The 39-min DVD depicts a variety of scenes of a house and yard. A voice labels common household objects, each of which is named three times, with several minutes intervening between the repetitions of a given label. In addition, during the first and last labeling of a given object, a person is shown producing a manual sign for the object.

Conditions

In the three experimental conditions, the experimenter made three home visits to each family. During the first visit, the experimenter gave detailed oral and written instructions to the parents. The experimental conditions included two video conditions: Video with interaction and video with no interaction. In both of these conditions, parents gave their children substantial experience with the DVD in their own homes over 4 weeks. To ensure that they followed the instructions, we asked them to complete a daily log of their child's experience with the video. Parents in the parent-teaching (non-video) condition estimated how often they had attempted to teach their children the target words. On the second and third home visits in all three of these conditions, the experimenter checked to make sure the parents had been following the protocol.

In the *video-with-interaction condition,* the child and a parent watched the DVD together at least five times a week over a 4-week period, for a total of 10 or more hours of viewing time in 20 or more viewing episodes. (Some advertisements for baby videos recommend that parents watch with their children.) Parents were instructed to interact with their child in whatever way seemed natural to them while viewing the video. This condition mimicked the common everyday experience of young children and parents watching television together.

In the *video-with-no-interaction* condition, the children watched the video alone, but had the same total amount of exposure to it as did the children in the video-with-interaction condition. (The parents were almost always in the room with their infants, but were not watching television with them.) This condition mimicked another common situation, in which young children watch television on their own while their parents are nearby, but engaged in other activities.

In the *parent-teaching* condition, the children were not exposed to the video at all. Instead, the parents were given a list of the 25 words featured on the video and were instructed simply to "try to teach your child as many of these words as you can in whatever way seems natural to you."

The fourth condition, in which there was no intervention, was the control condition. It provided a

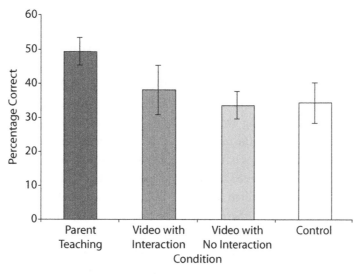

Fig. 1. Children's mean performance on the posttest as a function of group. Each child was tested on an individualized set of target words. Error bars represent standard errors of the mean.

baseline of normal vocabulary growth against which performance in the three intervention groups could be compared.

Testing

During the initial home visit, each child was tested for knowledge of 13 of the 25 words featured on the video in order to establish an individualized set of target words for that child. (As Table S1 in the Supplemental Material available online shows, children in the target age range perform around or below chance when tested for their knowledge of the majority of these words.) On each of 13 trials, the child was shown a pair of replica objects—a target representing an object featured in the video (e.g., clock, table, tree) and a distractor that did not appear in the video (e.g., fan, plate, fence). The experimenter named the target and asked the child to point to the appropriate object (e.g., "Can you show me the table?"). The names of the objects that a child failed to identify became that child's individualized set of target words. The number of target words ranged from 5 to 12; the mean number (6.4–6.9) did not differ across the four groups.

On the final visit, the child's knowledge of his or her target words was tested to determine how much word learning had taken place over the 4 weeks. The testing was conducted in the same way as in the initial visit, except that two trials were given for each of

the child's target words, with the words presented in one order for the first set of trials and in the reverse order for the second. To be credited with knowing a word, the child had to choose the correct object on both trials; this criterion minimized the likelihood that children would be counted as knowing a word after simply guessing correctly. Parents in the video conditions completed a brief questionnaire concerning their and their child's experience with the video.

RESULTS

Figure 1 shows the percentage of their target words that the children got correct on the posttest. Only the performance of the parent-teaching group was above chance ($p < .05$). The result of primary importance is clear: Children who had extensive exposure to a popular infant video over a full month, either with a parent or alone, did not learn any more new words than did children with no exposure to the video at all.

The absence of learning from experience with the video was not due to lack of attention to it. Representative comments from the logs of parents whose children were in the video groups include the following: "She was practically glued to the screen today;" "She was very quiet today—stared intently at the screen and ignored me when I asked her to talk;" "She loves the blasted thing. It's crack for babies!"

As Figure 1 shows, performance was highest in the parent-teaching group—those children who had no exposure to the video, but whose parents had attempted to teach them new words during everyday interactions. Preliminary examination of the individual scores indicated that the data were not normally distributed, so a median test was performed on the proportion of target words that the children in the four conditions identified on the posttest. There was a significant overall difference among the groups, $X^2(3, N = 72) = 10.03, p < .05$. Post hoc tests indicated that the performance of the parent-teaching group was significantly better than that of all three of the other groups—video-with-interaction group: $X^2(1, N = 36) = 4.0. p < ,05$; video-with-no-interaction group: $X^2(1, N = 36) = 11.11, p = .001$; and control group: $X^2(1, N = 36) = 4.0, p < .05$. Neither of the video conditions differed from the control condition. Thus, significantly more learning occurred in the context of everyday parent-child interactions than in front of television screens.

Finally, the parents' assessment of how much their children had learned from the DVD was unrelated to the children's performance on the posttest: Children whose parents thought that they had learned a substantial amount from their experience with the DVD performed no better than did children of less sanguine parents. There was, however, a significant correlation ($r = .64, p < .01$) between parents' own liking for the DVD and their estimate of how much their children had learned: The more a parent liked the DVD, the more he or she believed the child had learned from it.

DISCUSSION

The results of this study provide a clear answer to our original question: Infants between 12 and 18 months of age learned very little from a highly popular media product promoted for this age group. Even with the substantial amount of exposure that they had to the video, the infants learned only a few of the words featured on it. Because great care was taken to ensure that the video-viewing conditions were as natural as possible, the results should be generalizable to young children's everyday experience.

These results are consistent with a body of theory and research that has established that very young children often fail to use information communicated to them via symbolic media, including pictures, models, and video (e.g., DeLoache, 2004; Troseth, Pierroutsakos, & DeLoache, 2004). For example, 2-year-olds who watch a live video of an adult hiding a desirable toy in the room next-door fail to find the toy when encouraged to search for it immediately afterward (Troseth, 2003a, 2003b; Troscth & DeLoache, 1998). This and related results indicate that infants and very young children have difficulty understanding the relation between what they see on a screen and the real world.

An additional finding from this experiment is directly relevant to the possibility that parents may misattribute normal developmental progress to their infants' video exposure. Parents who had a favorable attitude toward the DVD thought that their children had learned more from it than did parents who were less positively disposed to the DVD. There was, in fact no difference in how many words were learned by the children of these two groups of parents. This result suggests that much of the enthusiasm expressed in parent testimonials about baby video products is misplaced.

In summary, the research reported here supports two important conclusions. First, parents whose infants have experience with baby videos tend to misattribute normal developmental change to that experience, thereby overestimating the impact of the videos on their children's development. Second, the degree to which babies actually learn from baby videos is negligible.

ACKNOWLEDGMENTS

We thank Monica Ehrbacher for her very helpful statistical advice.

Declaration of Conflicting Interests
The authors declared that they had no conflicts of interest with respect to their authorship or the publication of this article.

Funding

This research was supported by National Institutes of Health Grant HD-25271, as well as by National Science Foundation Grant 0819508, both to the first author.

Supplemental Material

Additional supporting information may be found at http://pss.sagepub.com/content/by/supplemental-data

REFERENCES

Anderson, D.R., & Penipek, T.A. (2005). Television and very young children. *American Behavioral Scientist, 48,* 505–522.

Barr; R., & Hayne, H. (1999). Developmental changes in imitation from television during infancy. *Child Development, 70,* 1067–1081.

Benedict, H. (1979). Early lexical development: Comprehension and production. *Journal of Child Language, 6,* 183–200.

DeLoache, J.S. (2004). Becoming symbol-minded. *Trends in Cognitive Sciences, 8,* 66–70.

DeLoache, J.S., & Chiong. C. (2009). Babies and baby media. *American Behavioral Scientist, 52.* 1115–1135.

Goldfield, B.A., & Reznick, J.S. (1990). Early lexical acquisition: Rate, content, and the vocabulary spurt. *Journal of Child Language, 17,* 171–184.

Hayne, H., Herbert. J., & Simcock, G. (2003). Imitation from television by 24- and 30-month-olds. *Developmental Science, 6,* 254–261.

Kremar, M., Grela, B., & Lin, K. (2007). Can toddlers learn vocabulary from television? An experimental approach. *Media Psychology, 10,* 41–63.

Kuhl, P.K.,Tsao, F.M., & Liu, H.M. (2003). Foreign-language experience in infancy: Effects of short-term exposure and social interaction on phonetic learning. *Proceedings of the National Academy of Sciences, USA, 100, 9096*–9101.

McCall, R.B., Parke, R.D., & Kavanaugh, R.D. (1977). Imitation of live and televised models by children one to three years of age. *Monographs of the Society for Research in Child Development, 42(5,* Serial No. 173).

Rideout, V. (2007). *Parents, children, and media.* Menlo Park, CA: Henry J. Kaiser Family Foundation.

Rideout, V.J., Vandewater, E.A., & Wartella, E.A. (2003). *Zero to six: Electronic media in the lives of infants, toddlers and preschoolers.* Menlo Park, CA: Henry J. Kaiser Family Foundation.

Robb, M., Richert, R., & Wartella, E. (2009). Just a talking book? Word learning from watching baby videos. *British Journal of Developmental Psychology, 27,* 27–45.

Schmidt, M.E., Rich, M., Rifas-Shiman, S.L., Oken, E., & Taverns, E.M. (2009). Television viewing in infancy and *child* cognition at 3 years-of age in a US cohort. *Pediatrics, 123,* 370–375.

Troseth, G.L. (2003a). Getting a clear picture: Young children's understanding of a televised image. *Developmental Science. 6,* 247–253.

Troseth, G.L. (2003b). TV guide: 2-year-olds learn to use video as a source of information. *Developmental Psychology, 39,* 140–150.

Troseth, G.L., & DeLoache, J.S. (1998). The medium can obscure the message: Young children's understanding of video. *Child Development, 69,* 950–965.

Troseth, G.L., Pierroutsakos, S.L., & DeLoache, J.S. (2004). From the innocent to the intelligent eye: The early development of pictorial competence. In R.V. Kail (Ed.), *Advances in child development and behavior. Volume 32* (pp. 1–35). New York, NY: Academic Press.

Zimmerman, F.J., Christakis, D.A., & Meltzoff, A. (2007). Television and DVD/video viewing in children younger than 2 years. *Archives of Pediatric* & *Adolescent Medicine, 69,* 473–479.

PRACTICAL APPLICATION ASSIGNMENTS

1. Let's return to Danika's birthday party to answer Susan's question regarding the educational benefits of infant-directed media programs. Explain the study results to Grandma Jones and Susan, Danika's mother. Be sure to describe how the study was conducted (type of research study, who the participants were, the four different conditions, and the dependent variable).

2. Parents often think that spurts in word learning are the result of exposure to infant-directed media programs. Given your understanding of the scientific method and the research findings from this study, first explain why parents may misattribute ordinary developmental progress to these infant-directed media programs. Second, explain why parents shouldn't give "credit" to these programs for the rapid increase in vocabulary between the first and second year of life. Third, based on this study, which parents are most likely to misattribute ordinary developmental progress to these programs?

3. Your best friend, Giselle, had a baby last year. Giselle and her husband are interested in buying several infant-directed DVDs to promote their baby's language development. They know that you are taking a psychology course, so they ask for your advice. How would you respond to your best friend and her husband?

Chapter 5

Biological Psychology: Exercise and the Brain

Exercise Training Increases Size of Hippocampus and Improves Memory

By Kirk I. Erickson, Michelle W. Voss, Ruchika Shaurya Prakash, Chandramallika Basak, Amanda Szabo, Laura Chaddock, Jennifer S. Kim, Susie Heo, Heloisa Alves, Siobhan M. White, Thomas R. Wojcicki, Emily Mailey, Victoria J. Vieira, Stephen A. Martin, Brandt D. Pence, Jeffrey A. Woods, Edward McAuley, and Arthur F. Kramer

EDITORS' INTRODUCTION

If you have interacted with a forgetful grandparent or older adult, these experiences may have left you wondering whether or not forgetfulness or memory decline are unavoidable as we age. Even if you understand that these changes are *not* an inevitable part of aging, you may wonder if there are interventions that can help reduce the likelihood of experiencing memory loss or reverse memory decline if it does occur. Recent research has found that the same physical exercise that keeps age-related physical impairments at bay may also be important for brain health and preventing specific kinds of memory decline.

Biological psychology is the area of psychology that studies the role of the brain and nervous system in behavior and mental processes. Researchers in this area of psychology are particularly interested in how changes in the brain can influence many different cognitive processes, such as learning and memory, or behaviors such as walking, talking, and eating. In this chapter, you will read about research in biological psychology that investigates a relationship between changes in the *anterior hippocampus* of the brain and a specific kind of memory in older adults.

Plasticity is an important concept in the areas of memory and biological psychology. Plasticity refers to the ability of the brain and nervous system to grow and change. Until about the 1970s, most psychologists believed that the brain stopped developing in adulthood and could not grow or repair itself after childhood. This contributed to the "brain myth" that age-related memory decline was inevitable, and that attempts to enhance cognition or increase brain volume were futile. Research on a region of the brain called the hippocampus eventually revealed a different story. It is now well established that the cells in the hippocampus that are involved in learning and memory continue to grow and change across a person's lifespan. Amazingly, interventions such as physical exercise can increase the size or number of cells in the hippocampus and improve performance on memory tasks (Kramer et al., 1999; van Pragg, Christie, Sejnowski, & Gage, 1999; van Pragg, Shubert, Zhao, & Gage, 2005). In this chapter, you'll learn more about how a basic intervention like aerobic exercise may help prevent memory decline, or even improve memory, as it did for some of the volunteers who participated in the study you'll read. Clearly, this research challenges the brain myth that memory loss is an unavoidable part of aging!

What is the *anterior hippocampus,* and how is it involved in memory? Psychologists have long known that the hippocampus is crucial for learning and the formation of memories. In one of the best-known case studies in psychology, a patient named Henry Molaison (or H. M. as he is known in many books and articles) lost the ability to form new memories (also known as *anterograde amnesia*) when parts of his hippocampus were removed during a surgery to treat epilepsy in 1954 (Scoville & Milner, 1957). Psychologists studied H. M. and his hippocampus for more than five decades until his death in 2008, and they learned a great deal about the importance of this brain region in memory (Carey, 2008).[1] More recently, researchers have discovered that the anterior hippocampus, which is the part of the hippocampus located closest to the front of the brain, is responsible for acquiring specific types of memory, such as spatial memory (Moser, Moser, Forrest, Andersen, & Morris, 1995). Spatial memory is the kind of memory that explains our ability to remember where things are located in three-dimensional space.

In general, the size of the hippocampus (including the anterior hippocampus) decreases with age, and this is associated with memory decline (including spatial memory) in older adults (Driscoll et al., 2003; Hackert et al., 2002; Raji, Lopez, Kuller, Carmichael, & Becker, 2009). It is important to note that these changes are associated with only one very specific type of cognition—spatial memory. We must be careful *not* to generalize from these findings to conclude that other cognitive functions (like decision making or the kind of thinking that driving a car requires, for example) are impaired in all older adults, that these types of memory decline are always inevitable, or that memory measures in a lab setting are always meaningful in the real world. For example, forgetting a list of nonsense words in a lab experiment may not be as meaningful in the real world where you can write lists down!

Exercise is emerging as one useful intervention for promoting brain health and plasticity in the hippocampus (Cotman & Berchtold, 2002; Olson, Eadie, Ernst, & Christie, 2006). Erickson and colleagues (2011), the authors of the article in this chapter, hypothesized that aerobic exercise (rather than nonaerobic exercise, like stretching and lifting moderate weights) could limit or reverse decline in the size of the hippocampus and improve spatial memory in older adults. The researchers used a simple intervention (walking) to improve the size and function of the hippocampus, which contributed to our understanding about how exercise improves brain structure and function by identifying a specific type of exercise that is most helpful.

As you read, think about how the results of this kind of research in plasticity and biological psychology might be applied to help improve the quality of life for older adults. Also consider whether or not the results of this study could be implemented in your community. One of the strengths of this research is that the intervention is inexpensive and readily available to most adults. Additional research will be needed to determine if this approach can be widely and successfully implemented, and if it can generalize to larger populations. If you were in a position to help older adults improve their memory, and banish the brain myth that memory loss is inevitable, would you be excited to read this research?

As you read the article in this chapter, notice how the format of the writing differs from other research articles in this book. While this article contains the sections Introduction, Methods, Results, and Conclusion, like many other articles in this book, the order and inclusion of details are a little different. Each journal requires authors to write using a specific format. Many psychology journals use the style of the *American Psychological Association* (or APA format); however, this article was published in the journal *Proceedings of the National Academy of Sciences* (PNAS) that has adopted a different style. Regardless of the specific format, you'll soon start to recognize that most research articles contain similar sections. As you practice reading research articles, you'll become more familiar with where to find information, such as the details about participants or reasons why the research was conducted.

ENDNOTE

1. To learn more about H. M. and to see pictures of his famous brain, visit The Brain Observatory website from the University of California San Diego School of Medicine: http://thebrainobservatory. ucsd.edu/hm

REFERENCES

Carey, B. (2008, December 5), H. M., an unforgettable amnesiac dies at 82. *The New York Times*. p. A1.

Cotman, C. W., & Berchtold, N. C. (2002). Exercise: a behavioral intervention to enhance brain health and plasticity. *Trends in Neurosciences, 25* (6), 295–301.

Driscoll, I., Hamilton, D. A., Petropoulos, H., Yeo, R. A., Brooks, W. M., Baumgartner, R. N., & Sutherland, R. J. (2003). The aging hippocampus: Cognitive, biochemical, and structural findings. *Cerebral Cortex, 13* (12), 1344–1351.

Erickson, K. I., Voss, M. W., Prakash, R. S., Basa, C., Szabo, A., Chaddock, L., Kim, J. S., Heo, S., Alves, H., White, S. M., Wojcicki, T. R., Mailey, E., Vieira, V. J., Martin, S. A., Pence, B. D., Woods, J. A., McAuley, E., & Kramer, A. F. (2011). Exercise training increases size of hippocampus and improves memory. *Proceedings of the National Academy of Sciences, 108* (7), 3017–3022.

Hackert V. H., den Heijer, T., Oudkerk, M., Koudstaal, P. J., Hofman A., & Breteler, M. M. B. (2002). Hippocampal head size associated with verbal memory performance in nondemented elderly. *Neuroimage, 17* (3), 1365–1372.

Kramer, A. F., Hahn, S., Cohen, N. J., Banich, M. T., McAuley, E., Harrison, C. R., Chason, J., Vakil, E., Bardell, L., Boileau, R. A., & Colcombe, A. (1999). Ageing, fitness, and neurocognitive function. *Nature, 400* (July 29), 418–419.

Moser, M. B., Moser, E. I., Forrest, E., Andersen, P., & Morris, R. G. (1995). Spatial learning with a mini-slab in the dorsal hippocampus. *Proceedings of the National Academy of Sciences, 92* (21), 9697–9701.

Olson, A. K., Eadie, B. D., Ernst, C., & Christie, B. R. (2006). Environmental enrichment and voluntary exercise massively increase neurogenesis in the adult hippocampus via dissociable pathways. *Hippocampus, 16* (3), 250–260.

Raji, C. A., Lopez, O. L., Kuller, L. H., Carmichael, O. T., & Becker, J. T. (2009). Age, Alzheimer disease, and brain structure. *Neurology, 73* (22), 1899–1905.

Scoville, W. B. & Milner, B. (1957). Loss of recent memory after bilateral hippocampal lesions. *Journal of Neurology, Neurosurgery, and Psychiatry, 20* (1), 11–21.

vanPragg, H., Shubert, T., Zhao, C., & Gage, F. H. (2005). Exercise enhances learning and hippocampal neurogenesis in aged mice. *The Journal of Neuroscience, 25* (38), 8680–8685.

vanPragg, H., Christie, B. R., Sejnowski, T. J., & Gage, F. H. (1999). Running enhances neurogenesis, learning, and long-term potentiation in mice. *Proceedings of the National Academy of Sciences, 96* (23), 13427–13431.

ABSTRACT

The hippocampus shrinks in late adulthood, leading to impaired memory and increased risk for dementia. Hippocampal and medial temporal lobe volumes are larger in higher-fit adults, and physical activity training increases hippocampal perfusion, but the extent to which aerobic exercise training can modify hippocampal volume in late adulthood remains unknown. Here we show, in a randomized controlled trial with 120 older adults, that aerobic exercise training increases the size of the anterior hippocampus, leading to improvements in spatial memory. Exercise training increased hippocampal volume by 2%, effectively reversing age-related loss in volume by 1 to 2 y. ... Hippocampal volume declined in the control group, but higher preintervention fitness partially attenuated the decline, suggesting that fitness protects against volume loss. ... These theoretically important findings indicate that aerobic exercise training is effective at reversing hippocampal volume loss in late adulthood, which is accompanied by improved memory function.

Deterioration of the hippocampus precedes and leads to memory impairment in late adulthood (1, 2). Strategies to fight hippocampal loss and protect against the development of memory impairment has become an important topic in recent years from both scientific and public health perspectives. Physical activity, such as aerobic exercise, has emerged as a promising low cost treatment to improve neurocognitive function that is accessible to most adults and is not plagued by intolerable side effects often found with pharmaceutical treatments (3). Exercise enhances learning and improves retention, which is accompanied by increased cell proliferation and survival in the hippocampus of rodents (4–6). ...

Hippocampal and medial temporal lobe volumes are larger in higher-fit older adults (13, 14), and larger hippocampal volumes mediate improvements in spatial memory (13). Exercise training increases ... [blood flow] (15) of the hippocampus (16), but the extent to which exercise can modify the size of the hippocampus in late adulthood remains unknown.

To evaluate whether exercise training increases the size of the hippocampus and improves spatial memory, we designed a singleblind, randomized controlled trial in which adults were randomly assigned to receive either moderate-intensity aerobic exercise 3 d/wk or stretching and toning exercises that served as a control. We predicted that 1 y of moderate-intensity exercise would increase the size of the hippocampus and that change in hippocampal volume would be associated with improved memory function.

Table 1. Characteristics for the Aerobic Exercise and Stretching Control Groups

Characteristic	Aerobic exercise	Stretching control
n	60	60
Age (y), mean (SD)	67.6 (5.81)	65.5 (5.44)
Sex (% female)	73	60
Attendance (%), mean (SD)	79.5 (13.70)	78.6 (13.61)
Fitness improvement (%), mean (SD)	7.78 (12.7)	1.11 (13.9)

Table 2. Means (SD) for Both Groups at All Three Time Points

Variable	Aerobic exercise group			Stretching control group		
	Baseline	6 mo	After intervention	Baseline	6 mo	After intervention
VO$_2$ max	21.36 (4.71)	22.25 (4.66)	22.61 (4.84)	21.75 (4.87)	21.87 (5.07)	21.87 (4.93)
L hippocampus	4.89 (0.74)	4.93 (0.71)	4.98 (0.69)	4.90 (0.80)	4.86 (0.80)	4.83 (0.80)
R hippocampus	5.00 (0.67)	5.03 (0.63)	5.09 (0.63)	4.92 (0.80)	4.89 (0.83)	4.86 (0.82)
L anterior hippocampus	2.86 (0.42)	2.88 (0.41)	2.93 (0.40)	2.84 (0.48)	2.82 (0.48)	2.78 (0.46)
R anterior hippocampus	2.90 (0.40)	2.93 (0.38)	2.99 (0.38)	2.88 (0.48)	2.87 (0.48)	2.84 (0.49)
L posterior hippocampus	2.03 (0.34)	2.04 (0.31)	2.05 (0.30)	2.05 (0.33)	2.03 (0.34)	2.03 (0.37)
R posterior hippocampus	2.05 (0.30)	2.09 (0.27)	2.09 (0.27)	2.03 (0.35)	2.02 (0.37)	2.01 (0.34)

VO$_2$ max was measured as ml/kg per min. Brain volumes were measured as cm^3. L, left; R, right.

RESULTS

Aerobic Exercise Training Selectively Increases Hippocampal Volume.

One hundred twenty older adults without dementia (Table 1) were randomly assigned to an aerobic exercise group ($n = 60$) or to a stretching control group ($n = 60$). Magnetic resonance images were collected before the intervention, after 6 mo, and again after the completion of the program. The groups did not differ at baseline in hippocampal volume or attendance rates (Table 2 and *SI Results*). We found that the exercise intervention was effective at increasing the size of the hippocampus. That is, the aerobic exercise group demonstrated an increase in volume of the left and right hippocampus by 2.12% and 1.97%, respectively, over the 1-y period, whereas the stretching control group displayed a 1.40% and 1.43% decline over this same interval (Fig. 1A). The moderating effect of aerobic exercise on hippocampal volume loss was confirmed by a significant Time × Group interaction for both the left [$F(2,114) = 8.25$; $P < 0.001$; $\eta_p^2 = 0.12$] and right [$F(2,114) = 10.41$; $P < 0.001$; $\eta_p^2 =$

0.15] hippocampus (see Table 2 for all means and SDs).

As can be seen in Fig. 2, we found that aerobic exercise selectively increased the volume of the anterior hippocampus that included the dentate gyrus, where cell proliferation occurs (4, 6, 8), as well as subiculum and CA1 subfields, but had a minimal effect on the volume of the posterior section. Cells in the anterior hippocampus mediate acquisition of spatial memory (17) and show more age-related atrophy compared with the tail of the hippocampus (18, 19). The selective effect of aerobic exercise on the anterior hippocampus was confirmed by a significant Time × Group × Region interaction for both the left [$F(2,114)=4.05$; $P < 0.02$; $\eta_p^2 = 0.06$] and right [$F(2,114) = 4.67$; $P < 0.01$; $\eta_p^2 = 0.07$] hippocampus. As revealed by t tests, the aerobic exercise group showed an increase in anterior hippocampus volume from baseline to after intervention [left: $t(2,58) = 3.38$; $P < 0.001$; right: $t(2,58) = 4.33$; $P < 0.001$] but demonstrated no change in the volume of the posterior hippocampus (both $P > 0.10$). In contrast, the stretching control group demonstrated a selective decline in volume from baseline to after intervention

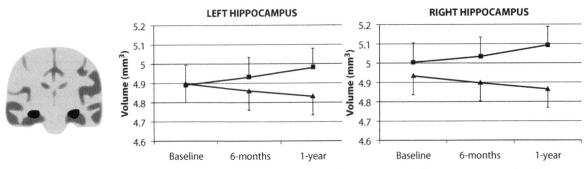

Fig. 1. Example of hippocampus segmentation and graphs demonstrating an increase in hippocampus volume for the aerobic exercise group and a decrease in volume for the stretching control group. The Time × Group interaction was significant ($P < 0.001$) for both left and right regions.

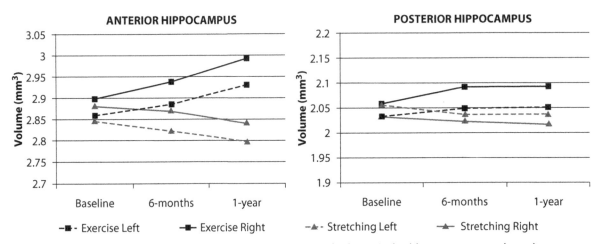

—■- Exercise Left   —■— Exercise Right   –▲- Stretching Left   —▲— Stretching Right

Fig. 2. The exercise group showed a selective increase in the anterior hippocampus and no change in the posterior hippocampus. See Table 2 for Means and SDs.

for the anterior hippocampus [left: $t(2,58) = -3.07$; $P < 0.003$; right: $t(2,58) = -2.45$; $P < 0.01$] but no significant change in volume for the posterior hippocampus (both $P > 0.20$). ...

Our results demonstrate that the size of the hippocampus is modifiable in late adulthood and that moderate-intensity aerobic exercise is effective at reversing volume loss. Increased volume with exercise occurred in a selective fashion, influencing the anterior hippocampus but not the posterior hippocampus. ...

Changes in Fitness Are Associated with Increased Hippocampal Volume.

The intervention was effective at increasing aerobic fitness levels. The aerobic exercise group showed a 7.78% improvement in maximal oxygen consumption (VO$_2$ max) after the intervention, whereas the

stretching control group showed a 1.11% improvement in VO$_2$ max (Table 1). This difference between the groups was confirmed by a Time × Group interaction [$F(2,111) = 4.42$; $P < 0.01$; $\eta_p^2 = 0.07$]. We examined whether improvements in fitness levels were associated with the magnitude of the change in hippocampal volume. We found that greater improvements in aerobic fitness level over the 1-y interval were associated with greater increases in hippocampal volume for the left ($r = 0.37$; $P < 0.001$) and right ($r = 0.40$; $P < 0.001$) hemispheres, suggesting that larger changes in fitness translate to larger changes in volume (Fig. 3 *A* and *B*). ... Improvements in VO$_2$ max were correlated with increases in both anterior (left: $r = 0.28$; $P < 0.001$; right: $r = 0.51$; $P < 0.001$) and posterior (left: $r = 0.32$; $P < 0.001$; right: $r = 0.39$; $P < 0.001$) hippocampal regions, indicating that changes in aerobic fitness have a global influence on hippocampal volume. ...

We reasoned that if higher physical fitness is protective against the loss of brain tissue, then higher fitness levels at baseline would be predictive of less volume loss over the 1-y period. We examined the participants that declined in volume in the stretching group to test this hypothesis, because the stretching group, and not the aerobic exercise group, showed a decline in hippocampal volume over the 1-y interval. We found results partially consistent with this prediction. That is, higher fitness levels at baseline were associated with less hippocampal volume loss over the 1-y interval, for the right ($r = 0.50$; $P < 0.002$) but not for the left ($r = 0.17$; $P < 0.30$) hippocampus. Further, consistent with our expectations, it was only the right anterior hippocampus ($r = 0.48$; $P < 0.003$) that was protected by higher fitness levels at baseline; the posterior hippocampus was not affected by baseline fitness ($r = 0.21$; $P > 0.20$). ...

Hippocampal Volume Is Related to Improvements in Spatial Memory.

Spatial memory (13, 22) was tested on both exercise and stretching groups at baseline, after 6 mo, and again after the completion of the 1-y intervention to determine whether changes in hippocampal volume translate to improved memory. Both groups showed improvements in memory, as demonstrated by significant increases in accuracy between the first and last testing sessions for the aerobic exercise [$t(2,51) = 2.08$; $P < 0.05$] and the stretching control [$t(2,54) = 4.41$; $P < 0.001$] groups. Response times also became faster for both groups between the baseline and postintervention sessions (all $P < 0.01$), indicating that improvements in accuracy were not caused by changes in speed–accuracy tradeoff. However, the aerobic exercise group did not improve performance above that achieved by the stretching control group, as demonstrated by a nonsignificant Time × Group interaction [$F(1,102) = 0.67$; $P < 0.40$; $\eta_p^2 = 0.007$]. Nonetheless, we found that higher aerobic fitness levels at baseline ($r = 0.31$; $P < 0.001$) and after intervention ($r = 0.28$; $P < 0.004$) were associated with better memory performance on the spatial memory task. Change in aerobic fitness levels from baseline to after intervention, however, was not related to

improvements in memory for either the entire sample ($r = 0.15$; $P < 0.12$) or when considering each group separately (both $P > 0.05$). ... Larger left and right hippocampi at baseline (both $P < 0.005$) and after intervention (both $P < 0.005$) were associated with better memory performance (12). Therefore, we reasoned that increased hippocampal volume after the exercise intervention should translate to improved memory function. In support of this hypothesis, we found that, in the aerobic exercise group, increased hippocampal volume was directly related to improvements in memory performance. The correlation between improvement in memory and hippocampal volume reached significance for left ($r = 0.23$; $P < 0.05$) and right ($r = 0.29$; $P < 0.02$) hemispheres (Fig. 3 E and F). This indicates that increases in hippocampal volume after 1 y of exercise augments memory function in late adulthood. ...

DISCUSSION

Hippocampal volume shrinks 1–2% annually in older adults without dementia (1), and this loss of volume increases the risk for developing cognitive impairment (2). We find results consistent with this pattern, such that the stretching control group demonstrated a 1.4% decline in volume over the 1-y interval. With escalating health care costs and an increased proportion of people aged >65 y, it is imperative that low-cost, accessible preventions and treatments for brain tissue loss are discovered. In this randomized controlled study of exercise training, we demonstrate that loss of hippocampal volume in late adulthood is not inevitable and can be reversed with moderate-intensity exercise. A 1-y aerobic exercise intervention was effective at increasing hippocampal volume by 2% and offsetting the deterioration associated with aging. Because hippocampal volume shrinks 1–2% annually, a 2% increase in hippocampal volume is equivalent to adding between 1 and 2 y worth of volume to the hippocampus for this age group. ...

Aerobic exercise increased anterior hippocampal volume but had little effect on the posterior hippocampus. Neurons in the anterior hippocampus are selectively associated with spatial memory acquisition (17) and show exacerbated age-related

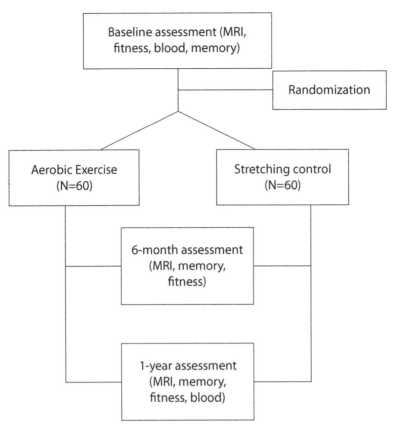

Fig. 4. Flow diagram for the randomization and assessment sessions for both exercise and stretching control groups.

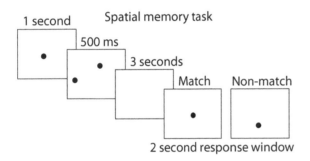

Fig. 5. Display of the spatial memory task used in this study. The spatial memory task load was parametrically manipulated between one, two, or three items (two-item condition shown here). Participants were asked to remember the locations of one, two, or three black dots. After a brief delay, a red dot appeared, and participants were asked to respond whether the location of the red dot matched or did not match one of the locations of the previously shown black dots. This task was administered to all participants at baseline, after 6 mo, and again after completion of the intervention.

atrophy compared with the posterior hippocampus (18, 19). It is possible that regions demonstrating less age-related decay might also be less amenable to growth. Thus, aerobic exercise might elicit the greatest changes in regions that show the most precipitous decline in late adulthood, such as the anterior hippocampus and prefrontal cortex (9). Overall, these data suggest that the anterior hippocampus remains amenable to augmentation.

In sum, we found that the hippocampus remains plastic in late adulthood and that 1 y of aerobic exercise was sufficient for enhancing volume. Increased hippocampal volume translates to improved memory function. ... We also demonstrate that higher fitness levels are protective against loss of hippocampal volume. These results clearly indicate that aerobic exercise is neuroprotective and that starting an exercise regimen later in life is not futile for either enhancing cognition or augmenting brain volume.

METHODS

Participants. Community-dwelling older adults (n = 842) were recruited, and 179 were enrolled. One hundred forty-five participants completed the intervention (81.0% of the participants originally enrolled). Five participants were excluded because they did not attend the 6-mo MRI session, owing to scheduling conflicts; eight participants were excluded because they did not attend the 12-mo follow-up MRI session; and 12 participants were excluded because they had excessive head motion that created inaccurate hippocampal, caudate nucleus, or thalamus segmentations. Therefore, 120 participants had complete MR data from all three sessions (82.7% of the enrolled sample) and were included in the analyses.

Eligible participants had to (*i*) demonstrate strong right handedness (35), (*ii*) be between the ages of 55 and 80 y, (*iii*) score ≥51 on the modified Mini-Mental Status Examination (36), (*iv*), score <3 on the Geriatric Depression Scale to rule out possible depression (37), (*v*) have normal color vision, (*vi*) have a corrected visual acuity of at least 20/40, (*vii*) have no history of neurological diseases or infarcts, including Parkinson's disease, Alzheimer's disease, multiple sclerosis, or stroke, (*viii*) have no history of major vasculature problems, including cardiovascular disease or diabetes, (*ix*) obtain consent from their personal physician, and (*x*) sign an informed consent form approved by the University of Illinois. In addition, all participants had to report being currently sedentary, defined as being physically active for 30 min or less in the last 6 mo. Participants were compensated for their participation.

After completion of the initial blood draw, MR session, and fitness assessment, participants were randomized to an aerobic walking group (*n* = 60) or a stretching control group (*n* = 60) (Fig. 4).

Fitness Assessments. Participants were required to obtain consent from their personal physician before cardiorespiratory fitness testing was conducted. Aerobic fitness (VO$_2$ max) was assessed by graded maximal exercise testing on a motor-driven treadmill. The participant walked at a speed slightly faster than their normal walking pace ($\approx$30–100m/min), with increasing grade increments of 2% every 2 min. A cardiologist and nurse continuously monitored oxygen uptake, heart rate, and blood pressure (see *SI Methods* for more detail).

MRI Parameters and Segmentation Algorithm. MR images were collected on all participants within 1 mo of the start of the intervention, after 6 mo, and within 2 wk after the completion of the intervention. High-resolution (1.3 mm × 1.3 mm × 1.3 mm) T1-weighted brain images were acquired using a 3D magnetization-prepared rapid gradient echo imaging protocol with 144 contiguous slices collected in an ascending fashion.

For segmentation and volumetric analysis of the left and right hippocampus, caudate nucleus, and thalamus we used the Oxford Centre for Functional MRI of the Brain (FMRIB)'s Integrated Registration and Segmentation Tool in FMRIB's Software Library version 4.1 (38–40) (see *SI Methods* for more detail).

Training Protocol. *Aerobic exercise condition.* For the aerobic exercise program, a trained exercise leader supervised all sessions. Participants started by walking for 10 min and increased walking duration weekly by 5-min increments until a duration of 40 min was achieved at week 7. Participants walked for 40 min per session for the remainder of the program. All walking sessions started and ended with approximately 5 min of stretching for the purpose of warming up and cooling down. Participants wore heart rate monitors and were encouraged to walk in their target heart rate zone, which was calculated using the Karvonen method (41) according to the resting and maximum heart rates achieved during the baseline maximal graded exercise test. The target heart rate zone was 50–60% of the maximum heart rate reserve for weeks 1 to 7 and 60–75% for the remainder of the program. Participants in the walking group completed an exercise log at each exercise session. Every 4 wk, participants received written feedback forms that summarized the data from their logs. Participants with low attendance and/or exercise heart rate were encouraged to improve their performance in the following month.

Stretching and toning control condition. For the stretching and toning control program, all sessions were led and monitored by trained exercise leaders. All classes started and ended with warm-up and cool-down stretching. During each class, participants engaged in four muscle-toning exercises using dumbbells or resistance bands, two exercises designed to improve balance, one yoga sequence, and one exercise of their choice. To maintain interest, a new group of exercises was introduced every 3 wk. During the first week, participants focused on becoming familiar with the new exercises, and during the second and third weeks they were encouraged to increase the intensity by using more weight or adding more repetitions. Participants in the stretching and toning control group also completed exercise logs at each exercise session and received monthly feedback forms. They were encouraged to exercise at an appropriate intensity of 13–15 on the Borg Rating of Perceived Exertion scale (42) and to attend as many classes as possible.

Spatial Memory Paradigm. To test memory function, all participants completed a computerized spatial memory task at baseline, after 6 mo, and again after completion of the intervention (13, 22, 43). …

A fixation crosshair appeared for 1 s, and participants were instructed to keep their eyes on the crosshair. After the fixation, one, two, or three black dots appeared at random locations on the screen for 500 ms. The dots were removed from the display for 3 s. During this time, participants were instructed to try and remember the locations of the previously presented black dots. At the end of the 3-s delay, a red dot appeared on the screen in either one of the same locations as the target dots (match condition) or at a different location (nonmatch condition). Participants had 2 s to respond to the red dot by pressing one of two keys on a standard keyboard—the "x" key for a nonmatch trial and the "m" key for a match trial (Fig. 5). Forty trials were presented for each set size (one, two, or three locations), with 20 trials as match trials and 20 trials as nonmatch trials. Participants were instructed to respond as quickly and accurately as possible. Several practice trials were performed before the task began to acquaint the participants with the task instructions and responses (see *SI Methods* for more detail). …

Analyses. All dependent variables were tested and met criteria for normality and skew before general linear model and Pearson correlations were conducted. Effects of the intervention on VO_2, … and the volume of the hippocampus, examined using an ANOVA with repeated measures with Group (aerobic exercise, stretching control) as a between-subjects factor and Time (baseline, 6 mo, and 1 y) as a within-subject factor. …

ACKNOWLEDGMENTS

We thank Susan Herrel, Edward Malkowski, Dawn Epstein, Zuha Warraich, Nancy Dodge, and Holly Tracy for help with data collection. This work was supported by National Institute on Aging, National Institutes of Health Grants RO1 AG25667 and RO1 AG25032. K.I.E. was supported by a Junior Scholar Award (P30 AG024827) from the Pittsburgh Claude D. Pepper Older Americans Independence Center and a seed grant (P50 AG005133) awarded through the University of Pittsburgh Alzheimer's Disease Research Center.

1. Raz N., et al. (2005) Regional brain changes in aging healthy adults: General trends, individual differences and modifiers. *Cereb Cortex* 15:1676–1689.
2. Jack C.R., Jr., et al.; Alzheimer's Disease Neuroimaging Initiative (2010) Brain beta-amyloid measures and magnetic resonance imaging atrophy both predict time-to-progression from mild cognitive impairment to Alzheimer's disease. *Brain* 133:3336–3348.
3. Hillman C.H., Erickson K.I., Kramer A.F. (2008) Be smart, exercise your heart: Exercise effects on brain and cognition. *Nat Rev Neurosci* 9:58–65.
4. van Praag H., Shubert T., Zhao C, Gage F.H. (2005) Exercise enhances learning and hippocampal neurogenesis in aged mice. *J Neurosci* 25:8680–8685.
5. Cotman C.W., Berchtold N.C. (2002) Exercise: A behavioral intervention to enhance brain health and plasticity. *Trends Neurosci* 25:295–301.
6. Creer D.J., Romberg C., Saksida L.M., van Praag H., Bussey T.J. (2010) Running enhances spatial pattern separation in mice. *Proc Natl Acad Sci USA* 107:2367–2372.
7. Vaynman S., Ying Z., Gomez-Pinilla F. (2004) Hippocampal BDNF mediates the efficacy of exercise on synaptic plasticity and cognition. *Eur J Neurosci* 20:2580–2590.
8. Li Y., et al. (2008) TrkB regulates hippocampal neurogenesis and governs sensitivity to antidepressive treatment. *Neuron* 59:399–412.
9. Colcombe S.J., et al. (2006) Aerobic exercise training increases brain volume in aging humans. *J Gerontol A Biol Sci Med Sci* 61:1166–1170.
10. Colcombe S.J., et al. (2004) Cardiovascular fitness, cortical plasticity, and aging. *Proc Natl Acad Sci USA* 101:3316–3321.
11. Rosano C., et al. (2010) Psychomotor speed and functional brain MRI 2 years after completing a physical activity treatment. *J Gerontol A Biol Sci Med Sci* 65:639–647.
12. Erickson K.I., et al. (2010) Physical activity predicts gray matter volume in late adulthood: The Cardiovascular Health Study. *Neurology* 75:1415–1422.
13. Erickson K.I., et al. (2009) Aerobic fitness is associated with hippocampal volume in elderly humans. *Hippocampus* 19:1030–1039.

14. Honea R.A., et al. (2009) Cardiorespiratory fitness and preserved medial temporal lobe volume in Alzheimer's disease. *Alzheimer Dis Assoc Disord* 23:188–197.

15. Pereira A.C., et al. (2007) An in vivo correlate of exercise-induced neurogenesis in the adult dentate gyrus. *Proc Natl Acad Sci USA* 104:5638–5643.

16. Burdette J.H., et al. (2010) Using network science to evaluate exercise-associated brain changes in older adults. *Front Aging Neurosci* 2:23.

17. Moser M.B., Moser E.I., Forrest E., Andersen P., Morris R.G. (1995) Spatial learning with a minislab in the dorsal hippocampus. *Proc Natl Acad Sci* USA 92:9697–9701.

18. Raji C.A., Lopez O.L., Kuller L.H., Carmichael O.T., Becker J.T. (2009) Age, Alzheimer disease, and brain structure. *Neurology* 73:1899–1905.

19. Hackert V.H., et al. (2002) Hippocampal head size associated with verbal memory performance in nondemented elderly. *Neuroimage* 17:1365–1372.

20. Neeper S.A., Gómez-Pinilla F., Choi J., Cotman C. (1995) Exercise and brain neurotrophins. *Nature* 373:109.

21. Holmes M.M., Galea L.A., Mistlberger R.E., Kempermann G. (2004) Adult hippocampal neurogenesis and voluntary running activity: Circadian and dose-dependent effects. *J Neurosci Res* 76:216–222.

22. Erickson K.I., et al. (2010) Brain-derived neurotrophic factor is associated with agerelated decline in hippocampal volume. *J Neurosci* 30:5368–5375.

23. Kramer A.F., et al. (1999) Ageing, fitness and neurocognitive function. *Nature* 400: 418–419.

24. Colcombe S.J., Kramer A.F. (2003) Fitness effects on the cognitive function of older adults: A meta-analytic study. *Psychol Sci* 14:125–130.

25. Smith P.J., et al. (2010) Aerobic exercise and neurocognitive performance: A metaanalytic review of randomized controlled trials. *Psychosom Med* 72:239–252.

26. Rasmussen P., et al. (2009) Evidence for a release of brain-derived neurotrophic factor from the brain during exercise. *Exp Physiol* 94:1062–1069.

27. Zoladz J.A., et al. (2008) Endurance training increases plasma brain-derived neurotrophic factor concentration in young healthy men. *J Physiol Pharmacol* 59 (Suppl 7):119–132.

28. Lee R., Kermani P., Teng K.K., Hempstead B.L. (2001) Regulation of cell survival by secreted proneurotrophins. *Science* 294:1945–1948.

29. Pencea V., Bingaman K.D., Wiegand S.J., Luskin M.B. (2001) Infusion of brain-derived neurotrophic factor into the lateral ventricle of the adult rat leads to new neurons in the parenchyma of the striatum, septum, thalamus, and hypothalamus. *J Neurosci* 21: 6706–6717.

30. Figurov A., Pozzo-Miller L.D., Olafsson P., Wang T., Lu B. (1996) Regulation of synaptic responses to high-frequency stimulation and LTP by neurotrophins in the hippocampus. *Nature* 381:706–709.

31. Kang H., Schuman E.M. (1996) A requirement for local protein synthesis in neurotrophin-induced hippocampal synaptic plasticity. *Science* 273:1402–1406.

32. Pang P.T., et al. (2004) Cleavage of proBDNF by tPA/plasmin is essential for long-term hippocampal plasticity. *Science* 306:487–491.

33. Black J.E., Isaacs K.R., Anderson B.J., Alcantara A.A., Greenough W.T. (1990) Learning causes synaptogenesis, whereas motor activity causes angiogenesis, in cerebellar cortex of adult rats. *Proc Natl Acad Sci USA* 87:5568–5572.

34. Redila V.A., Christie B.R. (2006) Exercise-induced changes in dendritic structure and complexity in the adult hippocampal dentate gyrus. *Neuroscience* 137:1299–1307.

35. Oldfield R.C. (1971) The assessment and analysis of handedness: The Edinburgh inventory. *Neuropsychologia* 9:97–113.

36. Stern Y., et al. (1987) Modified mini-mental state examination: Validity and reliability. *Neurology* 37:179.

37. Sheikh J.I., Yesavage J.A. (1986) Geriatric Depression Scale (GDS): Recent evidence and development of a shorter version. *Clinical Gerontology: A Guide to Assessment and Intervention.* (Haworth Press, New York), pp 165–173.

38. Patenaude B., et al. (2007) *Bayesian Shape and Appearance Models. Technical Report TR07BP1* (FMRIB Centre, Univ Oxford, UK).

39. Zhang Y., Brady M., Smith S. (2001) Segmentation of brain MR images through a hidden Markov random field model and the expectation-maximization algorithm. *IEEE Trans Med Imaging* 20:45–57.

40. Smith S.M., et al. (2004) Advances in functional and structural MR image analysis and implementation as FSL. *Neuroimage* 23 (Suppl 1):S208.

41. Strath S.J., et al. (2000) Evaluation of heart rate as a method for assessing moderate intensity physical activity. *Med Sci Sports Exerc* 32 (9 Suppl):S465–S470.

42. Borg G. (1985) An Introduction to Borg's RPE-Scale (Mouvement, Ithaca, NY). 43. Heo S, et al. (2010) Resting hippocampal blood flow, spatial memory and aging. *Brain Res* 1315:119–127.

43. Heo S., et al. (2010) Resting hippocampal blood flow, spatial memory and aging. *Brain Res* 1315: 119–127.

PRACTICAL APPLICATION ASSIGNMENTS

1. When she can't remember where cereal is located in her favorite grocery store, imagine that an older adult says to you, "I can't help it; older people just can't remember things." After reading the research presented in this chapter, how might you respond to that statement? Is memory loss, particularly spatial memory loss, an inevitable aspect of aging? Write a persuasive letter to an older adult who might hold this belief, explaining the concept of brain plasticity and why spatial memory decline may not be inevitable.

2. As your first job after college, you are hired to design and coordinate activities for the residents of a local nursing home. Your supervisor has asked you to plan a six-month schedule of events for the residents, and her only directive to you is "to include some type of physical exercise for the residents" in your schedule. You know that many of the residents suffer from memory deficits, and you would like to plan some physical activities that might help them improve their memory. According to the research presented in this article, not all types of physical exercise increase the volume of the hippocampus or are associated with improved memory. Plan a six-month calendar of activities to present to your supervisor, including a variety of activities intended to help improve residents' memory. List these activities, and include a brief explanation of why you chose the ones you did and any other reasoning that you used to formulate your plan.

3. As a volunteer at a local community center for older adults, you often observe a group of adults walking in laps around the center or practicing tai chi. You wonder if these sorts of activities are beneficial for improving memory. Based on the research presented in this chapter, do you believe these activities are beneficial for improving memory in these adults? Why or why not? Can you make some specific predictions about what types of memory may benefit from these activities?

Chapter 6

Industrial and Organizational Psychology: Is It Possible to Improve Job Satisfaction and Productivity?

Cognitive-Behavioural Training to Change Attributional Style

Improves Employee Well-Being, Job Satisfaction, Productivity, and Turnover

By Judith G. Proudfoot, Philip J. Corr, David E. Guest, and Graham Dunn

EDITORS' INTRODUCTION

Jessica owns one of the nation's biggest insurance companies, which employs thousands of people. Each year, she replaces 30 percent of the workforce because people keep quitting. As you can imagine, employee turnover is a huge problem for the company, as it is time-consuming and expensive to recruit, hire, and train new employees. Jack works for a government organization that provides services to older adults. Recently, Jack lost interest in his job, failed to show up for work for several days, and was experiencing high levels of work stress. He became so hopeless that he eventually quit his job. As a result, he is now experiencing financial problems and is struggling to find a new job.

Can psychological science help improve productivity? Fortunately, the answer is "yes". The field of Industrial and Organizational (I-O) Psychology is the scientific study of workplace behavior. I-O psychologists empirically investigate a variety of topics ranging from job satisfaction to productivity. (For more information about I-O Psychology, visit http://www.siop.org/) For example, I-O psychologists apply psychological science to help employers select employees best suited for particular jobs, which will lead to improved job satisfaction (Lauver & Kristof-Brown, 2001), increased psychological well-being of the employees in the workplace (Vartia, 2001), and improved supervisor-employee relationships (Gilbreath & Benson, 2004).

The article in this chapter investigates the effectiveness of psychological training (a modified form of cognitive-behavioral therapy) on employee well-being and productivity. For this purpose, the researchers randomly assigned workers in a large insurance company to a treatment or wait-list group. After assessing participants' well-being before the intervention, Proudfoot and her colleagues (2009) implemented a 21-hour training program. They assessed the effectiveness of their intervention right after the training and three months later by comparing the participants in the treatment group to those in the wait-list group. After the three-month follow-up assessment, the researchers provided the same training to participants in the wait-list group. Using this design helped the authors to further examine the effectiveness of their training. The authors relied on effect sizes to infer whether or not the changes in overall well-being and productivity observed before and after the intervention were meaningful.

Thinking back to Chapter 1, can you correctly identify the dependent and independent variables in the study? How many times did the researchers assess psychological outcomes in the initial training and wait-list control groups? Also, can you identify when those individuals in the wait-list control group received the seven-week intervention? Finally, by looking at Table 3, can you identify two variables with the two strongest intervention effects? What do these effects suggest?

REFERENCES

Gilbreath, B., & Benson, P. G. (2004). The contribution of supervisor behaviour to employee psychological well-being. *Work and Stress, 18* (3), 255–266.

Lauver, K. J., & Kristof-Brown, A. (2001). Distinguishing between employees' perceptions of person-job and person-organization fit. *Journal of Vocational Behavior, 59* (3), 454–470.

Proudfoot, J. G., Philip J. Corr, P.J., David E. Guest, D. E., and Graham Dunn, G. (2009). Cognitive-behavioural training to change attributional style improves employee well-being, job satisfaction, productivity, and turnover. *Personality and Individual Differences, 46* (2), 147–153.

Vartia M. A. (2001). Consequences of workplace bullying with respect to the well-being of its targets and the observers of bullying. *Scandinavian Journal of Work, Environment, and Health*, 27 (1), 63–69.

ABSTRACT

We report, for the first time in the literature, a cognitive-behavioural training waiting-list controlled study that changed employees' attributional style, reduced turnover, increased productivity, and improved a number of individual differences measures of well-being. One hundred and sixty-six financial services sales agents (98% male, mean age 36.2 ± 9 years) were randomly assigned to either (a) a seven-week cognitive-behavioural training program or (b) a waiting-list.

Significant improvements resulted in employees' attributional style, job satisfaction, self-esteem, psychological well-being and general productivity. A significant reduction in employee turnover over a 4.5 month period was observed. The waiting-list control group replicated these results when they subsequently went through the same program. These findings demonstrate that work-related attitudes and behaviours, especially in motivationally challenging occupations, can be changed with cognitive-behavioural training to improve attributional style. The study is also valuable for personality and individual differences research because it shows how psychological variables can be changed by effective intervention in applied settings.

INTRODUCTION

Factors affecting workplace well-being are a concern for organizations and national economies.

An intervention based on sound psychological principles and shown to improve employee well-being and productivity would be of considerable value. Here we report, for the first time in the literature, a cognitive-behavioural training waiting-list controlled study which reduced employee turnover, increased productivity, and improved a number of individual differences measures of well-being. This study is important for personality and individual differences research because it demonstrates the impact of effective interventions in applied settings and fulfills Cronbach's (1957) and Eysenck's (1997) call for a unification of experimental and individual differences research approaches (see Corr, 2007).

Employee turnover is a significant problem for many organizations. In the UK financial services industry, turnover among sales people has exceeded 40% annually with similar figures reported in the USA. High turnover rates also occur in commercial, governmental and military sectors, especially those where change is prevalent. Quitting has financial and psychological consequences for those who leave and, for those who remain there is often additional work pressure and unsettled work practices. The cost of replacing sales staff (recruitment, training, and business lost) is high, yet very few organizations have systematic policies and procedures to control turnover. One reason is the shortage of empirically-validated strategies. Generally, research has focused on constructing and testing theoretical models of the turnover process involving employee attributes such as commitment, job satisfaction, tenure and job withdrawal cognitions (Hom, Robertson, & Ellis, 2008; Huang, Lawler, & Lei, 2007). The few documented attempts to reduce employee turnover have focused on selection procedures (Phillips, 1998), work re-design (Glassop, 2002) or large-scale organizational interventions (Glisson, Dukes, & Green, 2006). Training programs have been scarce and of limited effect (Pazy, Ganzach, & Davidov, 2006; Waung, 1995).

In this paper, we report the impact on employee well-being, job satisfaction, productivity and turn-over of a training program based on principles of cognitive-behavioural therapy (CBT). The program was designed to help employees evaluate and, where indicated, change their work-related thoughts, attitudes and behaviours, and specifically to assess the accuracy and functionality of attributions they made for work-related events.

Attributional style is the characteristic way people attribute causes to events, particularly successes and failures. When negative events are consistently attributed to internal, stable and global factors, and positive events to external, temporary and specific causes, even in the face of contrary evidence (a "pessimistic attributional style"), hopelessness and giving up tends to result when failure, stress, rejection and other negative events are encountered (Abramson, Seligman, & Teasdale 1978; Alloy, Abramson, Metalsky, & Hartlage, 1988). The workplace equivalent of hopelessness and giving up is presenteeism, absenteeism, withdrawal cognitions and actual quitting. A study of 103 newly-appointed insurance sales agents demonstrated that those with an optimistic attributional style remained in their job at twice the rate and sold more insurance than those with a pessimistic attributional style (Seligman & Schulman, 1986). Optimistic attributional style correlates significantly with job satisfaction and performance (Corr & Gray, 1995, 1996). Yet, to our knowledge, there have been no organizational interventions to help employees evaluate the veridicality and functionality of the attributions they make for work-related events.

CBT modifies attributional style (Seligman et al., 1988), and is efficacious in the treatment of a variety of psychological disorders (Leahy, 2004), but its application to work-related issues has been limited. Proudfoot, Guest, Carson, Dunn and Gray (1997) demonstrated that a cognitive-behavioural intervention was associated with significant gains in well-being and job-finding among long-term unemployed people, and Ruwaard, Lange, Bouwman, Broek-steeg, and Schrieken (2007) showed that a cognitive-behavioural program conducted via email brought about improvements in employees' anxiety and stress. However, there have not been any direct attempts to apply cognitive-behavioural techniques to work variables.

In this study, we hypothesized that a training program based on CBT principles and aimed at changing employees' work-related attributional style, would improve work self-esteem, job satisfaction, psychological well-being, productivity and turnover.

We evaluated the program in a high-turnover occupation: Insurance selling.

METHODS

The training program

The program consisted of seven weekly sessions, 3 h per week (Table 1), a 6-week maintenance program at work, and a review session 3 months after the conclusion of the training. The program was written to conform to the average length of CBT, and consistent with adult learning procedures, it was conducted over a number of sessions to allow the skills to be practised at work between the sessions and consolidated. The program was designed on the CBT manual (Beck, Rush, Shaw, & Emery, 1979) and organizational training principles. It was inspired by a one-day course written by Martin Seligman and his colleagues, which they made available to us for pilot studies, and which was substantially modified and extended by the first author to form the 13-week (7 weeks training, 6 weeks maintenance) program.

Design

A waiting-list control group design was employed. Participants randomly allocated to the waiting-listed group received the attributional training program after the completion of 3-month follow-up (Fig. 1). Ethics approval for the study was granted by the Institute of Psychiatry Human Ethics Committee, and participants gave informed written consent.

Table 1 Schedule of attributional training program

Length	21 h
Structure	7 × 3-h sessions, one per week
	Assignments between sessions to promote experimentation with, and application of, strategies
Session content	
1	Introduction to cognitive model
2	Automatic thoughts, goal-setting, time management, task breakdown
3	Thought recording, thinking errors, activity scheduling
4	Changing unhelpful thinking
5	Accessing deeper beliefs, attributions
6	Attributional dimensions
7	Integration of strategies, action planning, relapse prevention
Training techniques	Socratic questioning, group discussions, self-observation, experimentation, individual and syndicate activities, assignments
Session format	Review of previous session
	Debrief assignments
	Introduce session topic(s)
	Individual and syndicate activities
	Feedback, discussion, reflection
	Outline weekly assignment
	Session summary
	Survey delegates' response to the session

Participants

Participants were recruited from a major British insurance company which had recently been acquired by a competitive, results-oriented organisation. Large-scale changes had been imposed and substantial numbers of employees were quitting. Sales agents from four Divisions in South-East England were invited to attend the program, particularly those deemed by their managers or themselves to be experiencing stress in their jobs.

Power calculations, based on independent *t*-tests of pre-post change scores between groups in a previous study (Proudfoot, 1996), showed that to detect a difference of 0.5 standard deviation at 80% power and with a 0.05 α, 64 participants were needed in each condition.

One hundred and sixty-six employees took part in the study. They were randomly assigned to the "initial" training group ($n = 81$, mean age 36.2 ±9 years, 98% male, mean years in job 6.6 ±6.7), or to the waiting-listed control group ($n = 81$, mean age 36.2 ± 9 years, 98% male, mean years in job 6.6 ± 6.7). Seventy one percent reported experiencing work-related stress in the three months prior to the study and performing poorly (that is, not reaching their sales or earnings targets).

Twelve courses were conducted: Six for the 81 sales agents randomly allocated to the initial courses, and six courses, 5 months later, for the remaining 75 in the waiting-listed group. (By the time the courses commenced for the waiting-list control group, the initial sample of 85 was reduced to 75.)

Outcomes

Psychological outcomes

Participants completed psychological questionnaires prior to their course, at its end, 3 months later to test for maintenance of effect and to provide a baseline for the waiting-list control courses (post-test 2); and at the end of the second series of courses (posttest 3) (see Fig. 1). The following measures were used.

Attributional style. The financial services attributional style questionnaire (FSASQ; Proudfoot, Corr, Guest, & Gray, 2001) is a domain-specific version of the attributional style questionnaire (ASQ; Peterson et al., 1982), which provides eight positive and eight negative hypothetical situations for which the respondent supplies causes and then rates each cause along dimensions of locus, permanence and pervasiveness. Scores range from 0 to 21, with a strong attributional style indicated by a high composite score for the positive events (CoPos) and low composite score for the negative events (CoNeg), respectively. The scale displays good internal reliability (α = 0.89 for CoPos and α = 0.91 for CoNeg), and good convergent validity with the attributional style questionnaire ($rs > 0.70$).

Psychological distress. The general health questionnaire 30 (GHQ-30; Goldberg, 1972) has been used extensively in the detection of non-psychiatric distress. Scores range 0–30, with high scores indicating a greater degree of psychological distress. A score of 5 or above indicates the incidence of acute or episodic distress warranting attention. The scale has been widely validated (Goldberg, 1978) and used in occupational studies (Wall & Clegg, 1981). The alpha coefficient in the present study was 0.93.

Job satisfaction. The overall job satisfaction scale (Warr, Cook, & Wall, 1979) is a 15-item measure in which respondents indicate on a seven-point scale their satisfaction with intrinsic and extrinsic features of their job. An unweighted total ranging from 15 to 105 is computed, with higher scores indicating higher job satisfaction. The scale has been used in a range of occupational settings and its alpha coefficient in this study was 0.85.

Self-esteem. The professional self-esteem scale (adapted from Beehr, 1976) is a three item scale designed to measure self-esteem in job-related contexts. The items are bipolar adjectival descriptors (successful—not successful; important—not important; doing my best—not doing my best) on a seven-point continuum. In this study, the scale was extended to include a further three items: (a) capable—not capable, (b) effective—not effective, and (c) confident—not confident. A post-hoc analysis of the six-item scale indicated that it possessed good internal consistency (α = 0.90).

Job withdrawal cognitions. The intention to quit scale (Guest, Peccei, & Thomas, 1993) consists of three items answered on a seven-point scale ranging from "strongly agree" to "strongly disagree", yielding a scale range of 3–21. The items have good internal consistency (α = 0.72) and that they cluster into one factor (Guest et al., 1993). The internal consistency of the scale in this study was acceptable ($\alpha = 0.68$).

Organisational outcomes

"Bottom-line" financial results were measured primarily by resignations from the company and by sales productivity. Resignations were monitored throughout the 8 months of the study and for a further 10 months, both for the two study groups and for a large group of non-participating employees ($n = 932$) from the same four company divisions, performing the same job and matched for length of service. Aggregated data were also provided by the company on participants' sales productivity, compared with other employees from the same four divisions, for 2 years after the program.

Analyses

Analysis of covariance (using the *regress* command of *Stata* release 10—StataCorp, 2008) was used to test for differences between the two study groups on each psychological variable (with separate analyses at each follow-up time). Covariates included division membership (four levels) and the corresponding baseline measure of the variable. Comparison of the pre- and post-training psychological data for the waiting-list control group was undertaken by *t*-tests (see Table 2). Resignation data were analyzed by χ^2 tests and survival analysis.

Mediational analyses were carried out using the procedure advocated by Baron and Kenny (1986)

again using Stata's regress command, with division, baseline measure of the putative mediator and the baseline measure of the relevant outcome measure being included as covariates at all three stages of the analyses. The stages were: (1) demonstrate an effect of the intervention on the outcome, (2) demonstrate an effect of the intervention on the proposed mediator, and (3) investigate the joint effects of intervention and proposed mediator on outcome. The purpose of stage 3 is to demonstrate a reduction in the size of the effect of the intervention after controlling for the mediator, and to demonstrate that there is an influence on the mediator on outcome after controlling for the initial intervention (i.e. there is evidence of a mediated effect). Stages 1 and 2 both investigate the effect of a randomized intervention and are therefore not subject to possible confounding. The estimates arising in stage 3, however, may be invalid. They are only valid if it is correctly assumed that there is not hidden confounding between the mediator and the outcome (highly unlikely). Statisticians have recently developed methods to overcome this problem (see Albert, 2008; Dunn, 2007; TenHave et al., 2007).

However, they are based on the validity of other assumptions: That there are group by covariate interactions in the model predicting the proposed mediator, but not in the effect of mediator on outcome or in the direct effect of intervention on the outcome (i.e. homogenous treatment effects). Here we use the methods described by Dunn (2007) and by Albert (2008) and refer to the method of analysis

'Initial' Group

T1_____T2...T3

7-week program   3-month follow-up

'Waiting-list' Group

T1.................T2..T3_____T4

7-week program

Fig. 1. *Research design, showing 'initial' training group sessions, 3 months interval, training courses for waiting-list group (five months later) and measurement points: T1 = before training; T2 = after training; T3 = 3 month follow-up (also baseline for waiting-list group); and T4 = after training for waiting-list group. Solid lines = training period.*

Table 2 Means and standard deviations for initial training group and waiting-list control group

Training conditions (M; SD)	Initial training group			Waiting-list control group			
	T1	T2	T3	T1	T2	T3	T4
CoPos	16.51; 2.0	17.95; 1.89	18.01; 2.02	16.52; 1.8	16.33; 2.29	16.54; 2.04	17.85; 1.99
CoNeg	14.73; 2.44	12.76; 3.07	12.98; 3.01	14.63; 2.37	14.91; 2.53	14.96; 92.39	13.05; 3.01
Self-esteem	3.85; 0.88	4.45; 0.85	4.46; 0.94	3.97; 0.85	3.94; 0.84	3.86; 0.75	4.47; 0.76
Job satisfaction	74.1; 11.57	77.12; 11.36	79.21; 11.65	72.32; 12.33	71.67; 13.19	73.36; 13.42	76.94; 11.56
Intention to quit	10.75; 3.89	9.01; 3.95	9.05; 4.05	10.73; 4.1	10.79; 4.19	10.39; 4.33	8.96; 3.63
Psychological distress	8.1; 7.67	2.64; 5.13	2.88; 6.57	7.09; 6.79	6.12; 7.20	4.37; 5.86	1.18; 1.29

Both groups completed psychological measures on three occasions: T1 before the first series of courses; T2 at the end of the first series; and T3 at the 3 month follow-up (which also provided a baseline for the waiting-list-control training). The waiting-list control group also completed measures after their training program (T4).

as an "extended instrumental variable regression:" the instrumental variables being the above covariate by intervention interactions. We use Stata's ivreg command.

RESULTS

Psychological outcomes

Table 2 shows summary statistics for psychological measures administered before and after the intervention. There was a consistent improvement in all psychological variables-attributional style, self-esteem, job satisfaction, intention to quit and psychological distress at the end of the first series of programs that was not seen in the waiting-list controls at that time. Furthermore, the improvements persisted: By the 3-month follow-up, there were still significant differences between the "initial" trained group and the "waiting-list" group on all the psychological variables. Results of the formal analyses of covariance for the various outcomes are provided in Table 3. Note that all of the intervention effects are statistically-significant and effect sizes are large. The same improvements occurred in the "waiting-list" group after their training (Fig. 2).

Notably, on the GHQ-30, there was a decline in the percentage of scores > 5 (indicative of psychological distress requiring attention), after training in both cohorts (χ^2 = 26.2, 10.72, respectively, df = 1, p < 0.01). Initially, 37% of the total sample experienced levels of psychological distress that were above this cut-off, which reduced to 10% after training. Further, there was statistically and occupationally significant change in participants' intention to quit from "probably" to "probably not."

Organizational outcomes

Employee turnover

Data were consistent with the indices of psychological improvement. There were three times as many resignations in the "waiting-list" group (10/85; 12%) as in the "initial" trained group (3/81; 4%) during the 4.5 months from the commencement of the first series of programs to the three-month follow-up point (χ^2 = 3.73, df = 1, p = 0.05). A similar reduction in turnover took place when the waiting-listed group underwent their training: By the end of the seven-week program, quitting was 1.3%. The equivalent figure in the "initial" group (i.e. at the end of their 7-week course) was 2.5%. As the rates did not differ (χ^2 < 1), the data from the two groups were combined and compared with the large cohort of non-participating controls (n

Table 3 Formal estimates of the impact of CBT on various outcomes

Variable	ITT/total effect (se) (difference in means)	95% Confidence interval	p-Value
Copos T2	+1.64(0.31)	+1.03 to +2.25	<0.001
Copos T3	+1.46(0.33)	+0.82 to +2.11	<0.001
Coneg T2	-2.10(0.45)	-0.65 to -0.28	<0.001
Coneg T3	-2.18(0.47)	-3.11 to -1.24	<0.001
Job satisfaction T2	+3.69(1.28)	+1.16 to +6.22	0.005
Job satisfaction T3	+4.52(1.64)	+1.27 to + 7.77	0.007
Intention to quit T2	-1.87(0.50)	-2.85 to -0.88	<0.001
Intention to quit T3	-1.16(0.57)	-2.28 to -0.04	0.043
Self-esteem T2	+1.45(0.49)	+0.48 to +2.43	0.004
Self-esteem T3	+0.74(0.12)	+0.50 to +0.99	<0.001
Psychological distress T2	-4.03(0.91)	-5.83 to -2.23	<0.001
Psychological distress T3	-2.21(1.02)	-4.22 to -0.20 .	0.031

= 932), revealing a significant reduction in turnover during the 8 months in which the training program took place: Non-participating controls 103/932 (11%), trained employees 7/156 (4%); $\chi^2 = 6.34$, df = 1, $p < 0.02$. There was no further change for the 10 months of follow-up, the rates of decline reverting to parallel, as verified by survival analysis (Wilcoxon statistic = 0.11 and 0.14, respectively, $p = 0.74$ and 0.71) (Fig. 3).

Productivity

Only aggregated annual sales figures were available from the company. In the 2 years post-training, 50% of the two trained groups had achieved sales figures that were above the average for their division, with a further 15% performing within 5% of the average.

Exploration of the role of attributional style as a mediator of the intervention effects on outcomes

Using the Baron and Kenny procedure, we see from Table 4(a) that there appears to be a mediating effect of Copos on job satisfaction. The estimated direct effect of the intervention is considerably smaller than the total effect (mediation is explaining about half of the total effect), consistent with the statistically-significant effect of the mediator on the outcome (note that the total effects differ slightly from those in Table 3, arising from the inclusion of an extra covariate, baseline value of the mediator). The use of the extended instrumental variable regression, however, suggests that this may not be a safe finding—see top rows of Table 2(b). It is possible that the apparent mediation found in the Baron and Kenny analysis is an artifact created by hidden confounding. Unfortunately, the instrumental variable regression results are very imprecise (a price we pay for

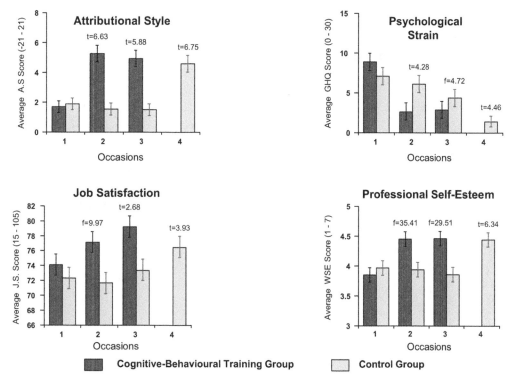

Fig. 2. *Comparison of 'initial' group with 'waiting-list' group: 1 = before 'initial' courses; 2 = after 'initial' courses; 3 = 3-month follow-up (also baseline for the 'waiting-list' group); and 4 = after training of 'waiting-list' group. Bars show standard errors of the mean calculated separately for each group on each occasion.*

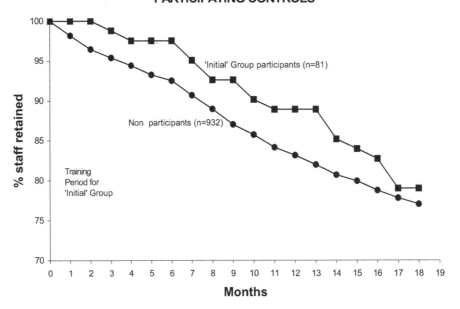

COMPARISON OF 'INITIAL' TRAINED GROUP WITH NON-PARTICIPATING CONTROLS

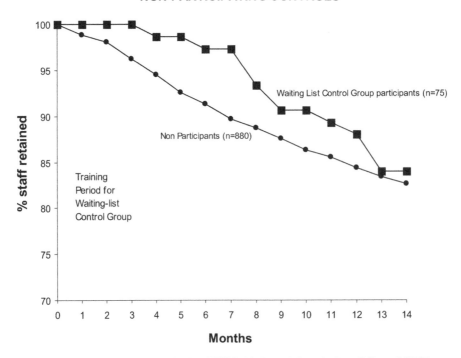

COMPARISON OF WAITING-LIST CONTROL GROUP WITH NON-PARTICIPATING CONTROLS

Fig. 3. *Staff retention analysis: CBT 'initial' participants (n = 81) and CBT 'waiting-list' participants (n = 75), each compared with non-participating employees (n = 932) in terms of percentage of staff retained throughout the period of the courses and for a further 10 months.*

Table 4 Estimates (and standard errors) of the total, direct and mediated effects of the intervention on job-related outcomes

Outcome variable	Putative mediator	Total effect[a] difference in means	Direct effect difference in means	Effect of mediator on outcome regression coefficient
(a) Standard regression/ANCOVA				
Job satisfaction T2	Copos T2	+3.89(1.37)	+2.39(1.48)	-0.79(0.38)
Job satisfaction T3	Copos T3	+4.60(1.74)	+2.45(1.81)	-1.88(0.48)
Intention to quit T2	Copos T2	-1.50(0.49)	-1.39(0.56)	+0.09(0.52)
Intention to quit T3	Copos T3	-1.28(0.60)	-0.91(0.64)	+0.39(0.17)
Self-esteem T2	Copos T2	+0.59(0.11)	+0.58(0.12)	-0.004(0.031)
Self-esteem T3	Copos T3	+0.53(0.14)	+0.53(0.14)	-0.15(0.03)
Psychological distress T2	Copos T2	-3.65(0.96)	-3.32(1.07)	+0.27(0.27)
Psychological distress T3	Copos T3	-2.49(1.07)	-2.47(1.16)	+0.38(0.29)
(b) Extended instrumental variable regression				
Job satisfaction T2	Copos T2	+3.89(1.37)	+4.43(2.54)	+0.54(1.38)
Job satisfaction T3	Copos T3	+4.60(1.74)	+3.01(3.17)	-1.48(1.93)
Intention to quit T2	Copos T2	-1.50(0.49)	-2.23(1.11)	-0.41(0.59)
Intention to quit T3	Copos T3	-1.28(0.60)	-1.97(1.15)	-0.33(0.65)
Self-esteem T2	Copos T2	+0.59(0.11)	+1.00(0.27)	+0.25(0.14)
Self-esteem T3	Copos T3	+0.53(0.14)	+0.93(0.25)	+0.13(0.14)
Psychological distress T2	Copos T2	-3.65(0.96)	-6.20(2.37)	-1.48(1.27)
Psychological distress T3	Copos T3	-2.49(1.07)	-3.51(2.20)	-0.68(1.25)

[a] From the standard regressions.

acknowledging that there may be hidden confounding) but provide no support for the conclusion that the direct effect is any smaller than the total effect of the intervention. The rest of Table 2 suggests that there is no convincing evidence of the mediating role of Copos. A similar series of analyses using Coneg as the putative mediator (not shown) also failed to reveal any evidence of mediation.

DISCUSSION

Significant improvements in employees' attributional style, psychological distress, self-esteem, job satisfaction and intention to quit resulted from the cognitive-behavioural training program. The improvements persisted to the 3-month follow-up point (the longest follow-up period possible due to organizational constraints), thereby indicating that the effect of the cognitive-behavioural training transferred to the day-to-day work of the employees and was maintained after the end of training. Symptoms of psychological stress warranting intervention reduced from 37% of the sample to 10% after training. Typically, 20% of employed samples are above the cut-off of psychological distress (Warr, 1984)—our results compare well therefore, considering the organization was undergoing a large-scale change, which many employees found distressing.

The psychological changes were accompanied by a 66% reduction in employee turnover, relative to the waiting-listed control group (4% vs. 12%, respectively). Further, our results indicated that the training program acted to prevent, not merely delay, resignations in employees many of whom, pre-training, were low performers and therefore likely to have a higher than average resignation rate. In the period following training, rates of resignation reverted to average. Such improvements in employee turnover represent a large saving for organizations in the cost of replacing staff, as well as minimizing disruption.

Participants' productivity also improved. Two years post-training, 65% of the sample achieved sales figures that were above the average or within 5% of the average for their division. Considering that before training, only 29% of the participants were deemed to be performing at an acceptable standard (that is,

reaching their sales or earnings targets), this result suggests that the cognitive-behavioural program had a positive impact on sales agents' productivity in addition to their job retention.

With regard to mediation, it is not possible to demonstrate that a variable B is a mediator of the effects of A on C. All we can do is see whether the data appear to be consistent with the hypothesis and to try to get valid estimates of the causal effects. One problem is that we cannot demonstrate that attributions changed earlier than the main outcomes. Although there is an effect of CBT on attribution and on the other psychological outcomes, there is no convincing evidence that attributions acted as mediators. Further research, therefore, is needed to isolate the mechanism(s) through which cognitive-behavioural interventions operate.

Nevertheless, our results fit with reviews demonstrating the link between occupational stress, well-being and performance, including withdrawal behaviours (Cotton & Hart, 2003). To our knowledge, our study is the first empirical evaluation of the effects of cognitive-behavioural training on organizational outcomes. Whilst cognitive-behavioural principles are now universally accepted in clinical contexts, this study demonstrates that the core principles and processes are translatable to non-clinical contexts, with measurable and organizationally significant benefits.

The follow-up period, which was restricted to 3 months for organizational reasons, is a major limitation of our study. Similarly, the fact that our sample was 98% male limits the generalisability of findings. Our results need to be replicated on different occupational samples, across a wide range of companies/industries. Nonetheless, our results show that the application of cognitive-behavioural training has important organizational outcomes; the process by which these outcomes is achieved remains for future research to delineate.

ACKNOWLEDGMENTS

We thank Legal & General Assurance Co., Ltd., for financial support (particularly generous as the research was not conducted in their organization) and the UK Economic and Social Research Council (ESRC). We also thank Prof. Martin Seligman and Foresight Inc., for laying the foundation for this research with their program Optimism ABC; Dr. Melanie Marks for help in developing our training program; Dr. Pat Shipley for advice; and A/Prof. Jane Goodman-Delahunty for comments on the manuscript.

This paper is dedicated to Professor Jeffrey Gray, our mentor colleague and collaborator on this study.

REFERENCES

Abramson, L.Y., Seligman, M.E.P., & Teasdale, J.D. (1978). Learned helplessness in humans: Critique and reformulation. *Journal of Abnormal Psychology*, 87, 49–74.

Albert, J.M. (2008). Mediation analysis via potential outcomes models. *Statistics in Medicine*, 27, 1282–1304.

Alloy, L.B., Abramson, L.Y., Metalsky, G.I., & Hartlage, S. (1988). The hopelessness theory of depression: Attributional aspects. *British Journal of Clinical Psychology*, 27, 5–21.

Baron, R.M., & Kenny, D.A. (1986). The moderator-mediator variable distinction in social psychological research: Conceptual, strategic, and statistical considerations. *Journal of Personality and Social Psychology*, 51, 1173–1182.

Beck, A.T., Rush, A.J., Shaw, B.F., & Emery, G. (1979). *Cognitive therapy of depression*. New York: The Guilford Press.

Beehr, T.A. (1976). Perceived situational moderators of the relationship between subjective role ambiguity and role strain. *Journal of Applied Psychology*, 61, 35–40.

Corr, P.J. (2007). Personality and psychology: Hans Eysenck's unifying themes. *The Psychologist*, 20, 666–669.

Corr, P.J., & Gray, J.A. (1995). Attributional style, socialisation and cognitive ability as predictors of sales success. *Personality and Individual Differences*, 18, 241–252.

Corr, P.J., & Gray, J.A. (1996). Attributional style as a personality factor in insurance sales performance in the UK. *Journal of Occupational and Organisational Psychology*, 69, 83–87.

Cotton, P., & Hart, P.M. (2003). Occupational well-being and performance: A review of organisational health research. *Australian Psychologist*, 38, 118–127.

Cronbach, L. (1957). The two disciplines of scientific psychology. *American Psychologist*, 12(11), 671–684.

Dunn, G., & Bentall, R. (2007). Modelling treatment effect heterogeneity in randomised controlled trials of complex interventions (psychological treatments). *Statistics in Medicine*, 26, 4709–4745.

Eysenck, H.J. (1997). Personality and experimental psychology: The unification of psychology and the possibility of a paradigm. *Journal of Personality and Social Psychology*, 73, 1224–1237.

Glassop, L. (2002). The organisational benefit of teams. *Human Relations*, 55, 225–249.

Glisson, C., Dukes, D., & Green, P. (2006). The effects of the ARC organizational intervention on caseworker turnover, climate, and culture in children's service systems. *Child Abuse and Neglect*, 30, 855–880.

Goldberg, D. (1972). The detection of psychiatric illness by questionnaire. *Maudsley Monograph* No. 21. London: Oxford University Press.

Goldberg, D. (1978). *Manual of the general health questionnaire*. Windsor: NFER Nelson.

Guest, D., Peccei, R., & Thomas, A. (1993). The impact of employee involvement on organisational commitment and "them and us" attitudes. *Industrial Relations Journal*, 24, 191–200.

Hom, P.W., Robertson, L., & Ellis, A. (2008). Challenging convention wisdom about who quits: Revelations from corporate America. *Journal of Applied Psychology*, 93(1), 1–34.

Huang, T., Lawler, J., & Lei, C.Y. (2007). The effects of quality of work life on commitment and turnover intention. *Social Behavior and Personality*, 35, 735–750.

Leahy, R.L. (2004). *Contemporary cognitive therapy: Theory, research and practice*. New York: Guildford Press.

Pazy, A., Ganzach, Y., & Davidov, Y. (2006). Decision-making training for occupational choice and early turnover: A field experiment. *Career Development International*, 11(1), 80–91.

Peterson, C., Semmel, A., Von Baeyer, C., Abramson, L.Y., Metalsky, G.I., & Seligman, M.E.P. (1982). The attributional style questionnaire. *Cognitive Therapy and Research*, 6, 287–300.

Phillips, J.M. (1998). Effects of realistic job previews on multiple organisational outcomes: A meta-analysis. *Academy of Management Journal*, 41, 673–690.

Proudfoot, J. (1996). The application of attributional training and cognitive therapy to occupational settings. Ph.D. Thesis. London: University of London.

Proudfoot, J.G., Corr, P.J., Guest, D.E., & Gray, J.A. (2001). The development and evaluation of a scale to measure occupational attributional style in the financial services sector. *Personality and Individual Differences*, 30, 259–270.

Proudfoot, J., Guest, G., Carson, J., Dunn, G., & Gray, J. (1997). Cognitive-behavioural training increases job-finding among long-term unemployed. *The Lancet*, 350, 96–100.

Ruwaard, J., Lange, A., Bouwman, M., Broeksteeg, J., & Schrieken, B. (2007). Emailed standardised cognitive-behavioural treatment of work-related stress: A randomised controlled trial. *Cognitive Behaviour Therapy*, 36, 179–192.

Seligman, M.E.P., Castellon, C., Cacciola, J., Schulman, P., Luborsky, L., Ollove, M., & Downing, R. (1988). Explanatory style change during cognitive therapy for unipolar depression. *Journal of Abnormal Psychology*, 97, 13–18.

Seligman, P., & Schulman, P. (1986). Explanatory style as a predictor of productivity and quitting among life insurance sales agents. *Journal of Personality and Social Psychology*, 50, 832–838.

StataCorp. *Stata Release 10*, 2008. College Station, Texas.

TenHave, T.R., Joffe, M.M., Lynch, K.G., Brown, G.K., Maisto, S.A., & Beck, A.T. (2007). Causal mediation analysis with rank preserving models. *Biometrics*, 63, 926–934.

Wall, T.D., & Clegg, C.W. (1981). Individual strain and organizational functioning. *British Journal of Clinical Psychology*, 20, 135–136.

Warr, P.B. (1984). Job loss, unemployment and psychological well-being. In E. VandeVliert & V. Allen (Eds.), *Role transition* (pp. 263–285). New York: Plenum.

Warr, P., Cook, J., & Wall, T. (1979). Scales for the measurement of some work attitudes and aspects of psychological well-being. *Journal of Occupational Psychology, 52,* 129–148.

Waung, M. (1995). The effects of self-regulatory coping orientation on newcomer adjustment and job survival. *Personnel Psychology, 48,* 633–650.

PRACTICAL APPLICATION ASSIGNMENTS

1. You just started working at a government agency that provides services to veterans. Within a few weeks, you realize that most of the staff members are not satisfied with their jobs and this is negatively influencing their productivity. In a private conversation, you tell your boss that using psychological interventions could improve your coworkers' job satisfaction. Your boss tells you that she does not believe in psychology and that psychological interventions are not effective. Write an official letter to your boss and her supervisor explaining why implementing a psychological intervention (Cognitive Behavioral Training) at the workplace has the potential to promote job satisfaction.

2. Your cousin, who has been working for a life insurance company for a year, called you to ask for your advice regarding a cognitive-behavioral training workshop that is being offered at his company. He is not sure if he should participate in this activity. Relying on the Proudfoot et al. (2009) article, try convincing him to participate by providing four potential benefits for participants in the cognitive-behavioral training workshop (e.g., less psychological distress).

3. You are the newly appointed CEO of an Internet company that serves 45 million people. One of the problems your company faces is a 35% employee turnover rate. As the CEO of the company, write a letter to the shareholders explaining why it is a good idea to fund psychological research that aims to promote employee well-being and productivity and reduce turnover. In your letter, make sure you convince the shareholders by providing two reasons relevant to the organizational outcomes expected by referring to psychological interventions discussed in the research.

Chapter 7

Social Psychology: Gratitude and Psychosocial Well-being

Benefits of Expressing Gratitude

Expressing Gratitude to a Partner Changes One's View of the Relationship

By Nathaniel M. Lambert, Margaret S. Clark, Jared Durtschi, Frank D. Fincham, and Steven M. Graham

EDITORS' INTRODUCTION

Imagine the following situations: Your best friend throws a surprise birthday party for you. Your close friend gives you the lecture notes for the classes you have missed when you were sick. Your friends nominate you for a prestigious university award in light of your dedication to volunteering in community social programs (e.g., Meals on Wheels). How would you feel if you were the beneficiary of these positive experiences? Most individuals, if not all, are likely to feel grateful. Gratitude is an emotion defined as the recognition and appreciation of meaningful and personally valuable things and experiences in which someone is the beneficiary of someone else's kindness (Emmons & McCullough, 2003).

There is no doubt that individuals from different walks of life all have something in their lives for which they are grateful. Yet, empirical research shows that individuals differ as to how often they feel or think about being grateful (e.g., Emmons, 2008). Some individuals might take the positive experiences in their lives for granted, whereas others continually engage in grateful thinking. Another area where people differ is the expression of gratitude to the providers of kind behaviors. Some individuals are more likely than others to go the extra mile and show their appreciation to the people in their social environment (e.g., writing a thank you card). While understanding individual differences in grateful thinking and expression of gratitude is important, an equally essential task is to investigate the implications of these specific behaviors and ways of thinking on the psychosocial well-being of the individual.

Psychologists in different sub-disciplines (e.g., developmental psychology, social psychology) have studied the effects of feeling gratitude, grateful thinking, and expressing gratitude on individual well-being. For instance, it has been shown that engaging in grateful thinking and counting one's blessings promote physical health (Emmons & McCullough, 2003) and individual happiness (Lambert, Fincham, Stillman, & Dean, 2009), and how they are associated with academic success (Froh, Emmons, Card, Bono, & Wilson, 2011). Importantly, the effects of grateful thinking on psychosocial well-being among adolescents and adults have been shown by employing a variety of research methods. For instance, correlational studies report a positive association between grateful thinking and happiness (Froh et al., 2011). Experimental studies, in which participants are randomly assigned to count their blessings (things they are grateful for) or write about their everyday life for a certain period of time, show that only those in the experimental condition (e.g., counting blessings) report higher levels of psychological well-being immediately after the study and a few months later (Froh,

Nathaniel M. Lambert, Margaret S. Clark, Jared Durtschi, Frank D. Fincham, and Steven M. Graham, "Benefits of Expressing Gratitude: Expressing Gratitude to a Partner Changes One's View of the Relationship," *Psychological Science*, vol. 21, no. 4, pp. 574–580. Copyright © 2010 by Sage Publications. Reprinted with permission.

Benefits of Expressing Gratitude | 89

Sefick, & Emmons, 2008; Sheldon & Lyubomirsky, 2006). Overall, a burgeoning body of empirical evidence highlights the benefits of grateful thinking. Do expressions of gratitude to a significant other impact relationship well-being?

Lambert, Clark, Durtschi, Fincham, and Graham (2010) test the hypothesis that expressing gratitude to a relationship partner is related to and promotes relationship closeness. They focus on communal strength as their outcome variable, which is one of the many indicators of perceived closeness in a personal bond. Specifically, it refers to the degree of responsibility one feels for and the motivation to respond to the needs and well-being of the relationship partner, such as a friend (Clark & Mills, 2011). The authors conducted three studies, each employing a different research method, when testing their hypothesis. Study 1 relies on questionnaires gathered from participants at one point. Study 2 follows the participants and assesses the study variables (e.g., communal strength, expression of gratitude) across time. Study 3 involves the random assignment of participants to experimental and control conditions. A critical aspect of the third study is that it compares the effects of the expression of gratitude to a close friend on communal strength to various cognitive activities (e.g., engaging in grateful thinking about one's friend).

Thinking back to Chapter 1, make sure you can identify the differences in the methods used in the three studies. For instance, what is the main difference between Study 1 and 2? What specific conclusions can one draw from the findings reported in each study? For example, which studies show that expressing gratitude is associated with and promotes communal strength? Which study provides the most convincing empirical evidence about the cause-and-effect relationship between the expression of gratitude and communal strength? In light of the effect sizes reported in the third study, which condition proved to be most effective in promoting relationship closeness?

REFERENCES

Clark, M. S., & Mills, J. (in press). A theory of communal (and exchange) relationships. In P. A. M. Van Lange, A. W. Kruglanski, & E. T. Higgins (Eds.), *Handbook of theories of social psychology* (Vol. 2, pp. 232–250). Thousand Oaks, CA: Sage Publications.

Emmons, R. A. (2008). Gratitude, subjective well-being, and the brain. In R. J. Larsen & M. Eid (Eds.), *The Science of Subjective Well-Being.* (pp. 469–489). New York, NY: Guilford Press.

Emmons, R. A., & McCullough, M. E. (2003). Counting blessings versus burdens: Experimental studies of gratitude and subjective well-being in daily life. *Journal of Personality and Social Psychology, 84* (2), 377–389.

Froh, J. J., Emmons, R. A., Card, N. A., Bono, G., & Wilson, J. A. (2011). Gratitude and the reduced costs of materialism in adolescents. *Journal of Happiness Studies, 12* (2), 289–302.

Froh, J. J., Sefick, W. J., & Emmons, R. A. (2008). Counting blessings in early adolescents: An experimental study of gratitude and subjective well-being. *Journal of School Psychology, 46* (2), 213–233.

Lambert, N. M., Clark, M. S., Durtschi, J., Fincham, F. D., & Graham, S. M. (2010). Benefits of expressing gratitude: Expressing gratitude to a partner changes one's view of the relationship. *Psychological Science, 21*(4), 574-580.

Lambert, N. M., Fincham, F. D., Stillman, T. F., & Dean, L. R. (2009). More gratitude, less materialism: The mediating role of life satisfaction. *The Journal of Positive Psychology, 4* (1), 32–42.

Sheldon, K. M., & Lyubomirsky, S. (2006). How to increase and sustain positive emotion: The benefits of expressing gratitude and visualizing best possible selves. *The Journal of Positive Psychology, 1* (2), 73–82.

ABSTRACT

This research was conducted to examine the hypothesis that expressing gratitude to a relationship partner enhances ones perception of the relationship's communal strength. In Study 1 (N = 137), a cross-sectional survey, expressing gratitude to a relationship partner was positively associated with the expresser's perception of the communal strength of the relationship. In Study 2 (N = 218), expressing gratitude predicted increases in the expresser's perceptions of the communal strength of the relationship across time. In Study 3 (N = 75), participants were randomly assigned to an experimental condition, in which they expressed gratitude to a friend, or to one of three control conditions, in which they thought grateful thoughts about a friend, thought about daily activities, or had positive interactions with a friend. At the end of the study, perceived communal strength was higher among participants in the expression-of-gratitude condition than among those in all three control conditions. We discuss the theoretical and applied implications of these findings and suggest directions for future research.

Research on gratitude has been burgeoning. Gratitude has been defined as an emotion or state resulting from an awareness and appreciation of that which is valuable and meaningful to oneself (Lambert, Graham, & Fincham, in press). Recent research has demonstrated that feeling grateful enhances physical health (Emmons & McCullough, 2003), promotes positive refraining of negative situations (Lambert, Graham, Fincham, & Stillman, in press), increases life satisfaction (Lambert, Fincham, Stillman, & Dean, 2009), and enhances comfort in voicing relationship concerns (Lambert & Fincham, 2010b).

Few people would argue with the proposition that it is a good idea to express gratitude for a relationship partner's supportive behaviors. Indeed, virtually every etiquette book advocates writing thank-you notes for gifts received or, at the very least, expressing verbal thanks. From an early age, children are urged to express thanks for courtesies extended to them. Doing so presumably conveys to benefactors that their efforts have been noticed and are appreciated, and presumably encourages them to act in a similar fashion in the future. Thus, not surprisingly, people report that expressing gratitude is important to the quality of their relationships (Algoe, Haidt, & Gable, 2008; Billingsley, Lim, Caron, Harris, & Canada, 2005; Greeff & Le Roux, 1999; Sharlin, 1996). Empirical evidence does show that expressing gratitude is positively linked with relationship satisfaction (Schramm, Marshall, Harris, & Lee, 2005). Also, expressions of gratitude have been linked to lowered perceptions of unfairness in household labor (Hawkins, Marshall, & Meiners, 1995; Klumb, Hoppmann, & Staats, 2006). Perhaps James (1890/1981) was correct in stating, "The deepest principle in human nature is the craving to be appreciated" (p. 313).

Yet several of these observations suggest that primarily the recipient of expressed gratitude will benefit from the expression of gratitude. Might people who express gratitude also benefit from so doing? We suspected they would and conducted three tests of that hypothesis. More specifically, we thought that the simple act of expressing gratitude to a partner would increase the expresser's perception that the relationship is characterized by high communal strength.

What Is Communal Strength?

A communal relationship is one in which an individual feels a sense of responsibility for meeting the needs of the partner, and in which benefits are given noncontingently in response to the partner's needs (Clark & Mills, 1979, in press). *Communal strength* refers to the degree of felt responsibility for a partner's welfare (Mills, Clark, Ford, & Johnson, 2004). People's motivation to respond noncontingently to a partner's needs differs greatly across different acquaintances, friends, and family members. For example, most people would have higher motivation to meet the needs of a close family member than to meet the needs of a casual friend, even though both kinship and friendship are communal relationships. In this example, the communal relationship with the close family member has a higher degree of communal strength than the communal relationship with the friend.

Mills et al. (2004) discussed three ways to conceptualize communal strength. First, communal strength can be conceptualized as referring to how much personal sacrifice or cost an individual is willing to incur to benefit the partner. Second, communal strength can be conceptualized as referring to how much distress or guilt a person would feel if unable to meet the partner's needs. The third conceptualization focuses on the person's hierarchy of communal relationships. People often have many communal relationships; a few are strong (a romantic partner, a close family member), a large number are moderate (close friends, more distant relatives), and an even greater number are weak (casual acquaintances and strangers). Where a partner falls within an individual's hierarchy of communal strength should predict whether or not this individual meets this partner's needs before other people's needs. The objective of the studies reported here was to examine how expressing gratitude to a relationship partner may enhance the expresser's perception of the relationship's communal strength.

OVERVIEW OF THE STUDIES

In Study 1, we explored whether there is a naturally occurring relationship between expression of gratitude and perceived communal strength. We hypothesized not only that there would be a relationship between these two variables, but also that the relationship would hold even when we controlled for relationship satisfaction and social desirability. In Study 2, we tested whether expressing gratitude would predict an increase in the expresser's perceptions of the communal strength of the relationship across time, controlling for Time 1 levels of communal strength, relationship satisfaction, and social desirability. In Study 3, we tested the direction and causality of this relationship by experimentally testing whether increasing the frequency and regularity of expressing gratitude to a friend influenced perceived communal strength of the relationship. We hypothesized that this manipulation would increase participants' perception of communal strength more than would having participants think grateful thoughts about the partner or interact positively with the partner.

STUDY 1

Given that no prior research had explored the relationship between expression of gratitude and perceived communal strength, we first sought to test for such a relationship. Fin-cham and Bradbury (1987) suggested that, in research on close relationships, care must be taken to ensure that relationship quality is distinguished from other constructs because spurious statistical relationships may arise from overlapping item content in the measures used to assess these constructs. Thus, we assessed and controlled for relationship satisfaction. In addition, because expressing gratitude and communal strength are both socially desirable, we controlled for the tendency to respond in a socially desirable way. We hypothesized that greater expression of gratitude would be associated with more communal strength and that this association would hold when we controlled for relationship satisfaction, social desirability, and demographic variables.

Method

Participants. In an introductory course on families and the life span, 137 participants (116 women, 21 men) completed an on-line survey for extra credit. Participants' ages ranged from 18 to 37, with a median of 19. Participants reported about a relationship with either a romantic partner or a close friend.

Measures. We assessed expression of gratitude with the three-item Expression of Gratitude in Relationships scale (Lambert & Fincham, 2010a; e.g., "I express my gratitude for the things that my partner/friend does for me;" $\alpha = .94$). To assess communal strength, we used a 10-item measure developed by Mills et al. (2004; e.g., "How happy do you feel when doing something that helps your partner/best friend?" $\alpha = .87$). The survey also included a 10-item short form of the Marlowe-Crowne Social Desirability scale (Strahan & Gerbasi, 1972). Reliability was not computed for this measure because it more closely resembles an index than a scale. We assessed relationship satisfaction using Funk and Rogge's (2007) four-item measure (e.g., "How rewarding is your relationship with your partner/friend?" $\alpha = .95$).

We also thought it would be important to control for other variables that might predict perceived communal strength. These variables included sex (1 = male, 2 = female), age, relationship status (1 = romantic relationship, 2 = best friend), and relationship length (from 1, less than 2 months, to 7, more than 3 years).

Results

First, we calculated a zero-order correlation between gratitude expression and communal strength and found them to be strongly correlated, $r(135) = .52$. Next, a hierarchical regression equation was computed to examine whether expression of gratitude accounted for variance in perceived communal strength of the relationship over and beyond the effects of relationship satisfaction, social desirability, sex, age, relationship status, and relationship length. All control variables were entered on the first step, and expression of gratitude was entered on the second step. As expected, higher scores for expression of gratitude significantly predicted higher scores for perception of communal strength ($\beta = .53$, $p < .01$) after controlling for relationship satisfaction, social desirability, sex, age, relationship status, and relationship length. None of the control variables were significant predictors of communal strength, and there were no interactions between gratitude expression and any of these other variables.

Discussion

Our hypothesis was confirmed. We found a link between expression of gratitude and communal strength, over and beyond any effects of relationship satisfaction and social desirability. However, the data from this study were cross-sectional. The results are consistent with and therefore support our hypothesis. In our next two studies, we sought to confirm the link between expression of gratitude and the expresser's felt communal strength and also to provide more convincing evidence for a potential causal link. First, by collecting longitudinal data, we were able to determine whether expressed gratitude predicts the expresser's subsequent perception of the relationship's communal strength (controlling for earlier perceived communal strength). Second, conducting a true experiment allowed us to determine whether a manipulation of expressed gratitude would influence the expresser's felt communal strength toward the target.

STUDY 2: LONGITUDINAL EVIDENCE

Method

Participants and procedure. This study included 218 undergraduates (171 women, 47 men), who participated for partial course credit. Participants ranged in age from 17 to 33, with a median of 19. They completed the measures at the beginning of the academic semester and then again 6 weeks later; the instructions indicated that they should answer all questions with reference to their romantic partner or the partner in their most important interpersonal relationship.

Measures. We used the same measures from Study 1; communal strength was measured at Time 1 ($\alpha = .87$) and Time 2 ($\alpha = .90$), and the following variables were measured at Time 1: Expression of gratitude ($\alpha = .83$), social desirability, relationship satisfaction ($\alpha = .93$), sex, age, relationship status, and relationship length.

Results and Discussion

We used hierarchical regression analysis to determine whether Time 1 gratitude expression predicted a participant's later perceived communal strength, controlling for that person's Time 1 perceived communal strength, relationship satisfaction, and social desirability. On the first step, we entered the control variables (all from Time 1) of perceived communal strength, relationship satisfaction, social desirability, sex, age, relationship status, and relationship length. On the second step, we entered Time 1 gratitude-expression scores. As predicted, higher gratitude expression at Time 1 was associated with higher communal-strength scores 6 weeks later, controlling for Time 1 communal strength, relationship satisfaction, social desirability, sex, age, relationship status, and relationship length ($\beta = 0.13$, $p < .01$; see Table 1).

Our hypothesis again was supported. Going beyond the previously established correlation between expression of gratitude and communal strength, these findings provide important support for a time-order relationship between these variables. They suggest that increased expression of gratitude predicts later increased perceptions of communal strength, after controlling for initial communal strength.

However, these longitudinal data are still correlational. Perhaps variables such as being especially attracted to a partner or especially committed to the relationship predict both expressing more gratitude toward the partner and working hard over time to establish a strong communal relationship. To firmly establish that expressing gratitude leads to greater perceived communal strength of a relationship, we needed to follow a true experimental design. We did this in Study 3.

STUDY 3

In the third study, we randomly assigned participants to an experimental condition or to one of three control conditions. Participants in the experimental condition were instructed to increase their expressions of gratitude to a partner (and report on their efforts and success twice a week) for a 3-week period. The most straightforward control condition involved a "neutral" control of paying particular attention to daily activities and reporting on them twice a week.

Table 1. Summary of the Hierarchical Regression Analysis for Variables Predicting Time 2 Perception of Communal Strength in Study 2

Variable	b	SE b	ß	P
Step 1				
Time 1 communal strength	0.60	0.06	0.52	.00
Sex	0.21	0.17	0.07	.22
Age	0.04	0.04	0.05	.33
Relationship status	-0.01	0.16	-0.01	.94
Relationship length	0.01	0.03	0.03	.66
Relationship satisfaction	0.14	0.07	0.11	.05
Social desirability	0.72	035	O.11	.04
Step 2				
Time 1 expression of gratitude	0.10	0.05	0.13	.05

Note. N = 218. R^2 = .42 for Step 1 ($p < .01$); ΔR^2 = .01 for Step 2 ($p < .05$).

Yet we wished to examine the effects of expressing gratitude specifically and therefore also wanted to control for merely thinking positive thoughts and, indeed, merely thinking about one's gratitude toward a partner. Therefore, we included two additional control conditions: One involved paying particular attention to memories of positive events in the relationship and bringing these up in conversation with a partner twice a week, and the other involved paying careful attention to events that made one feel grateful to the partner, but not expressing feelings of gratitude (and reporting on these efforts twice a week). We predicted that participants' perceptions of communal strength would be increased more by increasing expressions of gratitude than by attending to daily activities, discussing positive events in the relationship, or thinking about gratitude toward the partner.

Method

Participants. Ninety-seven participants enrolled in an introductory course on family development completed the study's Time 1 measures. However, in our final analysis, we included only those 75 undergraduates (60 women, 15 men) who both completed all relevant measures at both the start and conclusion of the study and indicated (on a measure described later) that they had taken the study seriously. Participants ranged in age from 18 to 23, with a median of 19.

Procedure. After participants completed relevant measures (Time 1), they began their assigned activity. They completed this activity twice a week for 3 weeks and reported on it using an on-line journal. We sent them a link every Monday and Thursday morning and instructed them to write about the completion of their assigned activity. As previously mentioned, there were four conditions, which focused on (a) expression of gratitude, (b) daily activities (neutral), (c) thoughts of gratitude, and (d) expression of positive memories. Participants in all conditions reported on a relationship with a close friend. The average length of the relationship was 2.45 years. Participants were instructed to engage in an assigned activity with their friend and to answer all relationship questions with this specific person in mind.

The *expression-of-gratitude* condition ($n = 19$) was the experimental condition and was designed to increase the frequency of participants' expression of gratitude. Participants assigned to this condition were given the following instructions:

> For the next 3 weeks I would like you to focus on trying to go the extra mile to express gratitude to your friend. Between now and Thursday, please do something you wouldn't normally do to express this gratitude verbally or through writing (e.g., perhaps write an e-mail, a kind note, tell him/her how much you appreciate something specific that he/she does). Make sure to record or remember what you did so that you can report about it on Thursday.

The *neutral* (daily-activities) condition ($n = 17$) was designed to provide a neutral comparison for the other conditions, as well as to rule out the unlikely possibility that simply engaging in a 3-week study could affect any of the dependent variables. Participants in this condition were given the following instructions:

> For the next 3 weeks I would like you to focus on trying to go the extra mile to think about your daily activities. Between now and Thursday, please think about something that happened to you and make sure to record or remember what you did so that you can report about it on Thursday.

The *thoughts-of-gratitude* condition ($n = 20$) was designed to rule out the possibility that simply thinking appreciative thoughts about a friend, rather than the behavior of actually expressing gratitude to him or her, could drive any posttest differences in the dependent variables. Participants in this condition were given the following instructions:

> For the next 3 weeks I would like you to focus on trying to go the extra mile to think about things that you appreciate about your friend. Between now and Thursday, please think about something you appreciate about your

friend. Make sure to record or remember what you thought so you can report about it on Thursday.

The *positive-interaction* condition ($n = 19$) was designed to help rule out the alternative hypothesis that being assigned to have positive interactions with a friend would lead to posttest differences in the dependent variables. Participants in this condition were given the following instructions:

> For the next 3 weeks I would like you to focus on thinking of positive memories you've had with your friend. Between now and Thursday, please think about a pleasant memory with this friend and bring it up with him/her in person, by phone, or by e-mail. Make sure to record or remember what you did so that you can report about it on Thursday.

Participants in all conditions were asked to report on their assigned activity twice per week (i.e., on Monday and Thursday) for 3 weeks. Thus, we had a record of whether or not they completed the activity. After completion of the sixth entry, participants completed another round of self-report measures (Time 2).

Measures. We again measured communal strength with the 10-item measure developed by Mills et al. (2004; $\alpha = .82$ at Time 1 and .84 at Time 2). To filter out participants who did not fully participate in the study, we asked all participants how often they had participated in their assigned activity and rated them as never, rarely, occasionally, fairly frequently, or always doing so. We excluded data from 4 participants who indicated they never or rarely took their assigned activity seriously.

We again measured Time 1 relationship satisfaction ($\alpha = .92$), sex, age, relationship status, social desirability, and relationship length. There were no differences between conditions on any of these variables (all $Fs < 1$, n.s.), so we did not include them in the analysis.

Results

Nineteen participants who completed all measures at Time 1 dropped out by Time 2. Time 1 communal strength did not differ between participants who were included in analyses and those who were excluded because they did not complete all measures or failed to participate in their assigned activity, $t(95) = 0.41$, n.s.

An analysis of covariance controlling for Time 1 communal strength revealed a significant main effect of condition on Time 2 communal strength, $F(3, 70) = 4.07$, $p = .01$. Planned comparisons revealed that Time 2 communal strength was higher for participants in the expression-of-gratitude condition ($M = 7.89$, $SD = 1.03$) than for those in the thoughts-of-gratitude condition ($M = 7.48$, $SD = 1.39$), $F(1,70) = 4.07$, $p = .01$, $d = 0.34$; the neutral condition ($M = 7.39$, $SD = 1.05$), $F(1, 70) = 3.96$, $p = .05$, $d = 0.48$; and the positive-interaction condition ($M = 7.00$, $SD = 1.56$), $F(1, 70) = 12.04$, $p < .001$, $d = 0.67$ (see Table 2).

Discussion

As hypothesized, increasing the regularity and frequency of expressing gratitude enhanced participants' perception of the communal strength of their relationship with their friend. Given that participants were randomly assigned to conditions and that we controlled for Time 1 communal-strength scores, the significant increase in perception of communal strength in the expression-of-gratitude condition is attributable to the intervention.

General Discussion

This research focused on whether openly expressing gratitude to a friend or romantic partner leads to increased perceived communal strength of the relationship in the expresser's eyes. In three studies, we demonstrated—cross-sectionally, longitudinally, and experimentally—a relationship between expressing gratitude and perception of communal strength. In Study 1, self-report of having expressed gratitude was associated with greater perceived communal strength of the relationship. In Study 2, expressing gratitude predicted increases in the perceived communal strength of the relationship across time, after controlling for Time 1 communal strength, relationship satisfaction, and social desirability. In Study 3, we obtained experimental support for the hypothesis

Table 2. Communal Strength at Time 1 and Time 2 in Study 3

Condition	Time 1		Time 2	
	M	SD	M	SD
Expression of gratitude ($n = 19$)	6.69	1.40	7.89	1.03
Thoughts of gratitude ($n = 20$)	7.06	1.06	7.48	1.39
Neutral ($n = 17$)	6.94	0.75	7.39	1.05
Positive interaction ($n = 19$)	7.07	1.35	7.00	1.56

that expressing gratitude to a partner increases the perceived communal strength of that relationship.

Limitations and Future Directions

One limitation of the study is our exclusive use of college student samples, which restricts the generalizability of these findings to more diverse populations. In addition, we used a general measure of social desirability in these studies, and a relationship-specific measure of social desirability may be more appropriate for such studies in the future (e.g., Edmonds, 1967).

Although our research focused on documenting that expressing gratitude does increase the perceived communal strength of a relationship, future research should examine potential mechanisms for this effect. Why should expressing gratitude to a partner increase the *expresser's* perceptions of the relationship's communal strength? We propose a three-component answer. First, expressing gratitude constitutes a communication not only to the partner, but to the self as well. Through self-perception (Bem, 1967, 1972) or dissonance reduction (Festinger, 1957), taking this action ought to convince expressers that they welcomed the partner's supportive action. In turn, this ought to convince expressers that they desire or have a communal relationship with the partner.

Second, the act of expressing gratitude can be seen as a responsive action directed toward the partner— an action indicating that one cares enough about the partner to reassure the partner that his or her actions were appreciated, appropriate, and desired. Again, through self-perception or dissonance reduction, being responsive to a partner should convince expressers that they have communal feelings toward the partner.

Finally, expressing gratitude is likely to have an actual impact on the partner. Conveying to the partner that his or her actions were appreciated and valued ought to encourage additional and possibly larger or more costly supportive acts on the partner's part. In this way, the actual communal strength of the relationship ought to be enhanced, and this effect also may be perceived and reciprocated by the participant.

In sum, we reiterate our beliefs that gratitude is a social emotion that serves important functions in relationships when it is expressed. Expression of gratitude signals to the target that his or her communal actions were both useful to and desired by the expresser. Thus, it validates the target's actions and encourages the target to repeat or even enhance efforts to be responsive to the partner; such efforts, in turn, should please the partner (increasing relationship satisfaction) and enhance the communal strength of the relationship. The present work supports our theorizing that expressing gratitude to a partner serves an important communication function for the expresser as well. The very act of expressing gratitude signals to the expresser (through self-perception) that he or she both recognizes the target's responsiveness and welcomes that responsiveness. Given that expressing gratitude conveys one's desire for such support and willingness to receive it, such expressions should also increase a sense of dependency on the relationship, which may trigger thoughts of trusting the partner and even dissonance-reduction processes, which themselves may enhance a sense of communal strength. It may also be the case that expressing gratitude increases the expresser's perceived communal strength through a more interpersonal route. That is, expressing gratitude may make the partner feel good, encourage the partner's further communal actions, and thereby increase the extent to which the expresser views the relationship as communal. We will be conducting research to investigate these proposed mediators in the future.

Conclusion

It is worthwhile to step back from the data and take a broader perspective on expressions of gratitude. What we have done is to establish a link between expressing gratitude to a partner and feeling increased communal strength in the relationship. Moreover, we have provided clean evidence that expressing gratitude can cause increased perception of communal strength. This evidence supports our initial hypothesis regarding the effect of expression of gratitude on the expresser, but it remains important to establish which (if any) of our proposed mechanisms mediate the effect.

On a practical level, regardless of what the mediating mechanisms are, we have provided additional documentation that expressing gratitude, an easily modifiable behavior, can strengthen a close relationship. Some past research suggests that it may do so by increasing the relationship satisfaction of the recipient; the current research suggests it may do so by increasing the expresser's felt communal strength. Thus, therapists may well want to suggest this behavior, perhaps along with other behaviors with documented beneficial effects on relationships (e.g., sharing good news: Gable, Reis, Impett, & Asher, 2004; sharing exciting activities: Aron, Norman, Aron, McKenna, & Heyman, 2000), to clients who seek ways to improve their relationships. Individuals not in therapy may be well advised to follow the same suggestion.

REFERENCES

Algoe, S., Haidt, J., & Gable, S. (2008). Beyond reciprocity: Gratitude and relationships in everyday life. *Emotion, 8,* 425–429.

Aron, A., Norman, C.C., Aron, E.N., McKenna, C, & Heyman, R.E. (2000). Couples' shared participation in novel and arousing activities and experienced relationship quality. *Journal of Personality and Social Psychology, 78,* 273–284.

Bem, D.J. (1967). Self-perception: An alternative interpretation of cognitive dissonance phenomena. *Psychological Review, 74,* 183–200.

Bem, DJ. (1972). Self-perception theory. In L. Berkowitz (Ed.), *Advances in experimental social psychology* (Vol. 6, pp. 1–62). New York: Academic Press.

Billingsley, S., Lim, M., Caron, J., Harris, A., & Canada, R. (2005). Historical overview of criteria for marital and family success. *Family Therapy, 32,* 1–14.

Clark, M.S., & Mills, J. (1979). Interpersonal attraction in exchange and communal relationships. *Journal of Personality and Social Psychology, 37,* 12–24.

Clark, M.S., & Mills, J. (in press). A theory of communal (and exchange) relationships. In P.A.M. Van Lange, A.W. Kruglanski, & E.T. Higgins (Eds.), *Handbook of theories of social psychology.* Thousand Oaks, CA: Sage.

Edmonds, V.H. (1967). Marital conventionalization: Definition and measurement. *Journal of Marriage and the Family, 29,* 681–688.

Emmons, R.A., & McCullough, M.E. (2003). Counting blessings versus burdens: An experimental investigation of gratitude and subjective well-being in daily life. *Journal of Personality and Social Psychology, 84,* 377–389.

Festinger, L. (1957). *A theory of cognitive dissonance.* Oxford, England: Row, Peterson.

Fincham, F.D., & Bradbury, T.N. (1987). The assessment of marital quality: A reevaluation. *Journal of Marriage and the Family, 49,* 797–809.

Funk, J.L., & Rogge, R.D. (2007). Testing the ruler with item response theory: Increasing precision of measurement for relationship satisfaction with the Couples Satisfaction Index. *Journal of Family Psychology, 21,* 572–583.

Gable, S.L., Reis, H.T., Impett, E.A., & Asher, E.R. (2004). What do you do when things go right? The intrapersonal and interpersonal benefits of sharing positive events. *Journal of Personality and Social Psychology, 87,* 1246–1265.

Greeff, A.P., & Le Roux, C.M. (1999). Parents' and adolescents' perceptions of a strong family. *Psychological Reports, 84,* 1219–1224.

Hawkins, A.J., Marshall, C.M., & Meiners, K.M. (1995). Exploring wives' sense of fairness about family work: An initial test of the distributive justice framework. *Journal of Family Issues, 16,* 693–721.

James, W. (1981). *The principles of psychology.* Cambridge, MA: Harvard University Press. (Original work published 1890)

Klumb, P., Hoppmann, C, & Staats, M. (2006). Division of labor in German dual-earner families: Testing equity theoretical hypotheses. *Journal of Marriage and the Family, 68,* 870–882.

Lambert, N.M., & Fincham, F.D. (2010a). *The potency of gratitude expression.* Manuscript submitted for publication.

Lambert, N.M., & Fincham, F.D. (2010b). *Expressing gratitude to a partner leads to more relationship maintenance behavior.* Manuscript submitted for publication.

Lambert, N.M., Fincham, F.D., Stillman, T.L., & Dean, L.R. (2009). More gratitude, less materialism: The mediating role of life satisfaction. *Journal of Positive Psychology, 4,* 32–42.

Lambert, N.M., Graham, S., & Fincham, F.D. (in press). A proto-type analysis of gratitude: Varieties of gratitude experiences. *Personality and Social Psychology Bulletin.*

Lambert, N.M., Graham, S.M., Fincham, F.D., & Stillman, T.F. (in press). A changed perspective: How gratitude can affect sense of coherence through positive reframing. *Journal of Positive Psychology.*

Mills, J., Clark, M.S., Ford, T.E., & Johnson, M. (2004). Measurement of communal strength. *Personal Relationships, II,* 213–230.

Schramm, D.G., Marshall, J.P., Harris, V.W., & Lee, T.R. (2005). After 'I do': The newlywed transition. *Marriage & Family Review, 38,* 45–67.

Sharlin, S.A. (1996). Long-term successful marriages in Israel. *Contemporary Family Therapy: An International Journal, 18,* 225–242.

Strahan, R., & Gerbasi, K.C. (1972). Short, homogeneous versions of the Marlowe-Crowne Social Desirability Scale. *Journal of Clinical Psychology, 28,* 191–193.

PRACTICAL APPLICATION ASSIGNMENTS

1. Imagine the following scenario: You have just been hired as a consultant for a documentary at a national news media station. The station is working on a documentary that claims that what individuals experience in their lives is based on random occurrences, and they should focus on what they want to do with their lives rather than trying to understand why these events happened. Prepare a brief report for your boss that includes two suggestions about how individuals might benefit from displaying grateful thinking in their lives as opposed to accepting occurrences as random.

2. Write an email to a psychotherapist working with a client who is experiencing relationship problems. The client would like to experience more closeness and intimacy in the relationship. Based on your understanding of this article, suggest two actions that the psychotherapist should encourage in order for the client to improve his/her relationships.

3. Your best friend's friend, Alex Souza, has been sick for two days, and Victoria Nina, his close friend, has been taking care of him. Your friend tells you that Alex took it for granted that Victoria brought him soup and checked his temperature regularly until he felt better while his other friends were out of town to attend a baseball game. A week later your best friend also informs you that Alex realized how generous and thoughtful Victoria had been to him. He has told Victoria how grateful he is. Tell your best friend about the benefits Alex might enjoy by expressing his gratitude to Victoria for their relationship.

Chapter 8

Conservation Psychology: The Role of Psychology in Promoting Sustainable Behavior

A Practitioner's Guide to the Psychology of Sustainable Behaviour

By Adam Corner

EDITOR'S INTRODUCTION

There is a sufficiency in the world for man's need but not for man's greed.
—Mohandas K. Gandhi

Most people know a few things they could do to help reduce their impact on the environment, such as driving less, eating organic foods, and hanging their clothes to dry rather than using a dryer. Yet many people are not engaging in these sustainable behaviors. Why not?

There are many factors that influence whether or not individuals engage in sustainable behaviors, such as knowledge about and attitudes toward sustainable issues. Another important factor that influences people's willingness to engage in sustainable behaviors is the way in which "green" behaviors and environmental issues are discussed. The Center for Research on Environmental Decisions (2009) stresses that in order for environmental information "to be fully absorbed by audiences, it must be actively communicated with appropriate language, metaphor, and analogy; combined with narrative storytelling; made vivid through visual imagery and experiential scenarios; balanced with scientific information; and delivered by trusted messengers in group settings" (p. 2). Effective communication about issues, such as sustainability, that are multifaceted, inexact, overwhelming at times, and often emotionally and politically loaded is essential to motivate people to change their behavior. The purpose of this chapter is to introduce you to strategies that can be used to help people communicate about and promote sustainability.

Sustainability refers to patterns of behaviors or a lifestyle that uses resources in such a way as to not deplete or permanently damage the environment. A common nonsustainable behavior that everyone can relate to is purchasing water in plastic bottles. People buy millions of plastic water bottles daily. After drinking the water, the plastic water bottle gets thrown away. Think about this: Drinking water from that plastic bottle takes a few minutes, yet the plastic water bottle, which is only used once in most cases, will last 1,000 years in our landfills! Despite the availability of recycling, most plastic water bottles are NOT recycled in the United States. Approximately 75 percent of the empty plastic bottles end up in our landfills, lakes, streams, and oceans. Even before the consumer drinks the bottled water, the environment is negatively affected, as fossil fuels are wasted in the production and transportation of the bottles. For example, in one year alone in the United States, the energy equivalent of 32 million barrels of oil were used to produce plastic water bottles and another 54 million barrels to transport them. That amount of energy could fuel approximately 1.5 million cars for a year (http://www.foodandwaterwatch.org). To learn more about the impact of bottled water, watch the short video at (http://storyofstuff.org/bottledwater/). How do we convince people to increase their sustainable behavior? Psychology can help us develop strategies.

Messages about sustainable behavior must be tailored to fit the audience you are addressing. People are more likely to "hear" a message if it is personally relevant and connects with their concerns and values (Manning, 2009). What we mean is that you, as the presenter, need to understand your audience's worldview. A *worldview* is a set of beliefs about what is important to an individual and how that person thinks the world works. World views act as a filter for the processing of new information in that they influence what we pay attention to and the likelihood that we will trust the new information. Similarly, we know that people are more likely to seek out and accept information that is consistent with (confirms) their worldview, and they are more likely to discredit or ignore information that is inconsistent with their already held beliefs about the world. This psychological concept is called a *confirmation bias*.

Let's look at another example related to conservation psychology. Given people's varying worldviews, the issue of global climate change must be framed or presented differently depending on the targeted audience's worldview. The scientific information doesn't change; rather the "packaging" of the message needs to highlight the issues that the audience values, such as human health, social justice, economic prosperity, national security, morality, etc. If you are trying to get people to drive their cars less and you are talking with people in a weight-loss clinic, you would focus on the health benefits of walking to work, rather than emphasizing the environmental impact of vehicle emissions. Alternatively, the message to a group of entrepreneurs would be more effective if the focus was on economic issues, for example, how they could save money by driving less. For an audience with a social-justice and human-rights worldview, a message that highlights the devastating effects of climate change for already disadvantaged people (i.e., people of color or people living in poverty) would be more likely to resonate than messages focused on health or national security. The more personally meaningful and relevant the message, the more likely people are to change their behavior (Cash et al., 2002).

The reading for this chapter by Adam Corner (2009) provides information learned through psychological science that can help people in their efforts to communicate better about sustainable living. It is important to recognize that the strategies and tips discussed are based on empirical research and can be applied to promote human and environmental well-being. "A practitioner's guide to the psychology of sustainable behavior" provides six concrete suggestions that can be used to more effectively persuade people to change their behaviors. As you are reading the article, think how you could apply this information to change someone's behavior regarding sustainability.

REFERENCES

Cash, D., Clark W., Alcock, F., Dickson, N, Eckley, N, & Jager, J. (2002). Salience, credibility, legitimacy, and boundaries: Linking research, assessment and decision making. John F. Cambridge, MA: Harvard University.

Center for Research on Environmental Decisions (2009). *The psychology of climate change communication. A guide for scientists, journalists, educators, political aides, and the interested public.* New York, NY: Columbia University. Retrieved from http://www.cred.columbia.edu/guide/

Corner, Adam. (2009). *A Practitioner's Guide to the Psychology of Sustainable Behaviour*, pp. 1–5. Oxford, UK: Climate Outreach and Information Network.

Freedman, J. L., & Fraser, S. C. (1966). Compliance without pressure: The foot-in-the-door technique. *Journal of Personality and Social Psychology, 4* (2), 195–202.

Manning, C. (2009). *The psychology of sustainable behavior: A handbook introducing research-based tips from psychology to help you in efforts to empower sustainability in your personal life, community, and workplace.* Retrieved from http://www.pca.state.mn.us/oea/ee/psychology.cfm

McKenzie-Mohr, D. (2007). *Fostering sustainable behavior: An introduction to community-based social marketing (3rd Edition).* Gabriola Island, BC: New Society Publishers.

There is an urgent need for social scientists, campaigners and policy makers to investigate and communicate everything they can about how to promote sustainable behaviour—how we think about our place in the world, the things that we value, and how we relate to other people[1]. Understanding the psychology of sustainable behaviour is a pressing task—and one that policy makers and campaigners are likely to be heavily engaged in over the coming years.

The following information is designed for practitioners to get a sense of what psychological research can tell us about sustainable behaviour. It focuses on practical messages—it is designed for people who communicate climate change and promote behaviour change. This information will help you think about the most effective ways of promoting sustainable behaviour—but the academic research needs translating into practical action.

START WITH THE RIGHT LANGUAGE

The language that you use to talk about climate change and promote sustainable behaviour has to engage people, not make them switch off. "Climate change" is vague, abstract and difficult to visualise. Most people in the UK don't feel personally threatened by climate change[2]. This means that doomsday scenarios and apocalyptic language are unlikely to work—studies show that although fear can motivate behaviour change, it only works when people feel personally vulnerable[3].

Clearly, exaggerating the threat of climate change is not an option. Many people already believe that the seriousness of climate change has been over-exaggerated by the media[4]. So how can climate change

be made more tangible and more relevant to people's lives?

The American think-tank EcoAmerica played people recordings of actors delivering speeches about climate change[5]. The version that people responded to the best talked about "air pollution" rather than "climate change"—because pollution is something visible that they can relate to, with strong connotations of dirtiness and poor health. Climate change is about much more than just dirty air—but finding ways of making climate change more visible is critical—people just don't worry about things they can't see (or even imagine)[6].

Of course, simply using different words isn't enough—messages will only work if they connect to people's underlying concerns. The most effective speech in the EcoAmerica research contrasted the dirty fossil fuels of the past with the clean energy of the future, and talked about "everlasting fuels" rather than "alternative energy." This is because a clean and plentiful future is something that has universal appeal. Using the right language is not about putting a "positive spin" on climate change. But it does mean talking less about "saving the planet" and more about the things that people care about—their health, their family and their happiness[7].

DON'T JUST BOMBARD PEOPLE WITH INFORMATION

There is certainly no shortage of information about climate change and sustainable behaviour. But time after time, studies have shown that information is not enough to change behaviour. Campaigns to tackle obesity, the spread of sexually transmitted diseases, smoking and teenage pregnancy have all moved past simply providing people with information—and campaigns to promote sustainable behaviour need to as well[8].

Why don't people change their behaviour when they find out more about a problem? One reason is that there is often a big gap between people's attitudes and their behaviour. So, although information campaigns might change attitudes and beliefs, they are unlikely to be an effective way of influencing behaviour. It is also important to be clear about which behaviours are most effective —unplugging a thousand phone chargers is no substitute for draught insulation, but lists of "101 ways to save the world" often don't reflect this[9]. It may also be that people don't know how to change their behaviour—and so at a minimum, campaigns that target sustainable behaviour need to show not only which behaviours to change, but *how* to change them. Because so much of our behaviour is *habitual,* this may mean learning to recognise deeply ingrained habits—something notoriously difficult to do.

One approach that has been used to successfully influence behaviour relating to speeding[10], consumer habits[11], and the amount that people use public transport[12], breaks down habits into simple "if…then" plans. To change a habitual behaviour, a person has to identify a goal (e.g. drive less), a behaviour they want to perform in pursuit of that goal (e.g. get the bus to work on Fridays) and the situation that will trigger the behaviour (e.g. having enough time to catch the bus). Learning how to respond to different situations allows habits to be identified and changed, and barriers to be removed. For example, IF its Thursday evening, THEN set the alarm for a different time; IF its Friday morning, THEN have a shower instead of a bath; IF an umbrella is left by the door THEN it won't matter if it's raining on the walk to the bus stop. This approach (of identifying a goal and possible barriers to achieving it) forms the basis of Community Based Social Marketing (CBSM)—a programme for delivering behaviour change strategies that has been developed in the US in response to the ineffectiveness of "information only" campaigns[13].

USE SOCIAL NORMS IN THE RIGHT WAY

Many environmental campaigns involve social norms—the standards that we use to judge the appropriateness of our own behaviour. People tend to act in a way that is socially acceptable, so if a particular behaviour (littering, for example, or driving a car with a large engine) can be cast in a socially unacceptable light, then people should be less likely to engage in it. However, the problem with appeals based on social norms is that they often contain a hidden message. So, for example, a campaign that focuses on the fact that too many people drive cars with large engines actually contains two messages— that driving cars with large engines is bad for the environment, and that *lots of people are driving cars with large engines.* This second message can give those who do not currently engage in that behaviour a perverse incentive to do so. Everyone else is doing it, so why shouldn't I?

In a recent experiment, Californian houses were picked at random and then divided into groups depending on whether their energy consumption was higher or lower than the average for that area[14]. Some low-energy-use households received only information about average energy usage—thereby setting the social norm. A second group of low-energy households had a positive "emoticon" (happy face) positioned next to their personal energy usage figure, conveying approval of their energy footprint. A third group of over-consuming households were shown their energy usage coupled with a negative emoticon (sad face), intended to convey disapproval of their higher-than-average footprint.

The researchers then measured energy consumption in the following months. As one might expect, the over-consuming households used the social norm as a motivation to reduce their energy use, but under-consuming households that had received only the social norm information actually *increased* their energy use. Crucially, though, the under-consuming households that had received positive feedback did not show this "boomerang" effect: The addition of a smiley face next to their energy usage made all the difference. Despite the simplicity of the feedback, households that felt their under-consumption was socially approved (rather than a reason to relax), maintained their small energy footprint. This suggests that using social norms can be effective—but only if they are used in the right way: If people are doing something positive, they need to know about it.

Making a public commitment to carry out a sustainable behaviour is a good way of generating a social norm—but it can also make people more likely to stick to their *own* behaviour. In one American neighbourhood, some residents were asked to take part in a recycling scheme, while other people were asked to recycle *and* put a sticker in their window saying that they recycled. The people who made a public commitment (as well as promoting the scheme to others) were more likely to be still be recycling months later[15].

PROMOTE PRO-ENVIRONMENTAL VALUES

A recent review of strategies for environmental behaviour change commissioned by the VWVF argued that the values targeted by pro-environmental campaigns may affect the likelihood of behaviour "spilling over" from one domain into another[16]. Drawing on well-established theories of social behaviour, they questioned whether focussing on non-environmental reasons for behaviour change was a help or a hindrance in the long term. While the prospect of saving money may motivate some energy saving behaviour, it does not trigger critical psychological mechanisms that make the performance of *other* pro-environmental behaviours more likely. In general, people like to avoid feeling hypocritical, and will take steps to avoid any *dissonance* between their actions. But people saving energy for financial reasons will feel no obligation to save energy when these reasons are absent—they might switch off appliances at home, for example, but leave things on at work. Similarly, saving energy for financial reasons does not encourage people to view themselves as "the sort of person who acts sustainably." Rather, it encourages people to view themselves as "the sort of person who saves money." Promoting the right sort of *self perception* is critical if changes in multiple behaviours are required.

Policy makers and campaigners aiming for spillover in sustainable behaviours should be clear about the environmental reasons for behaviour change—that is, they should promote pro-environmental values. Tellingly, experiments have shown that people who are highly materialistic are less likely to engage in sustainable behaviour[17]. While appealing to financial self interest may be the most effective way of motivating the greatest number of people to adopt a *particular* type of behaviour, this misses the bigger picture.

PROMOTE SUSTAINABLE CITIZENSHIP

The bigger picture is that life change for a sustainable Wales is likely to involve more than just changing consumer preferences and identifying habits—it will also involve promoting pro-environmental values and sustainable citizenship. While there are many different visions of what a sustainable future will be like, one thing seems clear: Business as usual is not an option. Citizen-led groups embracing this fundamental truth have started to spring up spontaneously around the country—for example, there are now hundreds of Transition Town groups across the UK and further afield. Typically though, these groups do more than just focus on how much energy they can save: They also invest time and energy into building social relationships and a sense of community. This is likely to have immediate non-environmental benefits (a sense of belonging etc), but it also creates the perfect environment for significant and sustained changes in behaviour. People who feel supported by friends and colleagues will be far more likely to change their behaviour than people who try to "go it alone."

Undoubtedly, asking questions about citizenship and how people see their place in society is more difficult than focussing on switching consumer preferences. But it seems unlikely that individual-level behaviour change will be enough to meet the challenge of a sustainable future.

HARNESS THE POWER OF PEER GROUPS AND SOCIAL NETWORKS

Social networks—people's friends, colleagues, peers or family—are a powerful influence on their behaviour, and some of the more sophisticated behaviour change work that's been done in the UK has used a group-based approach. For example, the charity Global Action Plan has used an approach called "Eco Teams,"[18] while the Climate Outreach and Information Network (COIN) has pioneered peer-to-peer learning as a pathway to behaviour change. This involves members of local communities holding meetings where they plan changes to household energy behaviour, share their experiences, and take decisive local action. The groups provide a support network for overcoming barriers and problems that people encounter when trying to make changes to their lives. Similarly, a six-month programme trialled with Women's Institute groups managed to substantially reduce the amount of food that was wasted by participants[19]. When asked what they enjoyed most about these projects, the Eco Teams, Women's Institute and COIN participants responded that the process of working together was what motivated them to keep going.

Of course, not everyone is interested in joining an "eco team." But everyone has a peer group and a social network. Finding ways of harnessing the power of these existing networks may hold the key to making sustainable behaviour the rule, rather than the exception. COIN has begun an ambitious project in partnership with the members of four of the UK's largest Trade Unions[20]. These firmly established networks provide fertile ground for new ideas and behaviours to take root. And crucially, working with existing social networks means that the effects of any behaviour change strategies will be amplified.

SUMMARY

Start with the right language—doomsday scenarios and apocalyptic language are unlikely to work, but making climate change more visible is critical. Talk less about saving the planet and more about the things that people care about.

Don't just bombard people with information—it's not enough to change behaviour. Changing habits is hard, but with the right approach it can be done.

Use social norms in the right way—if people are doing something positive, they need to know about it!

Promote pro-environmental values and sustainable citizenship—not economic self interest!

Harness the power of peer groups and social networks—people who feel supported by their friends and colleagues are far more likely to change their behaviour than people who "go it alone!"

REFERENCES:

[1] Hulme, M. (2009). *Why we disagree about climate change: Understanding controversy, inaction and opportunity.* Cambridge: Cambridge University Press.

[2] Lorenzoni, I., Nicholson-Cole, S. & Whitmarsh, L. (2007). Barriers perceived to engaging with climate change among the UK public and their policy implications. *Global Environmental Change, 17*, 445–459.

[3] Witte, K. & Allen, M. (2000). A meta-analysis of fear appeals: Implications for effective public health campaigns. *Health Education and Behaviour, 27* (5): 591–615.

[4] Gallup Environment Survey (2009). *US: Gallop.*

[5] Western Strategies & Lake Research Partners (2009). Climate and Energy Truths: Our Common Future. *Washington, US: EcoAmerica.*

[6] Hulme, M. & Lorenzoni, I. (2009). Believing is seeing: Laypeople's views of future socio-economic and climate change in England and Italy. *Public Understanding of Science, 18,* 323–400.

[7] Happy Planet Index 2.0. (2009). *New Economics Foundation.*

[8] Maio, G., Verplanken, B., Manstead, T., Stroebe, W., Abraham, C., Sheeran, P., & Conner, M. (2007). Social Psychological Factors in Lifestyle Change and the relevance to policy. *Social Issues & Policy Review, 1 (1)* 99–137.

[9] Gardner, G.T. & Stern, P.C. (2008). The Short List: The Most Effective Actions U.S. Households Can Take to Curb Climate Change. *Environment, 50 (5),* 12–24.

[10] Elliot, M.A. & Armitage, C.J. (2006). Effects of implementations on the self-reported frequency of drivers' compliance with speed limits. *Journal of Experimental Psychology: Applied 12,* 108–117.

[11] Verplanken, B. & Wood, W. (2006). Interventions to break and create consumer habits. *Journal of Public Policy and Marketing, 25,* 90–103.

[12] Bamberg, S. (2002). Effects of implementation intentions on the actual performance of new environmentally friendly behaviours —results of two field experiments. *Journal of Environmental Psychology 22,* 399–411.

[13] www.cbsm.com

[14] Schultz, P.W., Nolan, J.M., Cialdini, R.B., Goldstein, N.J., & Griskevicius, V. (2007). The Constructive, Destructive, and Reconstructive Power of Social Norms. *Psychological Science, 18* (5) 429–434.

[15] Cobern, M.K., Porter, B.E., Leeming, F.C., & Dwyer, W.O. (1995). The effect of commitment on adoption and diffusion of grass cycling. *Special Issue: Litter control and recycling. Environment and Behavior, 27* (2) 213–232.

[16] Crompton, T. & Thogersen, J. (2009). Simple and Painless? The limitations of spillover in environmental campaigning. *WWF*.

[17] Crompton, T. & Kasser, T. (2009). Meeting Environmental Challenges: The Role of Human Identity. *WWF*.

[18] Nye, M. & Burgess, J. (2008). Promoting durable change in household waste and energy use behaviour. *Defra*.

[19] http://www.lovefoodhatewaste.com/about food waste/love food champions.html

[20] http://coinet.org.uk/who-we-work-with/trade-unions

PRACTICAL APPLICATION ASSIGNMENTS

1. Pick one of the following sustainable behaviors (taking the bus to class, bringing a reusable water bottle instead of a disposable one, riding your bike to work) and attempt to change the behavior of one of your friends. Given the information provided, what steps would you take and why?

   Recall that if someone agrees to a small action, that person will be more likely to agree to a bigger action, especially if there is a connection between the two actions (known as the foot-in-the-door technique (Freedman & Fraser, 1966)). Be sure to use this technique to promote your friend's commitment to future sustainable behaviors.

2. Given that driving a car is the most air-polluting act an average citizen commits, it is important to reduce our reliance on personal cars for local transportation. Research has found that making a public commitment to engage in a behavior, especially a written commitment, increases the likelihood of continuing the behavior (McKenzie-Mohr, 2007). Write a letter to your congressional representative to persuade her/him to improve the public transportation system in your community in order to help reduce carbon emissions from cars. How would you frame your message?

3. Given the tremendous infrastructure and number of people connected to the daily use of a university, campuses have an enormous carbon footprint. Recognition of environmental problems has become a significant focus for most universities in the United States: More than 670 college and university presidents have signed the Presidents' Climate Commitment and made it a priority for their campus to conduct a greenhouse-gas inventory and write a Climate Action Plan (American College and University Presidents' Climate Commitment, 2011). You've been asked by the university president to organize a group of campus members to "roll out" a new sustainability program. Based on the information you learned in this chapter, what should you include in your sustainability program? Who would you want on your "sustainability committee?" Create a 10-minute presentation that highlights the key strategies that will need to be used to communicate the new sustainability program.

Chapter 9

Media Psychology: Violent Media and Helping Behavior

Comfortably Numb

Desensitizing Effects of Violent Media on Helping Others

By Brad J. Bushman and Craig A. Anderson

EDITORS' INTRODUCTION

How many times have you walked into a store or movie theater and noticed a person helpfully holding a door open for the person behind him or her? Do some individuals hold the door open all the time and some individuals none of the time? Or does helpful behavior change from situation to situation? This chapter explores the relationship between changes in an individual's experience (such as watching violent or nonviolent television or movies) and whether or not that person decides to help others.

Psychologists have been concerned about the effects of violence in media (including movies, television, and video games) for much of the past half century. Psychological research has documented a relationship between exposure to violent media and negative consequences, such as increased violence and aggression, and reduced helping behavior (Anderson & Bushman, 2001; Carnagey, Anderson, & Bushman, 2007). Two classic examples illustrate different aspects of this relationship. Bandura, Ross, and Ross's (1961) "Bobo the Clown" experiment demonstrated young children's tendency to imitate violent acts. In this experiment, children who watched an adult hit the inflatable clown Bobo on television engaged in similar behavior when they were later allowed to play with the toy. In contrast, children who had not been exposed to the violent example played with the toy in a nonviolent manner. The second classic example is based on a crime that occurred in 1964. In Queens, New York, several people saw or heard events related to the violent stabbing murder of Kitty Genovese, but they did not intervene to help the young woman. Social psychologists Bibb Latané and John Darley referenced this tragic event in their research describing the process people go through when deciding to offer help to others (Latané & Darley, 1968). Based on their research, Darley and Latané developed a model of a decision-making process to explain how or why individuals decide to help others. The Darley-Latané decision-making process first requires an individual to notice an incident; second, to interpret the incident as an emergency; and third, to assume responsibility for helping.

In the following article, Bushman and Anderson (2009) examine the impact that exposure to violent media has on the likelihood that an individual will notice an incident (first step in the Darley-Latané decision-making process) and interpret the incident as an emergency (second step; see Figure 2 in included article). The article refers to *desensitization* to violence, which is defined as "a reduction in emotion-related physiological reactivity to real violence" (Carnagey et al., 2007, p. 490). Individuals exposed to violent media (including video games) become desensitized and are less likely to respond to real violence. These "comfortably numb" individuals have a reduced heart rate and skin conductance (a measure of reaction to a stimulus) in response to real violence following exposure to violent media (Carnagey et al., 2007; Drabman, Horton, Lippincott, & Thomas, 1977). Desensitization to violence makes it less likely that individuals will help a victim. It seems that if our hearts aren't racing and our palms aren't sweaty, we don't interpret a situation as an emergency (the second step in the Darley-Latané decision-making process) and are therefore less likely to help.

The research article in this chapter describes two studies designed to evaluate the impact of violent media on helpfulness. As you read, pay attention to the differences in how these studies are conducted. Study 1 took place in a psychology research lab; therefore, the researchers were able to manipulate the study environment. The researchers randomly selected which participants were exposed to violence and which were not. Study 2 was a naturalistic field study. The researchers did *not* have control over which participants were exposed to violent media. As you read, think about what kinds of bias might be present in these studies.

One important concern in this area of research is the *causal relationship* between exposure to violent media and behavior such as aggression, violence, and reduced helpfulness. Does exposure to violent media *cause* violent behavior, or do individuals who already engage in violent behavior selectively *choose* to expose themselves to violent media? *Correlational research* investigates the relationship between two variables, but it cannot determine if one variable caused the outcome the researcher is studying. In *causal research*, the researcher designs a study to determine if an outcome depends directly on a manipulation the researcher used in the research. As you read, think about how the authors of this article address the issue of correlation versus causation. Are these studies correlational or causational? Does that change your thinking about this research?

Thinking back to Chapter 1, can you identify the *dependent* and *independent* variables in these studies? Do you think that the dependent variables included in these studies are appropriate for understanding the effects of violent media exposure on helping behavior? How would you evaluate the *effect sizes* in these studies? How does the *effect size* influence your interpretation of these studies?

REFERENCES

Anderson, C. A., & Bushman, B. J. (2001). Effects of violent video games on aggressive behavior, aggressive cognition, aggressive affect, physiological arousal, and prosocial behavior: A meta-analytic review of the scientific literature. *Psychological Science, 12* (5), 353–359.

Bandura, A., Ross, D., & Ross, S. A. (1961). Transmission of aggression through imitation of aggressive models. *Journal of Abnormal and Social Psychology, 63* (3), 575–582.

Bushman, B. J., & Anderson, C. A. (2009). Desensitizing effects of violent media on helping others. *Psychological Science, 20* (3), 273–277.

Carnagey, N. L., Anderson, C. A., & Bushman, B. J. (2007). The effect of video game violence on physiological desensitization to real-life violence. *Journal of Experimental Social Psychology, 43* (3), 489–496.

Latané, B. & Darley, J. M. (1968). Group inhibition of bystander intervention in emergencies. *Journal of Personality and Social Psychology, 10* (3), 215–221.

Manning, R., Levine, M., & Collins, A. (2007). The Kitty Genovese murder and the social psychology of helping. *American Psychologist, 62* (6), 555–562.

Thomas, M. H., Horton, R. W., Lippincott, E. C., & Drabman, R. S. (1977). Desensitization to portrayals of real-life aggression as a function of exposure to television violence. *Journal of Personality and Social Psychology, 35* (6), 450–458.

ABSTRACT

Two studies tested the hypothesis that exposure to violent media reduces aid offered to people in pain. In Study 1, participants played a violent or nonviolent video game for 20 min. After game play, while completing a lengthy questionnaire, they heard a loud fight, in which one person was injured, outside the lab. Participants who played violent games took longer to help the injured victim, rated the fight as less serious, and were less likely to "hear" the fight in comparison to participants who played nonviolent games. In Study 2, violent- and nonviolent-movie attendees witnessed a young woman with an injured ankle struggle to pick up her crutches outside the theater either before or after the movie. Participants who had just watched a violent movie took longer to help than participants in the other three conditions. The findings from both studies suggest that violent media make people numb to the pain and suffering of others.

Film is a powerful medium, film is a drug, film is a potential hallucinogen—it goes into your eye, it goes into your brain, it stimulates and it's a dangerous thing—it can be a very subversive thing.

— Oliver Stone (quoted in Dworkin, 1996)

If film is a drug, then violent film content might make people "comfortably numb" (borrowing the words of Pink Floyd). Specifically, exposure to blood and gore in the media might make people numb to the pain and suffering of others—a process called *desensitization*. One negative consequence of such physiological desensitization is that it may cause people to be less helpful to those in need.

The link between desensitization and helping behavior is provided by a recent model that integrates the pioneering work on helping by Latane and Darley (1968) with our work on physiological desensitization to aggression, illustrated in Figure 1. Several factors must be in place before someone decides to help a victim (Latane & Darley, 1970; see Fig. 2). Three of these factors are particularly relevant here. First, the individual must notice or attend to the violent incident. However, decreased attention to violent events is likely to be one consequence of desensitization. Second, the individual must recognize the event as an emergency. However, desensitization can reduce the perceived seriousness of injury and the perception that an emergency exists. Third, the individual must feel a personal responsibility to help. However, decreased sympathy for the victim, increased belief that violence is normative, and decreased negative attitudes toward violence all decrease feelings of personal responsibility.

Although previous research has shown that violence in the media can produce desensitization-related outcomes (e.g., Linz, Donnerstein, & Adams, 1989; Molitor & Hirsch, 1994; Mullin & Linz, 1995; Thomas, Horton, Lippincott, & Drabman, 1977), this model illuminates two gaps in the desensitization literature. First, there are no published studies testing the hypothesis that violent media stimuli known to produce physiological desensitization also reduce helping behavior. Second, there are no field experiments testing the effect of violent-entertainment media on helping an injured person. We recently found that playing a violent video game for just 20 min decreased skin conductance and heart

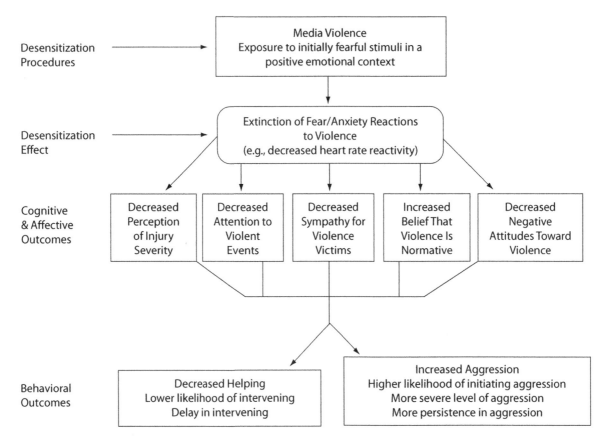

Fig. 1. Model of the effects of exposure to media violence. Such exposures serve as a desensitization procedure leading to increases in aggression and decreases in helping. Adapted from Carnagey, Anderson, and Bushman. (2007).

rate while watching real scenes of violence (Carnagey, Anderson, & Bushman, 2007). We conducted two studies to help fill these gaps: a lab experiment using violent video games (Study 1) and a field study using violent movies (Study 2).

STUDY 1

Participants played a violent or a nonviolent video game. Later, they overheard a staged fight leading to injury. We predicted that playing a violent video game, in comparison to playing a nonviolent game, would decrease the likelihood of help, delay helping, decrease the likelihood of noticing an emergency (the first step in the helping process), and decrease the judged severity of the emergency (the second step in the helping process).

METHOD

Participants

Participants were 320 college students (160 men, 160 women) who received extra course credit in exchange for voluntary participation.

Procedure

Participants were tested individually. They were told that the researchers were studying what types of people liked various types of video games. After giving consent, participants played a randomly assigned violent (*Carmageddon, Duke Nukem, Mortal Kombat, Future Cop*) or nonviolent (*Glider Pro, 3D Pinball, Austin Powers, Tetra Madness*) video game. We used the same violent and nonviolent video games and the same participant pool that Carnagey et al. (2007) used to demonstrate physiological desensitization to violence.

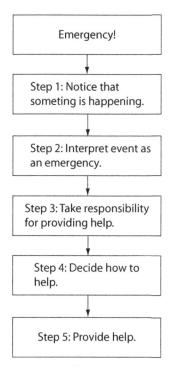

Fig 2. Five steps to helping. Adapted from Lalane and Darley (1970).

The experimenter set a timer for 20 min, handed the participant a lengthy questionnaire, and said,

After the timer goes off, please complete this questionnaire. I need to code some data for another study, but I promise to be back in about 40 min. Please don't leave the building until I get back. I have to ask you some questions about the video game before you leave. Okay?

The experimenter then departed.

After playing the video game for 20 min, participants rated on a 10-point scale (1 = *not at all*, 10 = *extremely*) how action-packed, enjoyable, fun, absorbing, arousing, boring, entertaining, exciting, involving, stimulating, addicting, and violent the video game was. The violence rating was used as a manipulation check. The other ratings were used as possible covariates in the analyses to control for differences in video games other than violent content. After reverse-scoring boring ratings, principal components factor analysis showed that the covariates loaded on a single factor (eigenvalue = 7.21), and were therefore combined (Cronbach a = .94). Because the results were virtually identical with and without the covariates, we only report the simpler analyses that excluded the covariates.

Next, participants indicated their favorite type of video game (i.e., education, fantasy, fighting with hands or weapons, skill, or sports). They also completed a lengthy bogus questionnaire (over 200 items), ostensibly to determine what types of people prefer various types of video games. The real purpose of the questionnaire was to keep participants busy while a recording of a staged fight was played outside the lab.

Three minutes after the participant finished playing the video game, the experimenter, who was outside of the lab, played an audio recording of a staged fight between two actors. The 6-min fight was professionally recorded using experienced actors. Two parallel versions of the fight involved male actors (used for male participants) or female actors (used for female participants). In the recording, the two actors were presumably waiting to do an experiment. They began by talking about how one stole the other's girlfriend (male version) or boyfriend (female version). The discussion quickly deteriorated into a shouting match (as indicated in the following script from the male version):

First actor: You stole her from me. I'm right, and you know it, you loser.

Second actor: Loser? If I'm a loser, why am I dating your ex-girlfriend?

First actor: Okay, that's it, I don't have to put up with this shit any longer.

When the recording reached this point, the experimenter threw a chair onto the floor, making a loud crash, and kicked the door to the participant's room twice.

Second actor: [groans in pain]
First actor: Ohhhh, did I hurt you?
Second actor: It's my ankle, you bastard. It's twisted or something.

First actor: Isn't that just too bad?

Second actor: I can't even stand up!

First actor: Don't look to me for pity.

Second actor: You could at least help me get off the floor.

First actor: You've gotta be kidding me. Help you? I'm outta here.

[slams the door and leaves]

At this point, the experimenter pressed the start button on the stopwatch to time how long it would take for participants to help the second actor—the violence victim. On the recording, the victim groaned in pain for about 1.5 min. Because the first actor had "left," there was no perceived danger to the participant in helping the second actor.

The experimenter waited 3 min after the groans of pain stopped to give participants ample time to help. If the participant left the room to help the victim, the experimenter pressed the stop button on the stopwatch and then debriefed the participant.

If the participant did not help after 3 min, the experimenter entered the room and said, "Hi, I'm back. Is everything going all right in here? I just saw someone limping down the hallway. Did something happen here?" The experimenter recorded whether the participant mentioned hearing the fight outside the room. Those who reported hearing the fight rated how serious it was on a 10-point scale (1 = *not at all serious*, 10 = *extremely serious)*. As justification for rating the severity of the fight, the experimenter explained the rating was required for a formal report that needed to be filed with the campus police. Finally, the participant was fully debriefed.

We conducted a pilot study involving 50 college students (25 men, 25 women) to test whether they thought the fight was real. Only 5 of the first 10 participants in the pilot study thought the fight was real. We therefore increased the realism of the fight (e.g., knocked over a chair and pounded on the door). After making these changes, all of the remaining 40 participants thought the fight was real.

RESULTS

Preliminary Analyses

As expected, violence ratings were higher for the violent games $(M = 7.89)$ than for the nonviolent games $(M = 1.51)$, $F(1, 316) = 823.13$, $p < .0001$, $p_{rep} > .99$, $d = 3.22$. We used four violent games and four nonviolent games to improve generalizability (Wells & Windschitl, 1999). Within each type of video game, we tested whether the four games produced different effects on any of the dependent variables. No significant differences were found among the four violent or the four nonviolent games. Thus, data were collapsed across exemplars of video game types for subsequent analyses.

Main Analyses

Helping. Although in the predicted direction, there was no significant difference in helping rates between violent and nonviolent video game players, 21% and 25%, respectively, $z = 0.88$, $p = .38$, $/p_{rep} > .59$, (j) = −.05. Participants who said their favorite type of video game involved "fighting with hands or weapons" were less likely to help than those who said their favorite video game was nonviolent, 11% and 26%, respectively, $z = 2.46$, $p < .02$, $p_{rep} > .92$, (j) = −.14.

Time to Help. When people who played a violent game did decide to help, they took significantly longer $(M = 73.3 s)$ to help the victim than those who played a nonviolent game $(M = 16.2 s)$, $F(1, 70) = 6.70$, $p < .02$, $p_{rep} > .92$, $d = 0.61$.

Heard Fight. The first step to helping is to notice the emergency. As expected, people who played a violent game were less likely to report that they heard the fight than those who played a nonviolent game, 94% and 99%, respectively, $z = 2,00$, $p < .05$, $p_{rep} > .87$, cj> = −.11.

Severity of Fight. The second step to helping is to judge the event as an emergency. As expected, people who played a violent game thought the fight was less serious $(M = 5.91)$ than did those who played a nonviolent game $(M = 6.44)$, $F(1, 239) = 4.44$, $p < .04$, $p_{rep} > .89$, $d = 0.27$. Men also thought the fight was less serious $(M = 5.92)$ than did women $(M = 6.49)$, $F(1, 239) = 5.43$, $p < .03$, $p_{rep}) > .90$, $d = 0.29$.

DISCUSSION

Violent video games known to produce physiological desensitization in a previous study (Carnagey et al, 2006) influenced helping behavior and related perceptual and cognitive variables in theoretically expected ways in Study 1. Participants who played a violent game took significantly longer to help, over 450% longer, than participants who played a nonviolent game. Furthermore, compared to participants who played a nonviolent game, those who played a violent game were less likely to notice the fight and rated it as less serious, which are two obstacles to helping.

STUDY 2

Participants in Study 2 were adult moviegoers. Our confederate, a young woman with a wrapped ankle and crutches, "accidentally" dropped her crutches outside a movie theater and struggled to retrieve them. A researcher hidden from view timed how long it took moviegoers to retrieve the crutches for the confederate. We expected that participants who had just watched a violent movie would take longer to help the confederate than would participants who had just watched a nonviolent movie or participants who had not yet seen a movie.

METHOD

Participants

Participants were 162 adult moviegoers.

Procedure

A minor emergency was staged just outside theaters that were showing either a violent movie (e.g., *The Ruins*, 2008) or a nonviolent movie (e.g., *Nim's Island*, 2008). The violent movies were rated "R;" the nonviolent movies were rated "PG." Participants had the opportunity to help a young woman with a wrapped ankle who dropped her crutches just outside the theater and was struggling to retrieve them. The confederate was told to pick up her crutches after 2 min

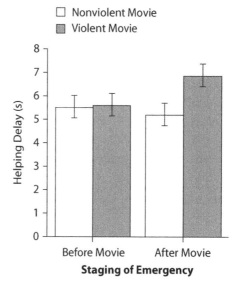

□ Nonviolent Movie
▣ Violent Movie

Fig. 3. Mean time elapsed before adults helped a confederate pick up her crutches as a function of whether they watched a violent or nonviolent movie before or after that staged emergency.

if nobody offered help, but she always received help in less than 11 s. After receiving help, she thanked the helper and then hobbled away from the theater. A researcher hidden from view timed with a stopwatch how long it took participants to help the confederate. The researcher also recorded the gender of the person offering help and the number of potential helpers in the vicinity.

The researcher flipped a coin in advance to determine whether the emergency was staged before or after the showing of a violent or nonviolent movie. Staging the emergency before the movie allowed us to test (and control) the helpfulness of people attending violent versus nonviolent movies. Staging the emergency after the movie allowed us to test the hypothesis that viewing violence inhibits helping. The confederate dropped her crutch 36 times, 9 times in each of the four experimental conditions.

RESULTS AND DISCUSSION

Although the helping delay increased as the number of bystanders increased, and women helped less often than men, these effects were not statistically significant and were not analyzed further. The data were analyzed using a model testing approach, in which a specific contrast representing our theoretical model and the residual between-groups variance are both tested for significance. If the theoretical model adequately accounts for differences among observed means, then the specific contrast should be significant and the residual between-groups variance should be nonsignificant. As predicted, participants who had just viewed a violent movie took over 26% longer to help ($M = 6.89$ s) than participants in the other three conditions ($M = 5.46$ s), $F(1, 32) = 6.20$, $p < .01$, $p_{rep} > .95$, $d = 0.88$ (see Fig. 3). Furthermore, the residual between-groups variance was not significant, $F < 1.0$, indicating that the theoretical model adequately accounted for the pattern of means. Indeed, the model accounted for 98% of the between-groups variance. The lack of a difference in helping before watching the movie rules out the possibility that less-helpful people were more likely to attend the violent movies.

GENERAL DISCUSSION

These two studies support the desensitization hypothesis linking media violence to decreased helping behavior. In Study 1, violent video games known to desensitize people caused decreases in helping-related behavior, perceptions, and cognitions. In Study 2, violent movies delayed helping in a wholly naturalistic setting. The person in need of help had an injured ankle in both studies. In Study 1, the injury resulted from interpersonal violence, whereas in Study 2, the cause of injury was unknown. The similar results across very different studies suggest that desensitization caused by media violence generalizes beyond failure to help victims of violence. Theoretically, we expect such generalization; one factor influencing helping behavior is judged severity of injury, and that judgment is influenced by one's own emotional and physiological reaction to the injury.

In sum, the present studies clearly demonstrate that violent media exposure can reduce helping behavior in precisely the way predicted by major models of helping and desensitization theory. People exposed to media violence become "comfortably numb" to the pain and suffering of others and are consequently less helpful.

ACKNOWLEDGMENTS

We thank Colleen Phillips for her help with Study 1 and Elizabeth Henley and Brad Gamache for their help with Study 2.

REFERENCES

Carnagey, N.L., Anderson, C.A., & Bushman, B.J. (2007). The effect of video game violence on physiological desensitization to real-life violence. *Journal of Experimental Social Psychology, 43*, 489–496.

Dworkin, A. (1996). *Slicing the baby in half.* Retrieved December 12, 2008, from the Times Higher Education Web site: http://www. timeshighereducation.co.uk/story. asp?storyCode=162012&section code=6

Latane, B., & Darley, J.M. (1968). Group inhibition of bystander intervention in emergencies. *Journal of Personality and Social Psychology 10*, 215–221.

Latane, B., & Darley, J.M. (1970). *The unresponsive bystander: Why doesn't he help?* New York: Appleton-Century-Crofts.

Linz, D., Donnerstein, E., & Adams, S.M. (1989). Physiological desensitization and judgments about female victims of violence. *Human Communication Research, 15*, 509–522.

Molitor, F., & Hirsch, K.W. (1994). Children's toleration of real-life aggression after exposure to media violence: A replication of the Drabman and Thomas studies. *Child Study Journal, 24*, 191–207.

Mullin, C.R., & Linz, D. (1995). Desensitization and resensitization to violence against women: Effects of exposure to sexually violent films on judgments of domestic violence victims. *Journal of Personality and Social Psychology, 69*, 449–459.

Thomas, M.H., Horton, R.W., Lippincott, E.C., & Drabman, R.S. (1977). Desensitization to portrayals of real life aggression as a function of television violence. *Journal of Personality and Social Psychology, 35*, 450–458.

Wells, G.L., & Windschitl, P.D. (1999). Stimulus sampling and social psychological experimentation. *Personality and Social Psychology Bulletin, 25*, 1115–1125.

PRACTICAL APPLICATION ASSIGNMENTS

1. You've just accepted a summer job as a counselor at a camp for boys who are identified to be at risk for violent behavior and aggression. One of the goals of the camp is to train these campers to act as peer mentors at their schools to help reduce fighting and violence. Before the campers arrive for the summer, the camp staff meets to discuss activities for the boys. One of the staff members has proposed spending some of the summer budget on a video-game system for the boys to use during their free time at camp. Based on your understanding of violent media and helpfulness, and keeping in mind the goal of the camp (to promote helpful peer-mentoring behavior), write an email memo to your supervisor that describes your recommendations for purchasing video games for the campers. Remember that your supervisor will be swayed only by well-supported recommendations.

2. You are a student intern working for the Red Cross this semester. You have been asked to help plan a media campaign intended to help victims of the 2011 earthquake and tsunami in Japan. You and a team of interns have designed a television advertisement intended to convince viewers to help these victims by volunteering or contributing to a fundraiser. The next big task for the team is to decide where and when to air the advertisement to increase the likelihood that viewers will help with the fundraiser either as volunteers or donors. Your supervisor has asked you to write a one-page report to identify television networks (such as networks devoted to music, news, sports, history, family, or cooking programming) and times of day that the advertisement should and should not be aired. In the report, your supervisor would like you to recommend five networks and times to air the advertisement, and five networks and times to *avoid* airing the advertisement, each with a short description explaining your recommendation. Base your recommendations on your understanding of Bushman and Anderson's (2009) research findings on the relationship between exposure to media and helping behavior.

3. As the president of your school's psychology club, you are responsible for recruiting volunteers to participate in a community-wide clean-up program. The psychology club thinks that it is important to get individuals involved in a program to clean up trash along sidewalks, maintain public spaces in your community, and involve residents in a community-wide effort to promote both sustainable behavior and a sense of community among residents. After reading the article in this chapter, you are inspired to recruit community volunteers at a local movie theater. The manager of the movie theater has allowed you to recruit outside of one movie each night. Which movies would you select to recruit from and why? Write a one-page email update to the psychology-club advisor outlining your ideas for recruitment at the theater.

Chapter 10

Psychology and the Law: Why Is Eyewitness Testimony Easily Distorted—And What Can We Do To Prevent It?

Current Issues and Advances in Misinformation Research

By Steven J. Frenda, Rebecca M. Nichols, and Elizabeth F. Loftus

EDITORS' INTRODUCTION

If you have watched television in the last decade, you have probably seen at least one plotline linking psychology and the law. On TV, psychologists work with police and district attorneys to "profile" perpetrators based on the patterns of their crimes, sometimes generating an uncannily accurate picture based on just a few shreds of evidence. Then, they guide detectives in the best ways to exploit suspects' weaknesses during the interrogation process. On the opposite side of the courtroom, psychologists serve as expert witnesses in the construction of "not guilty by reason of insanity" pleas, citing an exotic array of disorders calculated to get defendants off scot-free.

How do these TV portrayals stack up to reality? First, rather than just working for the prosecution or defense, psychologists involved in law fall into several distinct professional categories. *Forensic psychologists* are usually clinical psychologists who specialize in gathering and evaluating information to be used in legal proceedings, such as determining whether or not a defendant is competent to stand trial. *Legal psychologists* come from a variety of subfields including cognitive psychology, social psychology, and clinical psychology. This area is very diverse, but what legal psychologists have in common is a focus on understanding behavior and mental processes in legal contexts, often through empirical research. Legal psychologists may or may not directly participate in court cases; those who do often work as professional *trial consultants*, who advise attorneys in matters such as jury selection and how to determine the accuracy of eyewitness testimony. Legal psychology has grown tremendously in recent decades as legal professionals have become accustomed to using social science research (Monahan & Walker, 2011). Research in the field covers an amazing range of subjects: lie detection, recidivism, factors affecting award size in lawsuits, the role of mental illness in criminal behavior, interrogation tactics, confessions, jury instructions, and many more. Clearly, students who want to get involved in legal psychology have many juicy topics to choose from! (To learn more, visit the Student Information area of the web site of the American Psychology-Law Society, <http://www.ap-ls.org/aboutpsychlaw/InfoPsychLaw.php>.

Unlike what you see on TV, forensic psychologists do not typically spend large amounts of time dealing with "insanity defense" cases. In reality, these cases are far less common than TV plotlines suggest—according to one survey of legal cases in the United States., fewer than one percent of felony cases involved an insanity defense, and the majority were not successful (Callahan, Steadman, McGreevy, & Robbins, 1991). Nor do forensic psychologists focus strongly on criminal profiling: Although the FBI does maintain a behavioral analysis unit in which professionals do some profiling, there are serious questions about its effectiveness. Critics argue that profiling lacks scientific support, pointing to studies showing that professional profilers have little to no advantage over nonprofilers at predicting the characteristics of criminals based on crime-scene evidence (Snook, Eastwood, Gendreau, Goggin, & Cullen, 2007), and that profilers may look more accurate than they really are because media reports about profiling tend to focus only on successful profiling cases while ignoring unsuccessful ones (Snook, Cullen, Bennell, Taylor, & Gendreau, 2008; Snook, Taylor, Gendreau, & Bennell, 2009).

By contrast, one area where psychology has had a large and lasting impact is in memory research, specifically as it relates to eyewitness testimony. Eyewitness testimony encompasses a range of situations and issues, ranging from the straightforward, e.g., identifying suspects in a lineup, to the exotic, e.g., recovering a memory for a crime witnessed years previously. As you probably read in your textbook, psychologists have established that remembering events is more similar to piecing together scattered fragments—the so-called *reconstructive memory* process—than playing back a perfect recording. One major consequence of reconstructive memory is the *misinformation effect*, which is the subject of our psychology and law research article.

The misinformation effect takes many forms, but it can be loosely defined as a change in memory for a witnessed event caused by inaccurate information that comes in after the fact, such as a leading question or deliberately misleading suggestion. The misinformation effect is surprisingly easy to produce, even in eyewitnesses who feel quite confident that they remember an event accurately. It follows that eyewitness testimony is subject to contamination and distortion, particularly when eyewitnesses go through numerous interviews, which raises many concerns, given the importance of eyewitness testimony in the legal system. Take, as an example a hypothetical case where detectives repeatedly ask a witness to describe a knife they believe was used in a robbery. The witness may not have seen a knife at all, but may come to falsely remember seeing one based on what the detectives have suggested. This false recollection may then become part of the eyewitness's memory of the crime, and if the testimony is given weight in a court trial, could lead to the defendant's being convicted of armed robbery.

How vulnerable are different people to the misinformation effect, and is there any way that we can reduce its impact on eyewitness testimony? These are questions that Steven Frenda, Rebecca Nichols, and Elizabeth Loftus address in their brief review article titled *Current Issues and Advancements in Misinformation Research*. In it, the authors explain how researchers study the misinformation effect and describe the ways in which researchers have been able to manipulate memory in laboratory settings. They go on to discuss which circumstances, such as attention overload, tend to make the misinformation effect worse. In this same section, they point out that some groups of people are more susceptible to misinformation. Read this part very critically. Do you think it implies that testimony from certain types of people should be given less weight? Would such a practice be a fair or unfair application of misinformation research?

Frenda and coauthors (2011) continue with a thought-provoking section on what today's brain-scanning technology can tell us about the misinformation effect. Here again, consider critically whether you think brain scans will ever stand up as evidence in a court case, based on what these authors have to say. The article wraps up with two contrasting sections, one that describes positive steps that help prevent distortions to eyewitness memory, and a concluding section that describes other ways—besides the classic misinformation effect—in which eyewitness errors can arise. Once you have finished reading the entire article, ask yourself: Does this article suggest that cognitive research has helped reform the use of eyewitness testimony, or do we still have a tremendous amount left to do in order to address the problem?

REFERENCES

Callahan, L. A., Steadman, H. J., McGreevy, M. A., & Robbins, P. C. (1991). The volume and characteristics of insanity defense pleas: An eight-state study. *Bulletin of the American Academy of Psychiatry & the Law, 19* (4), 331–338.

Frenda, S. J., Nichols, R. M., & Loftus, E. F. (2011). Current issues and advances in misinformation research. *Current Directions in Psychological Science, 20* (1), 20–23.

Monahan, J., & Walker, L. (2011). Twenty-five years of social science in law. *Law and Human Behavior, 35* (1), 72–82.

Snook, B., Cullen, R. M., Bennell, C., Taylor, P. J., & Gendreau, P. (2008). The criminal profiling illusion: What's behind the smoke and mirrors? *Criminal Justice and Behavior, 35* (10), 1257–1276.

Snook, B., Eastwood, J., Gendreau, P., Goggin, C., & Cullen, R. M. (2007).Taking stock of criminal profiling: A narrative review and meta-analysis. *Criminal Justice and Behavior, 34* (4), 437–453.

Snook, B., Taylor, P. J., Gendreau, P., & Bennell, C. (2009). On the need for scientific experimentation in the criminal-profiling field: A reply to Dern and colleagues. *Criminal Justice and Behavior, 36* (10), 1091–1094.

ABSTRACT

Eyewitnesses are often called upon to report information about what they have seen. A wealth of research from the past century has demonstrated, however, that eyewitness memory is malleable and vulnerable to distorting influences, including the effects of misinformation. In this article, we review recent developments in research related to the misinformation effect, including individual differences in susceptibility, neuroimaging approaches, and protective interview procedures that may better elicit accurate event details. We conclude with a section on related false memory research.

Twenty-five people died when a Metrolink commuter train collided with a Union Pacific freight train near Los Angeles in September of 2008 (Steinhauer, 2008). With millions of dollars in lawsuit payouts at stake, federal accident authorities began an investigation of the deadly crash and had to decide a key issue: Did the conductor pass legally through a green light, as four eyewitnesses maintained? Or did he sail through a red light, distracted by sending and receiving text messages? The conductor died in the crash, so he could not be asked. If he were at fault, the railroad company that was responsible for hiring and supervising him would be liable. If the signal malfunctioned, another company would be on the hook. After an extensive investigation, the authorities decided the eyewitnesses were wrong. The signal was red, and the engineer's text messaging was a major contributor to the accident, is it possible that four eyewitnesses—including a conductor, a security guard, and two railroad enthusiasts—were all mistaken about such a crucial detail? The answer is yes. Eyewitnesses make mistakes, multiple eyewitnesses can all be wrong, and their erroneous testimony can have enormous consequences.

How is it possible that so many witnesses could all be so wrong? Eyewitnesses are called upon not only to remember details of events, but also to describe what people look like and to decide how confident they are in the accuracy of their memories. They are often asked to remember things they saw in extremely stressful circumstances, sometimes months or even years after the fact. They are frequently bombarded with information following the event they witnessed, such as other witnesses' reports, investigator feedback, leading questions, and pressures to be both accurate and helpful. In the face of these challenges, eyewitnesses misremember. In a recent discussion of the distorting effect witnesses have on the memory of other witnesses, Wright, Memort, Skagerberg, and Gabbert (2009) proposed three accounts of why eyewitnesses come to report incorrect information. First, a witness's report may be altered due to normative social influence. That is, a witness may decide that the cost of disagreeing with law enforcement—or with other witnesses—is too high, and so he adjusts his report accordingly. A second possibility is that through informational social influence processes, a witness comes to endorse a version of events that is different from what he remembers because he believes it to be truer or more accurate than his own memory. Finally, a witness's memory can become distorted, sometimes as the result of being exposed to incorrect or misleading information. This third possibility, known as the misinformation effect, is the focus of the current review. Advances in misinformation research concerning individual differences, neurophysiological correlates, cognitive interviewing, and related research paradigms are reviewed.

WHAT IS THE MISINFORMATION EFFECT?

In the wake of more than 30 years of research, an ever-growing literature continues to demonstrate the distorting effects of misleading postevent information on memory for words, faces, and details of witnessed events (see Loftus, 2005, for a review of the misinformation effect). In a typical misinformation experiment, research subjects are shown materials (e.g., photographs) and are then exposed to deliberately misleading information about what they saw. In a final testing phase, many subjects will inadvertently incorporate elements from the misleading information into their memory for the original source material. For example, Stark, Okado, and Loftus (2010) showed subjects a series of photographs that depicted a man stealing a woman's wallet and hiding it in his jacket pocket. Later, subjects heard recorded narratives describing the slides. Embedded in the narratives were several pieces of misleading information (e.g., "Then the man hid the wallet in his pants pocket"). Finally, subjects were asked questions about details from the photographs, such as "Where did the thief hide the woman's wallet?[1]" A substantial number of those subjects not only reported that the thief hid the wallet in his pants pocket, but they also reported that they remembered that information from the photographs, not the narratives.

WHO IS VULNERABLE?

Nobody is immune to the distorting effects of misinformation. Building on the adult literature, misinformation effects have been obtained in myriad subject samples, including infants (Rovee-Collier, Borza, Adler, & Boller, 1993), and even animals (e.g., Schwartz, Meissner, Hoffman, Evans, & Frazier, 2004). Nonetheless, there is evidence that certain types of people are especially vulnerable to misinformation effects. For instance, very young children and the elderly are more susceptible to misinformation than adolescents and adults (see Davis & Loftus, 2005). Also especially vulnerable are subjects who report lapses in memory and attention (Wright & Livingston-Raper, 2002). What do these findings tell us about the underlying mechanisms driving the misinformation effect? One argument is that a poverty of cognitive resources necessitates an increased reliance on external cues to reconstruct memories of events. As Loftus (2005) points out, misinformation effects are easier to obtain when subjects' attentional resources are limited. Similarly, people who perceive themselves to be forgetful and who experience memory lapses may be less able (or willing) to depend on their own memories as the sole source of information as they mentally reconstruct an event.

Recently, two major studies containing more than 400 subjects have explored cognitive ability and personality factors as predictors of susceptibility to misinformation. In each study, subjects viewed slides of two crimes and later read narratives of the crimes that contained misinformation. Those subjects who had higher intelligence scores, greater perceptual abilities, greater working memory capacities, and greater performance on face recognition tasks tended to resist misinformation and produce fewer false memories (Zhu et al., 2010a). Certain personality characteristics were also shown to be associated with false memory formation, particularly in individuals with lesser cognitive ability. Specifically, individuals low in fear of negative evaluation and harm avoidance, and those high in cooperativeness, reward dependence, and self-directedness were associated with an increased vulnerability to misinformation effects (Zhu et ah, 2010b). In other words, it seems that personality variables may be helpful in understanding the processes underlying memory distortion following exposure to misinformation, but less so in individuals with superior cognitive ability. These interactions may help explain why individual difference results have not always replicated in false memory research.

MISINFORMATION AND NEUROIMAGING

Relatively new, but increasingly popular tools for exploring the effects of postevent information on memory include a set of highly specialized neuroscientific methods which include functional magnetic resonance imaging, or fMRl. In a typical fMRI-based behavioral experiment, subjects undergo traditional experimental procedures in an MRI scanner, during which functional images of oxygenated blood flow in the brain are collected. The resulting images can be analyzed and interpreted as differential brain activation associated with particular tasks. Functional MRI, therefore, is a useful and noninvasive tool for examining the neurobiological correlates of behavior.

Scientists have begun to investigate brain activity associated with the misinformation effect. In a recent study (Stark et al., 2010), subjects were shown a series of photographs and later listened to an auditory narrative describing them, which included misleading information. Soon afterward, they were placed into an MRI scanner and given a test of their memory for the photographs. Functional neuroimaging data revealed similar patterns of brain activity for true and false memories, but the true memories (formed by visual information) showed somewhat more activation in the visual cortex while the false memories (derived from the auditory narrative) showed somewhat more activation in the auditory cortex. As the researchers noted, these results are congruent with the sensory reactivation hypothesis (Slotnick & Schacter, 2004, 2006), which in part proposes that the same sensory regions activated in the brain during encoding will be reactivated during retrieval. These results suggest that there may be differing brain activation patterns for true and false memories when they are encoded in different sensory modalities.

Research that involves neuroimaging and other neuroscientific measurement techniques are promising for discoveries about the effects of misinformation on memory: They can provide glimpses into how different neurological processes underlie true and false memories. At the present time, however, it would be wise to err on the side of caution in the application of these findings. Although some differences were found, the patterns of brain activation associated with true and false memories in Stark et al.'s (2010) study were not reliably distinct, and other small differences in brain activation (unrelated to the sensory reactivation hypothesis) were not fully accounted for. Furthermore, data from fMRI studies are often averaged both within and across participants, which makes interpretation at the individual level of analysis difficult. Although functional neuroimaging is elaborate and cutting edge, it has yet to provide a sure-fire way to confidently judge whether or not a particular person's memory is accurate.

PROTECTING AGAINST MISINFORMATION EFFECTS

Not surprisingly, some effort has been focused on ways to protect against the distorting effect of misinformation. One technique for improving the accuracy and completeness of an eyewitness's recollection is known as the *cognitive interview,* a set of rules and guidelines for interviewing eyewitnesses (see Wells, Memon, & Penrod, 2006, for a review). The CI recommends, for example, the use of free recall, contextual cues, temporal ordering of events, and recalling the event from a variety of perspectives (such as from a perpetrator's point of view). Also, the CI recommends that investigators avoid suggestive questioning, develop rapport with the witness, and discourage witnesses from guessing, in one recent study, subjects viewed an 8-minute film depicting a robbery (Memon, Zaragoza, Clifford, & Kidd, 2009). Later, subjects were given either a CI or a free-response control interview, followed by suggestive questioning about events not depicted in the film. Results indicated that, consistent with earlier findings, the CI produced more correct details than did the free-response procedure. One week after the interview procedure, subjects were given a recognition test for items in the video, and subjects incorporated details from the suggestive questioning into their memory for the event. Results showed that the CI deterred the effects of suggestion, but only when it came *before* the suggestive interview. Though the investigative process would ideally be free of all suggestive influence, a properly implemented cognitive interview may help protect the integrity of an eyewitness's memory.

RELATED LINES OF RESEARCH

In addition to the classic misinformation paradigm, researchers have developed other ways to demonstrate that even the subtlest suggestions can produce astonishing false witness reports. For instance, a handful of studies have emerged in which subjects are simply asked if they have seen video footage of well-known news events, when in fact no such video footage exists. One study found that 40% of a British sample was willing to report having seen nonexistent footage of a bus exploding in the 2005 London terrorist attacks (Ost, Granhag, Udell, & Hjelmsater. 2008). Of the subjects who claimed they saw the footage, 35% described memories of details that they could not have seen. Another study (Sjoden, Granhag, Ost, & Hjelmsater, 2009) found that 64% of a Swedish sample claimed to have seen nonexistent video footage of an attack on the Swedish foreign minister, and 19% went on to describe details in the form of written narratives. The ease with which these studies elicited blatantly false memory reports is striking.

Research has also shown that suggestion can also shape autobiographical memory. Beginning with Loftus and Piekrell's Lost in the Mall study (1995),

a series of studies have successfully used personalized suggestion (or other suggestive techniques) to plant false memories of traumatic childhood events (Porter, Yuille, & Lehman, 1999), receiving a painful enema (Hart & Schooler, 2006), and even impossible events such as meeting Bugs Bunny—a Warner Brothers character—at Disneyland (Bram, Ellis, & Loftus, 2002). These lines of research represent a broad area in their own right, with controversies and applications that are beyond the scope of this paper. However, they show that misleading postevent information has implications beyond merely mistaking a green traffic light for a red one or misremembering where a pickpocket hid a woman's wallet. If suggestion can cause us to remember experiences that never occurred, what does this say about the reliability of eyewitness evidence in general? If merely asking people if they have seen events they could not possibly have witnessed represents a strong enough suggestion to cause such staggering errors, what are the implications for witnesses who were present at a crime scene but never saw a perpetrator's face, only to hear it described later? Researchers continue to investigate what conditions lead to memory distortion, which types of people are most susceptible, and how best to prevent the distorting effects of postevent information. Unfortunately, in spite of recent scientific advances, many eyewitness errors continue to go undetected and can have devastating consequences.

Declaration of Conflicting Interests

The authors declared that they had no conflicts of interest with respect to their authorship or the publication of this article.

Recommended Reading

Brainerd, C.J., & Reyna, V.F. (2005). *The science of false memory*. New York; Oxford University Press. A book, over 500 pages long, that describes nearly everything a reader would want to know about false memories.

Loftus, E.F. (2005). (See References). Summarizes some of the key studies that have contributed to more than three decades' worth of research on the misinformation effect.

REFERENCES

Braun, K.A., Ellis, R., & Loftus, E.F. (2002). Make my memory: How advertising can change our memories of the past. *Psychology & Marketing, 19,* 1–23.

Davis, D., & Loftus, E.F. (2005). Age and functioning in the legal system: Perception memory and judgment in victims, witnesses and jurors, in I. Noy & W. Karwowski (Eds.), *Handbook of forensic human factors and ergonomics.* London, England; Taylor & Francis.

Hart, R.E., & Schooler, J.W. (2006). Increasing belief in the experience of an invasive procedure that never happened: The role of plausibility and schematicity, *Applied Cognitive Psychology, 20,*661–669.

Loftus, E.F. (2005). Planting misinformation in the human mind: A 30-year investigation of the malleability of memory. *Learning and Memory, 12,* 361–366.

Loftus, E.F., & Pickrell, J.E. (1995). The formation of false memories. *Psychiatric Annals, 25,* 720–725.

Memon, A., Zaragoza, M., Clifford, B.R., & Kidd, L. (2009). Inoculation or antidote? The effects of cognitive interview timing on fake memory for forcibly fabricated events. *Law and Human Behavior, 34,* 105–117.

Ost, J., Granhag, P., Udell, J., & Hjelmsater, E.R. (2008). Familiarity breeds distortion: The effects of media exposure on false reports concerning media coverage of the terrorist attacks in London on 7 July 2005. *Memory, 16,* 76–85.

Porter, S., Yuille, J.C., & Lehman, D.R. (1999), The nature of real, implanted, and fabricated memories for emotional childhood events: Implications for the recovered memory debate. *Law and Human Behavior, 23,* 517–537.

Rovee-Collier, C., Borza, M.A., Adler, S.A., & Boller, K. (1993). Infants' eyewitness testimony: Effects of postevent information on a prior memory representation. *Memory and Cognition, 21,* 267–279.

Schwartz, B.L., Meissner, C.M, Hoffman, M.L., & Evans, S., & Frazier, L.D, (2004). Event memory and information effects in a gorilla. *Animal Cognition, 7,* 93–100.

Sjoden, B., Granhag, P.A., Ost, J., & Hjelmsater, E.R. (2009). Is the truth in the details? Extended narratives help distinguishing false "memories" from false "reports." *Scandinavian Journal of Psychology, 50,* 203–210.

Slotnick, S.D., & Schacter, D.L. (2004). A sensory signature that distinguishes true from false memories. *Nature Neuroscience, 7,* 664–672.

Slotnick, S.D., & Schacter, D.L. (2006). The nature of memory related activity in early visual areas. *Neuropsychohgia, 44,* 2874–2886.

Stark, C.E.L., Okado, Y., & Loftus, E.F. (2010). Imaging the reconstruction of true and false memories using sensory reactivation and the misinformation paradigms. *Learning and Memory, 77,* 485–488.

Steinhauer, J. (2008, September 12). At least 18 killed as trains collide in Los Angeles. *The New York Times.* Retrieved from http://www.nytimes.com/2008/09/13/us/13crash.html

Wells, G.L., Memon, A., & Penrod. S.D, (2006). Eyewitness evidence: improving its probative value. *Psychological Science in the Public Interest, 7,* 45–75.

Wright, D.B., & Livingston-Raper, D. (2002). Memory distortion and dissociation: Exploring the relationship in a non-clinical sample. *Journal of Trauma & Dissociation, 3,* 97–109.

Wright, D.B., Memon, A., Skagerberg, E.M., & Gabbert, F. (2009). When eyewitnesses talk. *Current Directions in Psychological Science, 18,* 174–178.

Zhu, B., Chen, C., Loftus, E.F., Lin, C., He, Q., Chen, C., et al. (2010a). Individual differences in false memory from misinformation: Cognitive factors. *Memory,* 543–555.

Zhu, B., Chen, C., Loftus, E.F., Lin, C., He, Q., Chen, C., et al. (2010b). Individual differences in false memory from misinformation: Personality characteristics and their interactions with cognitive abilities. *Personality and Individual Differences, 48,* 889–894.

PRACTICAL APPLICATION ASSIGNMENTS

1. Prepare a report for your school's office of career services on career opportunities for legal and forensic psychologists. Start by going to the web site for the American Psychology-Law Society<http://www.ap-ls.org/index.php> and navigating to the section titled Job Listings. Choose one of the major job categories—academic, professional, or post-doctoral—and read each of the available listings. Based on these listings, write a description of what the job market is like for this kind of career, being sure to include the following: 1) specific job titles currently available, 2) typical work settings (university, hospital, etc.), 3) typical job activities and responsibilities, and 4) required qualifications (education, experience, etc.). Conclude with a paragraph that offers general advice to college students who want a career in legal or forensic psychology.

2. Write a report to a TV producer who has hired you to consult on a new legal drama about eyewitnesses. Summarize what psychologists currently know about false memory, and make some specific suggestions about plotlines that would accurately capture some of the important debates and developments in the study of eyewitness memory.

3. Write an email to a local police detective who has received conflicting information about a crime based on different eyewitnesses and corroborating evidence. The detective wants advice on how to weigh this conflicting information and how he should proceed with his investigation. In your email, describe and explain the different factors that affect the accuracy of eyewitness testimony. Then, make three to five specific suggestions about how the detective should proceed with the case.

Chapter 11

School Psychology:
School-Based Relational
Aggression Interventions

A Review of Existing Relational Aggression Programs

Strengths, Limitations, and Future Directions

By Stephen S. Leff, Tracy Evian Waasdorp, and Nicki R. Crick

EDITORS' INTRODUCTION

"Last winter I became the victim of relational aggression. One morning I awoke to find that my house had been 'egged.' There was a rumor started that I had gone out on a date with a senior boy that Friday, so his girlfriend decided that she would throw eggs at my house, as a pay-back. In fact, I had only been at dinner with my family. The girls egged our house two more times and in school, in the halls, I would hear them shout hurtful and embarrassing things to me.

One night at a basketball game they approached me, and verbally harassed me in front of everybody. I remember going home that night and crying to my parents. I felt like the entire school was against me. I was hurt, and I felt completely alone. I became more and more isolated as the harassment continued; I had never realized how vulnerable I was.

I did make it through the school year, but I had almost completely withdrawn from most school functions. This fall I transferred to another school." (Personal story from The Ophelia Project)

It is clear to most people that maliciously hitting someone is a case of aggression. Did you know that spreading rumors in order to hurt someone or telling someone that you will no longer be her friend if she doesn't do what you want are also forms of aggression? More specifically, these are examples of relational aggression. Coined by Crick and Grotpeter (1995), the term *relational aggression* is defined as nonphysical aggression in which one person manipulates or harms another person's social standing or reputation through direct or indirect actions. Other behaviors considered to be relationally aggressive include exclusion, ignoring, spiteful gossip, taunts and insults, malicious teasing, intimidation, alliance building, cyberbullying, and manipulative affection (using affection as a reward or a punishment to get what you want).

Contrary to popular perception, relational aggression is not limited to female relationships (Archer, 2004; Card, Stucky, Sawalani, & Little, 2008; Leff, Waasdorp, & Crick, 2010). While girls engage in relational aggression more than physical aggression and more girls than boys describe being hurt by relational aggression, boys also use relational aggression to harm others and experience its painful consequences. Just think back to the distressing accounts of boys in recent years who went on killing rampages in their schools after being rejected and humiliated by their peers and exposed to other traumatic experiences, such as physical abuse (Garbarino, 1999). It is clear that relational aggression is not just a girl phenomenon, as both boys and girls use relational aggression and experience its negative effects.

Relational aggression has been associated with social problem-solving challenges, emotion-regulation deficits, peer-relationship difficulties, academic struggles, teacher-student conflicts, anxiety, depression, and loneliness, and it is predictive of future psychosocial maladjustment (e.g., dropping out of college) (Card et al., 2008; Crick,Ostrov, & Kawabata, 2007). Past research has found that relationally aggressive girls often exhibit hostile attribution bias, the tendency to assume behaviors are hostile (Crick, Grotpeter, & Bigbee, 2002). For example, a relationally aggressive girl may overhear two classmates talking about having a sleepover and assume she has been deliberately excluded. In contrast, a girl who does not engage in relationally aggressive behavior is more likely to ignore the conversation or think that there was a legitimate reason why she wasn't invited to the sleepover.

Given the serious consequences linked with relational aggression, school-based professionals, especially school psychologists, must develop, implement, and evaluate school-based interventions to address relational aggression. *School psychologists* are scientific practitioners (i.e., helping professionals who base their activities on empirical research) who focus on children, families, and the schooling process.

In the research article for this chapter, Stephen Leff and colleagues (2010) summarize the correlates of relationally aggressive behaviors, but in the original, full-length article, they reviewed nine prevention programs. For this chapter, we have included one of the reviewed programs (the Friend-to-Friend Program) because it focused on the development of a social problem-solving/social-skills intervention for inner city 3rd- to 5th-grade urban, African American, relationally aggressive girls. The purpose of the intervention was to decrease the girls' relational and physical aggression, tendency to display hostile attributional biases, and internalization of symptoms, such as feelings of loneliness and sadness. One of the goals of this study was to develop an intervention that the participating girls and teachers would accept. As you read the article, think about why it is important to develop a culturally appropriate intervention. Do you think the researchers were successful in meeting their goal? Did the participants accept the intervention? Think back to the definitions of *field experiment* and *laboratory experiment* described in Chapter 1. Is this study a good example of a field experiment? Why or why not? Could the scientists answer their specific research questions if they had conducted the study in a laboratory?

REFERENCES

American Psychological Association (2011). *Division 16—School Psychology.* Retrieved from http://www. apa.org/about/division/div16.aspx

Archer, J. (2004). Sex differences in aggression in real-world settings. A meta-analytic review. *Review of General Psychology, 8* (4), 291–322.

Card, N. A., Stucky, B. D., Sawalani, G. M., & Little, T. D. (2008). Direct and indirect aggression during childhood and adolescence: A meta-analytic review of gender differences, intercorrelations, and relations to maladjustment. *Child Development, 79* (5), 1185–1229.

Crick, N. R., & Grotpeter, J. K. (1995). Relational aggression, gender, and social-psychological adjustment. *Child Development, 66* (3), 710–722.

Crick, N. R., Grotpeter, J. K., & Bigbee, M. A. (2002). Relationally and physically aggressive children's intent attributions and feelings of distress for relational and instrumental peer provocations. *Child Development, 73* (4), 1134–1142.

Crick, N. R., Ostrov, J. M., & Kawabata, Y. (2007), Relational aggression and gender: An overview. In D. J. Flannery, A. T. Vazsonyi, & I. D. Waldman, (Eds.), *The Cambridge handbook of violent behavior and aggression* (pp. 245–259). New York, NY: Cambridge University Press.

Garbarino, J. (1999). *Lost Boys: Why our sons turn violent and how we can save them.* New York: Free Press.

Leff, S. S., Waasdorp, T. E., & Crick, N. R. (2010). A review of existing relational aggression programs: Strengths, limitations, and future directions. *School Psychology Review, 39* (4), 508–535.

The Ophelia Project (2011). Retrieved from http://www.opheliaproject.org/main/ra_stories.htm

ABSTRACT

Research suggests that involvement in relational aggression is associated with serious adjustment problems, including concurrent and future social maladjustment (e.g., problematic friendships; rejection), internalizing problems (e.g., depressive symptoms), and school avoidance. Despite the burgeoning literature focusing on the harmful and damaging nature of relationally aggressive behavior, this research has only recently begun to be used to inform school-based prevention and intervention programming. This article reviews the developmental research related to relational aggression and presents a systematic examination of nine published school-based prevention and intervention programs to prevent relational aggression. Programs reviewed target preschool through eighth-grade students. Strengths and limitations of each program are discussed. Recommendations are offered for future research to develop and validate school-based programming for relational aggression, and implications for school psychologists are discussed.

Physical aggression, defined as the intent to harm another through physical force or dominance, has been studied extensively for many years (Dodge, Coie, & Lynam, 2006). As a result, research has shown that physical aggressors have many social problem-solving and emotional regulation deficits (Crick & Dodge, 1994; Vasey, Dangleish, & Silverman, 2003), extensive peer relationship difficulties, and a number of adjustment difficulties as they get older (Leff, Power, Manz, Costigan, & Nabors, 2001). In the past two decades, researchers have developed a broadened conceptualization of aggression to include nonphysical behaviors that damage one's status or social standing within the peer group (Crick, Ostrov, & Kawabata, 2007). Crick and Grotpeter (1995) coined the term *relational aggression* to describe these behaviors. Relational aggression is defined as nonphysical aggression in which one manipulates or harms another's social standing or reputation. Relationally aggressive behaviors can be direct, such as when peers indicate that they will no longer be a person's friend if that person does not do what they say, or indirect, such as when peers spread rumors behind a person's back so that others will not like that person. Relational aggression is a serious concern for youth, as it has been associated with a range of deficits including social problem-solving and emotion regulation deficits, peer relationship difficulties, internalizing problems such as anxiety, depression, and loneliness, and is predictive of future psychosocial maladjustment (Card, Stucky, Sawalani, & Little, 2008; Crick et al., 2007). Despite this, relatively little attention has been paid to how developmental research on relational aggression can inform the development and validation of evidence-based prevention and intervention programming (Leff, Gullan et al., 2009).

The goals of the current article are to: (a) briefly review the developmental research on relational aggression and associated features that may inform development of prevention/ intervention programs, (b) conduct a thorough review of the strengths and limitations of selected published intervention programs that address relational aggression, and (c) discuss recommendations and implications for future research and school psychology practice.

CORRELATES OF RELATIONALLY AGGRESSIVE BEHAVIORS

Adjustment Difficulties

Studies have demonstrated that relational aggression is moderately stable during both early childhood (Crick, Ostrov, Burr, Cullerton-Sen, Jansen-Yeh, & Ralston, 2006; Ostrov, Woods, Jansen, Casas, & Crick, 2004) and middle childhood (Zimmer-Gembeck, Geiger, & Crick, 2005); further, it significantly predicts peer rejection one year later, even after accounting for youths' levels of physical aggression (Crick, 1996). Relational aggression is also related to a number of other difficulties including behavioral challenges, internalizing problems, academic deficits, teacher-student conflicts, lack of school engagement (Crick & Grotpeter, 1995; Murray-Close, Ostrov, & Crick, 2007; Prinstein, Boergers, & Vernberg, 2001), and later mental health disorders among girls such as mood and eating disorders (Werner & Crick, 1999). In addition, relational aggression is highly associated with physical aggression for some children (Card et

al., 2008; Cillessen & Mayeux, 2004), which may compound the complexity of the problems. In sum, programs addressing relational aggression may need to use strategies that have been effective for the reduction of physical aggression and may benefit by addressing the extensive social and emotional difficulties related to relational aggression.

Social Processing and Emotional Arousal Deficits

A combination of biological vulnerabilities, sociocultural contexts, and life experiences interact with social and emotional processing skills to determine children's responses to social situations (Dodge & Petit, 2003). Along with emotional processing, youth progress through a series of social information processing (SIP) steps that likely mediate between biological/psychological risk factors and aggressive behaviors. These steps include (1) encoding environmental cues, (2) interpreting cues, (3) selecting social goals, (4) generating possible alternative responses, and (5) making decisions to enact a behavioral response. Many studies have shown that youth who are physically aggressive demonstrate deficits in these SIP steps (Vasey et al., 2003). Other studies suggest that relationally aggressive youth demonstrate some of the same social processing deficits as physical aggressors. For instance, relational aggressors tend to attribute hostile intentions to others in relationally provocative social situations (SIP Step 2; Crick, Grotpeter, & Bigbee, 2002; Leff, Kupersmidt, & Power, 2003), and evaluate aggressive solutions more favorably (SIP Step 4; Crick & Werner, 1998) as compared to nonrelational aggressive children. Although more research is needed to determine whether relational aggressors have additional processing deficits, a number of researchers advocate for the use of social cognitive reframing interventions with relationally aggressive youth, similar to interventions commonly used with physical aggressors (Fraser et al, 2005; Leff, Gullan et al., 2009).

Perceived Popularity

Despite the wide range of social processing, peer relationship, and social adjustment difficulties experienced by relational aggressors, a number of these youth may also have considerable social influence within the peer group (Cillessen & Mayeux, 2004; Puckett, Aikins, & Cillessen, 2008). Although this initially seems counterintuitive, it appears that some relationally aggressive youth reap benefits through being adept at social manipulation. For instance, studies have found that although relationally aggressive youth are often disliked by their peers, some are also viewed as quite influential and popular (Cillessen & Mayeux, 2004; Prinstein & Cillessen, 2003). Further, the association between high social status and relationally aggressive behavior has been found for both boys and girls (Hoff, Reese-Weber, Schneider, & Stagg, 2009; Puckett et al., 2008). To deal with popularity issues, programming for relationally aggressive youth may need to include opportunities for relational aggressors to demonstrate their influence and leadership in a prosocial manner.

DIFFERENCES IN THE EXPRESSION OF RELATIONAL AGGRESSION

Developmental Differences

Although relational aggression has largely been depicted in the popular press as a complicated and manipulative process used during adolescence, research demonstrates that relatively simple forms of relational aggression can be detected among children as young as 3 years of age (Ostrov et al., 2004). Relationally aggressive actions for preschoolers tend to be direct, with the victim usually present. For instance, children may put their hands over their ears as a way to indicate that they are ignoring a peer. Thus, relational aggression is more easily observed at this young age than it is among older children. Some research suggests that preschoolers' relationally aggressive actions may be influenced by their early experiences within the home with older siblings and parents (Stauffacher & De-Hart, 2006). The implication is that prevention/intervention programs for young children may need to address direct forms of relational aggression and include parent programming whenever possible.

As children progress through elementary and early middle school, relationally aggressive actions can be direct or indirect and begin to manifest in a more complex manner. For example, exclusionary behaviors are often seen at this age. Also, the importance of the peer group and specifically of peer reputations takes on increasing salience during these years (Leff et al., 2003), making it more difficult to change relationally aggressive behaviors. Thus, not only is it important to help relationally aggressive perpetrators and/or victims learn new and more adaptive behavioral repertoires, but it may also be important to change the peer group culture that supports and maintains relational aggression (Leff et al., 2003). Similarly, programs for school-age youth are likely to be more effective if they take into account the broader social-ecological contexts in which aggression occurs, such as the unstructured school settings of the playground, lunchroom, hallways, and bus stops (Leff, Costigan, & Power, 2004).

As youngsters approach adolescence, relationally aggressive actions continue to become more complex and subtle. In addition, with the increased use of electronic media (e.g., e-mail, text messaging, Facebook) during adolescence, youth can also use this as a medium for relationally aggressive behaviors (Williams & Guerra, 2007). Researchers have also started to study relational aggression within the context of romantic relationships (Ellis, Crooks, & Wolf, 2009). For instance, Ellis and colleagues found that girls who were relationally aggressive in both their peer and dating relationships were much more likely to display delinquent behaviors than girls who display relational aggression in only the peer context. Thus, prevention and intervention programs designed for adolescents may need to include ways in which to address the effect of electronic media on the expression of aggression and to potentially address the romantic relationship as another important aspect of the social-ecological context.

Gender Differences

Over the past few decades there has been a growing recognition that girls and boys express their anger differently, with boys tending to display aggression in a physical manner related to dominance, in contrast to girls tending to use relationally manipulative behaviors (Björkqvist, Osterman, & Kaukiainen, 1992; Crick et al., 2007; Galen & Underwood, 1997). Given research showing that girls place more importance on close dyadic peer relationships than boys (Crick & Grotpeter, 1995), it is not surprising that girls express much of their aggression in a form that involves damage to peer relationships. As a result, girls are more distressed by relational conflicts than are boys (Crick, 1995; Crick, Grotpeter, & Bigbee, 2002) and experience a substantially higher physiological response (systolic blood pressure) to relational situations as compared to boys (Murray-Close & Crick, 2007).

While recognizing the salience and meaning of relationally aggressive behaviors among girls, it has become clear that relational aggression also affects boys and the broader context in which it occurs. For example, research indicates that relational aggression occurs quite frequently among boys (Card et al., 2008; Swearer, 2008), and boys who display relational aggression (as opposed to physical aggression) experience greater psychosocial maladjustment than boys who display gendernormative expressions of aggression (Crick, 1997). With regard to the effect of relational aggression on the broader context, research has found that students feel less safe in schools in which relational aggression is frequent (Kuppens, Grietens, Onghena, Michiels, & Subramanian, 2008). Given that relational aggression occurs quite often among both boys and girls and has an effect on the school environment, it appears that school-based programming for relational aggression is needed for both girls and boys.

Taken together, the research focusing on relational aggression underscores the importance of targeting this form of aggression when designing programs for aggressive youth (Leff, Angelucci, Goldstein, Cardaciotto, Paskewich, & Grossman, 2007). The scientific literature has been relatively slow to inform relational aggression interventions; however, several researchers have begun to use this burgeoning literature base to update ongoing interventions that did not include relational aggression in prior trials, as well as to develop new programs with a concentrated focus on relational aggression. ...

Friend to Friend (F2F)

The goal of the school-based F2F program (Leff, Gullan et al., 2009) is to decrease relationally and physically aggressive behaviors, improve problem-solving skills, and increase prosocial behaviors among urban third-through fifth-grade relationally aggressive girls. A preliminary study across two large inner-city elementary schools was undertaken using a random assignment procedure with control group (treatment as usual/referral to counselor; Leff, Gullan et al., 2009). Relational aggressors were identified using an unlimited peer nomination process, and girls from classrooms with two or more relational aggressors were randomly assigned to F2F or a treatment-as-usual control group. Reliable and valid teacher- and self-report measures were used and both content and process integrity were measured and found to demonstrate strong inter-rater agreement (98% for content and 96% for process) by an observation team that was blind to study hypotheses (Leff, Gullan et al., 2009). Results suggest that relationally aggressive girls who were randomized to F2F had extremely large improvements in teacher-reported peer likeability ($d = 1.73$), large decreases in relational aggression ($d = 0.74$), and moderate reductions in physical aggression ($d = 0.43$), hostile attributions ($d = 0.61$), and loneliness ($d = 0.45$) as compared to relationally aggressive girls in the control condition. In contrast, F2F did not find clinically meaningful reductions in depression ($d = 0.22$), although girls' preprogram scores were not particularly elevated. Finally, the program was rated as quite acceptable by participating students and teachers.

One strength of F2F is that the program and materials were developed using a participatory action research framework by adapting best practice social cognitive violence prevention programs for urban physically aggressive youth through feedback from urban girls, parents, teachers, and community members (Leff et al., 2007). The program was judged to be culturally sensitive and highly acceptable by participants and their teachers. Further, F2F is theoretically based and capitalizes on the social influence that relationally aggressive youth may have (Cillessen & Mayeux, 2004; Prinstein & Cillessen, 2003) by including these girls as cofacilitators in the classroom component of the program. Also, F2F can be implemented with high levels of both content and procedural integrity (Leff, Gullan et al., 2009). Finally, groups are comprised of both high-risk relationally aggressive girls and prosocial role models, thereby reducing the potential deleterious effects of grouping aggressive youth (Dishion et al., 1999). A limitation is that this study was underpowered with an unequal number of youth in the treatment versus control conditions. Therefore, replication across more urban schools through a clinical trial is an important next step for the research. An additional limitation is that F2F was designed for urban, predominately African American girls, and thus the program is likely not generalizable beyond this target population. ...

DIRECTIONS FOR FUTURE RESEARCH AND IMPLICATIONS FOR PRACTICE

Given that relationally aggressive behaviors are quite complex, programming to reduce relational aggression must take into account important developmental, cultural, gender, and contextual considerations. From the review of the nine programs, it is clear that although prevention and intervention programs for relational aggression are still in the early stages of development and evaluation, a number of these programs show quite a bit of promise and help direct the field in terms of future research and practice implications. The recommendations that follow are based on the review of these programs and the relevant literature.

APPRECIATING THE COMPLEXITY OF RELATIONAL AGGRESSION

Programming for different developmental ages. Adjustment challenges and the experience and expression of relational aggression differ depending upon the age of the child. For instance, prevention programs for very young children need to have concrete and visual activities to help address the direct manifestations of relational aggression. Promising programs for preschoolers and kindergartners addressed the direct nature of relational aggression through developmentally appropriate visual and concrete strategies that taught and reinforced positive peer interactions. For example, the Early Childhood Friendship Project (Ostrov et al., 2009) and You Can't Say You Can't Play (Harrist & Bradley, 2003) have very brief teaching sessions using puppets or the reading out loud of fairy tales, respectively. Further, given programs for slightly older children such as

WITS and ICPS showed success in incorporating a parent generalization component, it would be especially beneficial for programs for young children to incorporate such components so that parents can reinforce learned strategies in the home and with siblings.

A number of the promising programs discussed have been designed and initially evaluated for late elementary and/or early middle school children. Given research indicating that the way youth approach and evaluate social cues affects their behavior (Crick & Dodge, 1994), most of these programs incorporate a social problem-solving model (e.g., MC; Fraser et al., 2004; Fraser et al., 2005; F2F, Leff et al., 2009; Second Step, Van Schoiack-Edstrom et al., 2002). Many of these same programs also recognize the importance of taking a systemic approach to prevention, incorporating a broader perspective to enhance the school and community context. Given recent research suggesting that adolescents use electronic media as an additional means of aggressing (William & Guerra, 2007) and that relational aggression may occur within the context of a romantic relationship (Ellis et al., 2009), future relational aggression intervention programs need to take these issues into account for adolescents.

Programming sensitive to gender and cultural contexts. Given developmental research indicating that girls and boys experience relational aggression differently (Murray-Close et al., 2007; Werner & Crick, 2004), perhaps some of the nonsignificant program effects are because of the lack of sensitivity to the qualitative gender differences. Therefore, it is recommended that more research be conducted to determine whether treatment approaches for relational aggression should be tailored to meet the specific needs of girls versus boys. Similarly, future research could focus on whether the experience of relational aggression differs across various racial and cultural contexts and if interventions should subsequently be tailored accordingly. Two programs reviewed in this article were designed with a concerted effort in making the program culturally sensitive to the specific needs of the participants (F2F, Leff et al, 2007; Sisters of Nia, Belgrave et al., 2004). The field could benefit from learning more about the sufficiency and necessity of these efforts.

Programming addressing the complex social-ecological contexts. Relational aggressors often exhibit peer relationship challenges and psychosocial adjustment difficulties (Card et al,, 2008), while at the same time being viewed as quite popular and influential within their peer group (Cillessen & Mayeux, 2004). Given this, intervention programs should integrate more opportunities for these youth to demonstrate their social influence and potential leadership in a prosocial manner. However, this was only emphasized in two programs, the F2F program (Leff et al., 2007) and the Sisters of Nia program (Belgrave et al., 2004).

Drawing from research documenting the relatively high correlations between relational and physical aggression and some of the similar maladjustment profiles experienced by these youth, it is recommended that future interventions for relational aggression build on empirically supported programs for physical aggression. Second Step (Grossman et al., 1997) and ICPS (Shure, 2001) are examples of nationally known and well-respected programs that have added curriculum and/or evaluations related to relational aggression. More research is needed on the cost-effectiveness and efficacy of this approach.

Given the extremely complex nature of relational aggression, it is also important that key individuals within the school and community are integrated into the intervention team. This approach is most clearly evident in the WITS program in which teachers, counselors, administrators, and school police officers serve as key implementation leaders (Leadbeater et al., 2003) and in the MC program in which teachers and/or parents are included in the combined treatment group (Fraser et al., 2004; Fraser et al., 2005). How well a program is integrated within a school and wider community may also be a crucial factor for the program's sustainability and long-term success (Leff, Gullan et al., 2009).

EVALUATING PROGRAMS THROUGH SYSTEMATIC RESEARCH

None of the nine promising programs reviewed met the stringent criteria for being efficacious according to the new standards set forth by the Society for Prevention Research (2006). Clearly, even the most promising relational aggression programs still require more systematic investigations using random assignment procedures in which alternative programs are used to control for nonspecific treatment factors. In fact, only the SAPP used a randomized trial with an active control group (Capella & Weinstein, 2006). Further, program reviews highlighted several methodological limitations, including some studies having difficulty achieving full randomization because teachers withdrew their students from the study if assigned to the control group. Other investigations were limited by psychometric properties of their outcome measures. For example, many outcome measures had reliability assessed only by internal consistency and not test-retest or inter-rater reliability. Others used extremely brief outcome measures for the primary constructs of relational aggression (e.g., two items). It is essential that outcome measures, including teacher reports and student self-reports, have well-demonstrated reliability and validity for measuring relational aggression. In general, we recommend that these newer relational aggression intervention programs be evaluated using more extensive multi-method, multi-informant measures across multiple time periods (Leff et al., 2001). Notably, several of the programs adequately monitored treatment fidelity and program acceptability (e.g., F2F, Leff et al., 2009; Early Childhood Friendship Project, Ostrov et al., 2009), which are extremely important aspects of effectiveness research (Society for Prevention Research, 2006).

THE ROLE OF SCHOOL PSYCHOLOGISTS

This review suggests a number of implications for school psychologists. First, school psychologists can provide school-wide workshops and trainings raising awareness that children's aggression includes both physical and nonphysical manifestations (e.g., social exclusion, gossip, ignoring). Second, school psychologists can take a central role in the implementation and evaluation of intervention programs. For example, because school psychologists are trained in data-based decision making, they could be part of an administrative team that reviews potential programs for adoption in their schools, help in the selection of an evidence-based program, collect data on outcomes and treatment fidelity for a selected program, and be part of the team that analyzes the outcome data. Specifically, it is suggested that school practitioners consider their school's needs and resources in conjunction with the mode of operation, target population, and preliminary findings for each of the promising existing programs in order to determine which program would best serve their school. Notably, although many general bullying programs may target relationally aggressive behaviors, this systematic review did not reveal any programs that have fully examined their effectiveness on relational aggression. Until more programs target and measure outcomes specifically related to relational bullying and victimization, it is important to recognize that general bullying programs require systematic evaluations related to relational bullying and victimization before large-scale implementation to address relational aggression.

Finally, school psychologists can be incorporated into implementation of interventions for relational aggression by serving as teacher trainers or co-implementers with teachers in classrooms. School psychologists can help ensure that for whichever program is selected, teachers and other program facilitators are well trained, are continuously supported, and follow appropriate implementation guidelines (see Leff et al., 2009). Although there are many challenges ahead, the findings from developmental research and some innovative intervention studies suggest that the field is moving in the right direction for preventing and reducing relational aggression and related challenges.

REFERENCES

Asher, S.R., Hymel, S., & Renshaw, P. D. (1984). Loneliness in children. *Child Development, 55,* 1456.

Asher, S.R., & Wheeler, V.A. (1985). Children's loneliness: A comparison of rejected and neglected status. *Journal of Consulting and Clinical Psychology, 53,* 500–505.

Belgrave, F.Z., Reed, M.C., Plybon, L.E., Butler, D.S., Allison, K.W., & Davis, T. (2004). An evaluation of Sisters of Nia: A cultural program for African American girls. *Journal of Black Psychology, 30,* 329–343.

Björkqvist, K., Österman, K., & Kaukiainen, A. (1992). The development of direct and indirect aggressive strategies in males and females. In K. Björkqvist & P. Niemelä (Eds.), *Of mice and women: Aspects of female aggression* (pp. 51–64). San Diego: Academic Press.

Boldizar, J.P. (1991). Assessing sex typing and androgyny in children: The children's sex role inventory. *Developmental Psychology, 27,* 505.

Boyle, D., & Hassett-Walker, C. (2008). Reducing overt and relational aggression among young children: The results from a two-year outcome evaluation. *Journal of School Violence, 7,* 27–42.

Caldwell, C.B., & Pianta, R.C. (1991). A measure of young children's problem and competence behaviors: The Early School Behavior Scale. *Journal of Psycho-educational Assessment, 9,* 32–44.

Cappella, E., & Weinstein, R. (2006). The prevention of social aggression among girls. *Social Development, 15,* 434–462.

Card, N.A., Stucky, B.D., Sawalani, G.M., & Little, T.D. (2008). Direct and indirect aggression during childhood and adolescence: A meta-analytic review of gender differences, intercorrelations, and relations to maladjustment. *Child Development, 79,* 1185–1229.

Cillessen, A.H.N., & Mayeux, L. (2004). From censure to reinforcement: Developmental changes in the association between aggression and social status. *Child Development, 75,* 147–163.

Cohen, J. (1988). *Statistical power analysis for the behavioral sciences* (2nd ed.). Hillsdale, NJ: Erlbaum.

Coie, J.D., & Dodge, K.A. (1983). Continuities and changes in children's social status: A five-year longitudinal study. *Merrill-Palmer Quarterly, 29,* 261–282.

Crick, N.R. (1995). Relational aggression: The role of intent attributions, feelings of distress, and provocation type. *Development and Psychopathology, 7,* 313–322.

Crick, N.R. (1996). The role of overt aggression, relational aggression, and prosocial behavior in the prediction of children's future social adjustment. *Child Development, 67,* 2317–2327.

Crick, N.R. (1997). Engagement in gender normative versus non-normative forms of aggression: Links to social-psychological adjustment. *Developmental Psychopathology, 33,* 610–617.

Crick, N.R., & Bigbee, M.A. (1998). Relational and overt forms of peer victimization: A multiinformant approach. *Journal of Consulting & Clinical Psychology, 66,* 337–347.

Crick, N.R., Casas, J.F., & Mosher, M. (1997). Relational and overt aggression in preschool. *Developmental Psychology, 33,* 579–588.

Crick, N.R., & Dodge, K.A. (1994). A review and reformulation of social information-processing mechanism in children's social adjustment. *Psychological Bulletin, 115,* 74–101.

Crick, N.R., & Grotpeter, J.K. (1995). Relational aggression, gender, and social-psychological adjustment. *Child Development, 66,* 710–722.

Crick, N.R., & Grotpeter, J.K. (1996). Children's treatment by peers: Victims of relational and overt aggression. *Development and Psychopathology, 8,* 367–380.

Crick, N.R., Grotpeter, J.K., & Bigbee, M.A. (2002). Relationally and physically aggressive children's intent attributions and feelings of distress for relational and instrumental peer provocations. *Child Development, 73,* 1134–1142.

Crick, N.R., Ostrov, J.M., Burr, J.E., Cullerton-Sen, C, Jansen-Yeh, E., & Ralston, P. (2006). A longitudinal study of relational and physical aggression in preschool. *Journal of Applied Developmental Psychology, 27,*254–268.

Crick, N.R., Ostrov, J.M., & Kawabata, Y. (2007). Relational aggression and gender: An overview. In D.J. Flannery, A.T. Vazsonyi, & I D. Waldman (Eds.), *The Cambridge handbook of violent behavior and aggression* (pp. 245–259). New York: Cambridge.

Crick, N.R., & Werner, N.E. (1998). Response decision processes in relational and overt aggression. *Child Development, 69,* 1630–1639.

Dishion, T.J., McCord. J., & Poulin, F. (1999). When interventions harm: Peer groups and problem behavior. *American Psychologist, 54,* 755–764.

Dodge, K.A. (1980). Social cognition and children's aggressive behavior. *Child Development, 51,* 162–170.

Dodge, K.A. (1986). A social information processing model of social competence in children. In M. Perlmutter (Ed.), *Minnesota symposia on child psychology* (Vol. 18, pp. 77–125) Hillsdale, NJ: Erlbaum.

Dodge, K., Coie, J., & Lynam, D. (2006). Aggression and antisocial behavior in youth. In N. Eisenberg, W. Damon, & R. Lerner (Eds.), *Handbook of child psychology: Vol. 3, Social, emotional, and personality development* (6th ed., pp. 719–788). Hoboken, NJ: John Wiley & Sons.

Dodge, K.A., & Pettit, G.S. (2003). A biopsychosocial model of the development of chronic conduct problems in adolescence. *Developmental Psychology, 39,* 349–371.

Ellis, W.E., Crooks, C.V., & Wolfe, D.A. (2009). Relational aggression in peer and dating relationships: Links to psychological and behavioral adjustment. *Social Development, 18,* 253–269.

Evertson, C.M., Emmer, E.T., Sanford, J.P., & Clements, B.S. (1983). Improving classroom management: Good Behavior Game manual. *Elementary School Journal, 83,* 173–188.

Farrell, A.D., Meyer, A.L., Kung, E.M, & Sullivan, T.N. (2001). Development and evaluation of school-based violence prevention programs. *Journal of Clinical Child Psychology, 30,* 207–220.

Fraser, M., Day, S., Galinsky, M., Hodges, V., & Smokowski, P. (2004). Conduct problems and peer rejection in childhood: A randomized trial of the Making Choices and Strong Families Programs. *Research on Social Work Practice, 14,* 313–324.

Fraser, M., Galinsky, M., Smokowski, P., Day, S., Terzian, M., Rose, R., et al. (2005). Social information-processing skills training to promote social competence and prevent aggressive behavior in the third grades. *Journal of Consulting and Clinical Psychology, 73,* 1045–1055.

Frey, K.S., Nolen, S.B., Van Schoiack Edstrom, L., & Hirschstein, M.K. (2005). Effects of a school-based social-emotional competence program: Linking children's goals, attributions, and behavior. *Journal of Applied Developmental Psychology, 26,* 171–200.

Galen, B.R., & Underwood, M. (1997). A developmental investigation of social aggression among children. *Developmental Psychology, 33,* 589–599.

Grossman, D.C., Neckerman, H.J., Koepsell, T.D., Liu, P., Asher, K.N., Beland, K., et al. (1997). Effectiveness of a violence prevention curriculum among children in elementary school: A randomized controlled trial. *Journal of the American Medical Association, 277,* 1605–1611.

Harrist, A.W., & Bradley, K.D. (2003). "You can't say you can't play": Intervening in the process of social exclusion in the kindergarten classroom. *Early Childhood Research Quarterly, 18,* 185–205.

Harter, S., & Pike, R. (1984). The pictorial scale of perceived competence and social acceptance for young children. *Child Development, 55,* 1969–1982.

Hoff, K.E., Reese-Weber, M., Schneider, W.J., & Stagg, J.W. (2009). The association between high status positions and aggressive behavior in early adolescence. *Journal of School Psychology, 47,* 395–426.

Kovacs, M. (1985). Children's Depression Inventory. *Psychopharmacology Bulletin, 21,* 995–998.

Kuppens, S., Grietens, H., Onghena, P., Michiels, D., & Subramanian, S.V. (2008). Individual and classroom variables associated with relational aggression in elementary-school aged children: A multilevel analysis. *Journal of School Psychology, 46,* 639–660.

LaFrenière, P.J., Dumas, J.E., Capuano, F., & Dubeau, D. (1992). Development and validation of the Preschool Socioaffective Profile. *Psychological Assessment, 4,* 442–450.

Leadbeater, B.J., & Hoglund, W. (2006). Changing the social contexts of peer victimization. *Journal of Canadian Academy of Child and Adolescent Psychiatry, 15,* 21–26.

Leadbeater, B., Hoglund, W., & Woods, T. (2003). Changing contexts? The effects of a primary prevention program on classroom levels of peer relational and physical victimization. *Journal of Community Psychology, 31,* 397–418.

Leff, S.S., Angelucci, J., Goldstein, A.B., Cardaciotto, L., Paskewich, B., & Grossman, M.B. (2007). Using a participatory action research model to create a school-based intervention program for relationally aggressive girls: The Friend to Friend Program. In J.E. Zins, M.J. Elias, & C.A. Maher (Eds.), *Bullying, victimization, and peer harassment: A handbook of prevention and intervention* (pp. 199–218). New York: Haworth.

Leff, S.S., Costigan, T.E., & Power, T.J. (2004). Using participatory-action research to develop a playground-based prevention program. *Journal of School Psychology, 42,* 3–21.

Leff, S.S., Crick, N.R., Angelucci, J., Haye, K., Jawad, A.F., Grossman, M., & Power, T.J. (2006). Social cognition in context: Validating a cartoon-based attributional measure for urban girls. *Child Development, 77,* 1351–1358.

Leff, S.S., Gullan, R.L., Paskewich, B.S., Abdul-Kabir S., Jawad, A.F., Grossman, M., et al. (2009). An initial evaluation of a culturally-adapted social problem solving and relational aggression prevention program for urban African American relationally aggressive girls. *Journal of Prevention and intervention in the Community, 37,* 260–274.

Leff, S.S., Hoffman, J.A., & Gullan, R. L. (2009). Intervention integrity: New paradigms and applications. *School Mental Health, 1,* 103–106.

Leff, S.S., Kupersmidt, J.B., & Power, T.J. (2003). An initial examination of girls' cognitions of their relationally aggressive peers as a function of their own social standing. *Merrill Palmer Quarterly, 49,* 28–53.

Leff, S.S., Power, T.J., Manz, P.H., Costigan, T.E., & Nabors, L.A. (2001). School-based aggression prevention programs for young children: Current status and implications for violence prevention. *School Psychology Review, 30,* 343–360.

Lochman, J.E., & Dodge, K.A. (1994). Social-cognitive processes of severely violent, moderately aggressive, and nonaggressive boys. *Journal of Consulting & Clinical Psychology, 62,* 366–374.

Macgowan, M.J., Nash, J.K., & Fraser, M. W. (2002). The Carolina Child Checklist of Risk and Protective Factors for Aggression. *Research on Social Work Practice, 12,* 253–276.

Morrison, F.J., Bachman, H.J., & Connor, C.M. (2005). Improving literacy in America: Guidelines from research. *Current Perspectives in Psychology.* New Haven, CT: Yale University Press.

Murray-Close, D., & Crick, N.R. (2007). Gender differences in the association between cardiovascular reactivity and aggressive conduct. *International Journal of Psychophysiology, 65,* 103–113.

Murray-Close, D., Ostrov, J.M., & Crick, N.R. (2007). A short-term longitudinal study of growth of relational aggression during middle childhood: Associations with gender, friendship intimacy, and internalizing problems. *Development and Psychopathology, 19,* 187–203.

Ostrov, J., & Keating, C. (2004). Gender differences in preschool aggression during free play and structured interactions: An observational study. *Social Development, 13,* 255–277.

Ostrov, J.M., Massetti, G.M., Stauffacher, K., Godleski, S.A., Hart, K.C, Karch, K.M., et al. (2009). An intervention for relational and physical aggression in early childhood: A preliminary study. *Early Childhood Research Quarterly, 24,* 15–28.

Ostrov, J.M., Woods, K.E., Jansen, E.A., Casas, J.F., & Crick, N.R. (2004). An observational study of delivered and received aggression, gender, and social-psychological adjustment in preschool: "This White Crayon Doesn't Work." *Early Childhood Research Quarterly, 19,* 355–371.

Paley, V.G. (1992). *You Can't Say You Can't Play.* Cambridge: Harvard University Press.

Perry, D.G., Perry, L.C., & Rasmussen, P. (1986). Cognitive social learning mediators of aggression. *Child Development, 57,* 700–711.

Prinstein, M.J., Boergers, J., & Vernberg, E.M. (2001). Overt and relational aggression in adolescents: Social-psychological adjustment of aggressors and victims. *Journal of Clinical Child Psychology, 30,* 479–491.

Prinstein, M.J., & Cillessen, A.H.N. (2003). Forms and functions of adolescent peer aggression associated with high levels of peer status. *Merrill-Palmer Quarterly, 49,* 310–342.

Puckett, M.B., Aikins, J., & Cillessen, A. (2008). Moderators of the association between relational aggression and perceived popularity. *Aggressive Behavior, 34,* 563–576.

Shure, M.B. (2001). *I Can Problem Solve (ICPS). An interpersonal problem-solving program (kindergarten/primary grades)* (2nd ed.). Champaign, IL: Research Press.

Shure, M.B. (2002). *Hahnemann Behavior Rating Scale.* Unpublished. Hahnemann University.

Slaby, R.G., & Guerra, N.G. (1988). Cognitive mediators of aggression in adolescent offenders: 1. Assessment. *Developmental Psychology, 24,* 580–588.

Smith, E.P., & Brookins, C.C. (1997). Toward the development of an ethnic identity measure for African American youth. *Journal of Black Psychology, 23,* 358–377.

Society for Prevention Research. (2006). *Standards of evidence: Criteria for efficacy, effectiveness and dissemination.* Retrieved from http://www.preventionscience.org/StandardsofEvidencebook.pdf

Stauffacher, K., & DeHart, G.B. (2006). Crossing social contexts: Relational aggression between siblings and friends during early and middle childhood. *Journal of Applied Developmental Psychology, 27,* 228–240.

Swearer, S.M. (2008). Relational aggression: Not just a female issue. *Journal of School Psychology, 46,* 611–616.

Van Schoiack-Edstrom, L., Frey, K.S., & Beland, K. (2002). Changing adolescents' attitudes about relational and physical aggression: An early evaluation of a school-based intervention. *School Psychology Review, 31,* 201–216.

Vasey, M., Dangleish, T., & Silverman, W. (2003). Research on information-processing factors in child and adolescent psychopathology: A critical commentary. *Journal of Clinical Child & Adolescent Psychology, 32,* 81–93.

Werner, N.E., & Crick, N.R. (1999). Relational aggression and social-psychological adjustment in a college sample. *Journal of Abnormal Psychology, 108,* 615–623.

Werner, N.E., & Crick, N.R. (2004). Maladaptive peer relationships and the development of relational and physical aggression during middle childhood. *Social Development, 13,* 495–514.

Williams, K.R., & Guerra, N.G. (2007). Prevalence and predictors of Internet bullying. *Journal of Adolescent Health, 41,* S14-S21.

Zimmer-Gembeck, M.J., Geiger, T.C., & Crick, N.R. (2005). Relational and physical aggression, prosocial behavior, and peer relations: Gender moderation and bidirectional associations. *The Journal of Early Adolescence, 25,* 421–452.

PRACTICAL APPLICATION ASSIGNMENTS

1. According to the American Psychological Association (2011), school psychologists participate in the following activities:

    - <u>Consult</u> with parents, educators, and other interested parties regarding:

        - academic, behavioral, cultural, social, and emotional assessments and supports that help meet the needs of all students.

        - appropriate, culturally sensitive, and comprehensive interventions within schools and other settings.

    - <u>Intervene</u> by developing instructional and behavioral strategies and methods to improve academic, social-emotional, and vocational outcomes.

    - <u>Assess</u> children, adolescents, and young adults to better understand abilities and areas of concern, including learning and behavioral difficulties and various disabilities.

    - <u>Conduct</u> and <u>translate</u> research for practice.

    - <u>Promote</u> social justice and children's rights across the globe.

    - <u>Collaborate</u> with various professionals to ensure equal opportunities for services to all children, adolescents, and young adults.

    For this task, think back to the scenario at the beginning of this chapter. Remember that the teenage girl transferred to a different school because she was being harassed by a group of girls. An intervention could have saved this student a lot of grief. After reading this chapter, the Leff et al. research article, and the list of activities that school psychologists engage in, you should have a solid understanding of how the local school psychologist and other school officials could have responded to this situation. Describe what the local school psychologist should have done in response to the initial harassing behaviors by applying at least four of the activities listed above to the scenario.

2. Imagine that you are an intern with a school psychologist as part of your undergraduate training in psychology. You are thrilled that you earned this coveted placement, as you will have the opportunity to work with the school psychologist at two middle schools, one in the wealthy suburbs of Chicago and the other in a lower-income area of inner-city Chicago. The school psychologist hopes to implement the exact same relational aggression intervention in these two very different schools. Based on your understanding of this article, explain why this may be problematic and how the interventions should be adapted for each group of students.

3. Oral presentation skills are an important part of your liberal arts education. As partial fulfillment of this requirement, you need to give a 20-minute presentation on relational aggression to a group of high school teachers. Create an outline of your presentation by identifying the major components that you think you should cover. Be sure to include the definition of relational aggression, consequences of relational aggression for perpetrators and victims, and important components that should be included in an intervention to reduce relational aggression in high schools.

Chapter 12

Health Psychology: Social Networks and Physical Health

Can We Improve Our Physical Health by Altering Our Social Networks?

By Sheldon Cohen and Denise Janicki-Deverts

EDITORS' INTRODUCTION

Can a person ever be "sick with worry," or can mental states really contribute to physical illness? The answer to both of these questions from the field of health psychology is a definite "yes."

The field of *health psychology* focuses on scientific relationships among psychological factors, behavior, and physical health and illness. Health psychologists can be employed in research or clinical settings. They may conduct research or work with clients to implement psychologically based practices to improve physical health. For example, health psychologists apply research-based therapies to help people stop smoking, manage their weight, control symptoms of diabetes, reduce migraine headaches, manage chronic pain, or improve cardiovascular health following a heart attack. (For a review of the science of health psychology, see Taylor, 1990.) For more information about health psychology, visit <*www.health-psych.org*>.

In this review article, Sheldon Cohen and Denise Janicki-Deverts specifically address the role of social networks in improving physical health. They summarize a wide variety of research about the role of social networks in recovery of heart-attack patients, HIV-AIDS patients, breast-cancer survivors, and healthy individuals to determine if we can improve our physical health through social networks (Cohen & Janicki-Deverts, 2009). In their article, Cohen and Janicki-Deverts summarize diverse research findings that range from the association between social integration (or membership in a diverse social network) and greater resistance to infections (Cohen, Doyle, Skoner, Rabin, & Gwaltney, 1997) to the relationship between greater social network diversity and a decreased risk for cancer recurrence (Helgeson, Cohen, & Fritz, 1998).

This review article only begins to address the wealth of research conducted in the field of psychology. Research linking psychological factors to physical health continues to accumulate. For example, did you know that researchers have recently studied whether or not living alone is associated with recovery from heart attacks? It turns out that living alone is associated with decreases in quality of life due to angina (chest pain) after a heart attack (Bucholz et al., 2011). Thinking back to Chapter 1, does this example of a review article do a good job of introducing a broad range of research in health psychology? Does it summarize many studies and present the cumulative results in a relatively concise and easy-to-understand format?

Similar to other research articles presented in this anthology, the authors of this article carefully highlight the difference between *correlation* and *causation*, as they explore the relationship between healthy social networks and improved physical health. While a great deal of helpful information can be gathered from well-designed correlational research, the authors describe a need for more *experimental-intervention studies* to firmly establish whether or not changing social networks can directly *cause* improved health. As you read, think of ways that an intervention could be designed to help determine if there are causal relationships between social networks and health. Does social integration cause better health? Does better health allow you to maintain relationships and therefore cause you to have improved social networks? Could there be another reason that physical health and social networks may be related? This is sometimes called a *third variable* situation—when there is another reason (the third variable) that accounts for the relationship between two things.

REFERENCES

Bucholz, E. M., Rathore, S. S., Gosch, K., Schoenfeld, A., Jones, P. G., Buchanan, D. M., Spertus, J. A., & Krumholz, H. M. (2011). Effect of living alone on patient outcomes after hospitalization for acute myocardial infarction. *American Journal of Cardiology, 108* (7), 943–948.

Cohen, S., Doyle, W. J., Skoner, D. P., Rabin, B. S., & Gwaltney, J. M., Jr. (1997). Social ties and susceptibility to the common cold. *The Journal of the American Medical Association, 277* (24), 1940–1944.

Cohen, S., & Janicki-Deverts D. (2009). Can we improve our physical health by altering our social networks? *Perspectives on Psychological Science, 4* (4), 375–378.

Hawkley, L. C., & Cacioppo, J. T. (2003). Loneliness and pathways to disease. *Brain, Behavior, and Immunity, 17* (Suppl 1): S98–S105.

Helgeson, V. S., Cohen, S., & Fritz, H. L. (1998). Social ties and cancer. In J. C. Holland (Ed.), *Psychooncology* (pp. 99–109). New York, NY: Oxford University Press.

Taylor, S. E. (1990). Health psychology: The science and the field. *American Psychologist, 45* (1), 40–50.

ABSTRACT

Persons with more types of social relationships live longer and have less cognitive decline with aging, greater resistance to infectious disease, and better prognoses when facing chronic life-threatening illnesses. We have known about the importance of social integration (engaging in diverse types of relationships) for health and longevity for 30 years. Yet, we still do not know why having a more diverse social network would have a positive influence on our health, and we have yet to design effective interventions that influence key components of the network and in turn physical health. Better understanding of the role of social integration in health will require research on how integrated social networks influence health relevant behaviors, regulate emotions and biological responses, and contribute to our expectations and worldviews.

Over the last 30 years, there has been substantial interest in defining the role that social environments and supports play in health maintenance and disease etiology (e.g., Cohen, 2004; Uchino, 2004). Researchers have found the most consistent and provocative results in a group of studies focusing on *social integration*—one's membership in a diverse social network. Prospective community studies indicate that those with more types of relationships—for example, being married; having close family members, friends, and neighbors; and belonging to social, political and religious groups—live longer (reviewed by Berkman, 1995; Berkman & Glass, 2000; Seeman, 1996). More socially integrated people also have less cognitive decline with aging (reviewed by Fratiglioni, Pallard-Borg, & Winblad, 2004), less dementia (reviewed by Fratiglioni et al., 2004), and greater resistance to upper respiratory infections (Cohen, Doyle, Skoner, Rabin, & Gwaltney, 1997).

It is not only studies of community samples that suggest that social integration has health benefits. More diverse networks are also associated with better prognoses among those facing chronic life threatening illnesses. For example, in longitudinal-prospective studies, more socially integrated individuals at high risk for or suffering from cardiovascular disease develop less arterial calcification (Kop et al., 2005), have a lower incidence of stroke (Rutledge et al., 2008), and live longer (Rutledge et al., 2004) than do their less integrated counterparts. Greater social network diversity is also associated with a decreased risk for the recurrence of cancer (reviewed by Helgeson, Cohen, & Fritz, 1998).

A graded relation between integration and better health was found in many of these studies (e.g., Berkman & Syme, 1979; Cohen et al., 1997; Seeman et al., 1993), but in some cases the association was attributed primarily to poorer health among the most isolated (see review by House, Landis, & Umberson, 1988). It has been proposed that associations between social integration and health may be driven by two separate processes: One associated with being isolated versus having some minimum number of contact types (common threshold is between one and three), and the other associated with incremental increases in network diversity (Cohen, 2004).

The most striking and consistent evidence for associations between social relationships and physical health derives from the social integration studies. However, there is also evidence that those who report that others will provide them with aid when they are in need (perceived social support) are protected from the pathogenic effects of life stress (Cohen, 2004). For example, there is some evidence for perceived emotional support protecting against the increased risk for mortality associated with high levels of stressful life events (Rosengren, Orth-Gomer, Wedel, & Wilhelmsen, 1993) and work stress (Falk, Hanson, Isacsson, & Ostergren, 1992). There is also evidence for perceived support delaying the progression of chronic life-threatening illnesses. For example, greater levels of perceived social support are associated with longer survival following heart attacks (reviewed by Lett et al., 2005) and possibly with survival from breast cancer (Gidron & Ronson, 2008; Soler-Vila, Kasl, & Jones, 2003) and HIV-AIDS (Lee & Rotheram-Borus, 2001; Patterson et al., 1996). Presumably, this protective effect occurs because perceived support reduces the stress associated with having a potentially fatal disease.

Finally, negative aspects of social relationships including social losses (Stroebe, Schut, & Stroebe, 2007), negative interactions (Kiecolt-Glaser & Newton, 2001; Rook, 1984), and loneliness (Cacioppo, Hawkley, & Berntson, 2003) may be detrimental to health. For example, the loss of close others through divorce or death is associated with greater morbidity and mortality risk (reviewed by Stroebe et al., 2007), and both conflicts with close others (reviewed by Kiecolt-Glaser & Newton, 2001) and feelings of loneliness (Cacioppo et al., 2003) have been associated with cardiovascular, endocrine, and immune changes thought to be detrimental to health.

The size, consistency, and range of the established relationships between our social networks and morbidity and mortality often lead us to talk about them as if they were causal. However, the truth is, we do not know this. This literature is based on prospective correlational research. Good prospective studies eliminate the possibility of reverse causality (illness causing deterioration of social networks). They accomplish this by assessing social characteristics and then following people to measure subsequent changes in health (controlling for baseline health). These studies also tend to control for spurious "third" factors such as age, sex, ethnicity, and socioeconomic status that could influence both the nature of our social networks and our health. Even so, there are still many psychosocial, environmental, and biological factors that could account for a correlation between a social factor and health outcomes.

Experimental-intervention studies (randomized clinical trials), the gold standard for both the psychological and medical communities, could provide the critical causal evidence. However, there are surprisingly few experimental studies testing the possibility that interventions that increase the diversity of our social networks, increase our social support, or decrease conflict and loneliness would be beneficial to our health. Moreover, the intervention studies that do exist seldom draw inspiration from the evidence reported in the correlational literature. In particular, although the correlational studies have found that characteristics of natural social networks were protective, intervention studies have generally manipulated support by facilitating interactions with strangers facing the same or similar threats (cf.

Helgeson & Cohen, 1996). Most of the intervention studies have been done with cancer patients comparing participation in therapy groups with other cancer patients to usual care. Because the therapy is conducted in groups, these studies are generally referred to as tests of the effectiveness of social support. Although two early studies did find beneficial effects of group psychotherapy on survival (Fawzy et al., 1993; Spiegel, Bloom, Kramer, & Gottheil, 1989), this work has been criticized in terms of design and data interpretation (Coyne, Stefanek, & Palmer, 2007; Fox, 1998). Moreover, more recent work (Cunningham et al., 1998; Ilnyckyj, Farber, Cheang, & Weinerman, 1994) including studies conducted at multiple sites with larger samples (Goodwin et al., 2001; Spiegel et al., 2007) has failed to replicate the early results.

Attempts to reduce the recurrence of heart attacks by increasing patients' perceived social support have also been unsuccessful. One multisite trial in which nurses regularly called and visited patients to provide social support actually found negative effects of the intervention on women and no benefit to men (Frasure-Smith et al., 1997). Another trial used cognitive behavioral therapy in an attempt to increase perceptions of social support from existing natural networks (Berkman et al., 2003). Although patients in the intervention group reported greater support, there was no effect on disease recurrence.

Why is it important to know if altering our social networks will improve physical health? From the health perspective, the benefits of engineering healthier social environments are obvious. Helping people maintain good health and address bad health has potential for controlling health care costs, as well as promoting happier and healthier lives. The role of social environments may be especially important for older persons who commonly experience major social transitions such as retirement, bereavement, and inability to participate in social activities because of disability or lack of mobility (Pillemer, Moen, Wethington, & Glasgow, 2000). However, they are also essential for those with chronic life threatening illnesses such as heart disease, cancer, and HIV. What may be most interesting is that the social integration literature suggests that social environments may play an essential role in the health and well-being of people who are neither challenged by major life stressors nor by serious disease.

What is less obvious is that both good health and disease are powerful outcomes that may provide insights and tools to pursue more basic social psychological questions. Particularly, how do characteristics of our social networks influence our cognitive, behavioral, and physiological responses? To understand how social environments influence one's health, we need to consider the potential roles of social control (social norms and pressures), regulation of emotions and biological responses, and the social environment's contribution to our expectations and world views, including our life goals and feelings of control, optimism, purpose, trust, and self-esteem (e.g., Brissette, Cohen, & Seeman, 2000; Cohen, 2004; Cohen & Lemay, 2007). If our social environments do influence our health, some or all of these processes may operate as key mechanistic pathways.

What should the field be doing? Clearly, this is a domain in which psychologists have the potential to make scientific and practical contributions to health care. It is also a domain that will allow us to investigate how the nature of our social networks influences basic psychological processes such as motivation, social influence, decision making, and emotional regulation.

We have documented a strong and reliable association between the diversity of our social networks and our longevity and risk for disease. Even though the basic association was first reported 30 years ago (Berkman & Syme, 1979), we still do not know why it happens, we still do not have convincing causal evidence, and we still have not designed interventions that influence the key components of the network and, in turn, physical health. The provocative associations between social integration and physical health are derived primarily from the work of social epidemiologists and draw on their expertise in assessing the distribution of disease in the population. However, the goals we present here draw on the strengths of psychological theory and methodology. This includes designing and testing social experiments and developing theory and empirical tests of how our social networks "get under the skin" to influence disease and mortality.

Our intent here is not to spin elaborate theory, but to frame a set of questions about the psychological meaning of social integration and how that meaning might explain its importance for health (cf. Cohen, 1988). What are the psychological characteristics of socially integrated people that help to prevent or cope successfully with disease? Do socially integrated people interact on a more regular schedule, more often, or with more people? Do they have different expectancies, perceptions, and outcomes of social interactions? Do they feel more responsible for other people in their network? Do they perceive that people in their networks feel more responsible for them? Are they more or less subject to social influence? Does belonging to a diverse network enhance their ability to regulate their emotions? Does a more diverse network provide a broader range of effective support resources? Is network diversity more important than numbers of people per se as a determinant of loneliness? Is it the behavior of their networks that influences their health, or is it their beliefs about the meaning of belonging to a diverse network?

Although not studied in the context of social integration, psychologists have contributed significantly to our understanding of the potential role of other social constructs in health, particularly in regard to their effects on psychological well-being. As alluded to earlier, it is possible that social integration operates through other social constructs. For example, the associations of social integration and health could be mediated by perceived social support. Socially integrated people may also have fewer negative interactions (interpersonal stressors) and at least part of the social integration effect may be attributable to feelings of loneliness on the part of the most isolated (Cacioppo et al., 2003; Sorkin, Rook, & Lu, 2002). Future work examining these constructs simultaneously with social integration can help answer these questions.

How can we effectively intervene in natural social networks to make them more diverse? Changing natural networks is challenging (cf. Gottlieb, 2000). It might involve activating dormant but existing domains (e.g., bringing persons together with estranged family members), adding additional domains (e.g., facilitating joining of a social or recreational group consistent with the person's interests), or providing social skills-training to facilitate maintenance of current relationships and creation of new ones. On the other hand, a better understanding of why social integration is so closely tied to health might alternatively suggest intervening in the more proximal causes whether it be increasing feelings of belonging, engagement, self-confidence, control, or purpose; promoting positive health practices and discouraging negative health practices; encouraging emotional regulation; or increasing social support.

Our argument is a simple one. There is an extremely provocative and reliable association between the nature of an individual's social network and their health. This association has implications for both the basic understanding of how social environments control cognition, behavior, and physiology and for prevention of disease and maintenance of good health. We believe that psychologists have the unique skills and knowledge base to address these questions.

ACKNOWLEDGMENT

Work on this article was supported in part by grants to the Pittsburgh Mind–Body Center from the National Heart, Lung and Blood Institute (HL65111 and HL65112).

REFERENCES

Berkman, L.F. (1995). The role of social relations in health promotion. *Psychosomatic Medicine, 57,* 245–254.

Berkman, L.F., Blumenthal, J., Burg, M., Carney, R.M., Catellier, D., Cowan, M.J., et al. (2003). Effects of treating depression and low perceived social support on clinical events after myocardial infarction: The Enhancing Recovery in Coronary Heart Disease Patients (ENRICHD) randomized trial. *Journal of the American Medical Association, 289,* 3106–3116.

Berkman, L.F., & Glass, T. (2000). Social integration, social networks, social support, and health. In L.F. Berkman & I. Kawachi (Eds.), *Social epidemiology* (pp. 137–173). New York: Oxford University Press.

Berkman, L.F., & Syme, S.L. (1979). Social networks, host resistance and mortality: A nine year follow-up study of Alameda County residents. *American Journal of Epidemiology, 109,* 186–204.

Brissette, I., Cohen, S., & Seeman, T.E. (2000). Measuring social integration and social networks. In S. Cohen, L. Underwood, & B. Gottlieb (Eds.), *Measuring and intervening in social support* (pp. 53–85). New York: Oxford University Press.

Cacioppo, J.T., Hawkley, L.C., & Berntson, G.G. (2003). The anatomy of loneliness. *Current Directions in Psychological Science, 12,* 71–74.

Cohen, S. (1988). Psychosocial models of social support in the etiology of physical disease. *Health Psychology, 7,* 269–297.

Cohen, S. (2004). Social relationships and health. *American Psychologist, 59,* 676–684.

Cohen, S., Doyle, W.J., Skoner, D.P., Rabin, B.S., & Gwaltney, J.M., Jr. (1997). Social ties and susceptibility to the common cold. *Journal of the American Medical Association, 277,* 1940–1944.

Cohen, S., & Lemay, E. (2007). Why would social networks be linked to affect and health practices? *Health Psychology, 26,* 410–417.

Coyne, J.C., Stefanek, M., & Palmer, S.C. (2007). Psychotherapy and survival in cancer: The conflict between hope and evidence. *Psychological Bulletin, 133,* 367–394.

Cunningham, A.J., Edmonds, C.V., Jenkins, G.P., Pollack, H., Lockwood, G.A., & Warr, D. (1998). A randomized controlled trial of the effects of group psychological therapy on survival in women with metastatic breast cancer. *Psycho-Oncology, 7,* 508–517.

Falk, A., Hanson, B.S., Isacsson, S.O., & Ostergren, P.O. (1992). Job strain and mortality in elderly men: Social network, support, and influence as buffers. *American Journal of Public Health, 82,* 1136–1139.

Fawzy, F.I., Fawzy, N.W., Hyun, C.S., Elashoff, R., Guthrie, D., Fahey, J.L., & Morton, D.L. (1993). Malignant melanoma: Effects of an early structured psychiatric intervention, coping, and affective state on recurrence and survival 6 years later. *Archives of General Psychiatry, 50,* 681–689.

Fox, B.H. (1998). A hypothesis about Spiegel et al.'s 1989 paper on psychosocial intervention and breast cancer survival. *Psycho-Oncology, 7,* 361–370.

Frasure-Smith, N., L'Esperance, F., Prince, R.H., Verrier, P., Garber, R., Juneau, M., et al. (1997). Randomized trial of home-based psychosocial nursing: Intervention for patients recovering from myocardial infarction. *Lancet, 350,* 473–479.

Fratiglioni, L., Pallard-Borg, S., & Winblad, B. (2004). An active and socially integrated lifestyle in late life might protect against dementia. *Lancet Neurology, 3,* 343–353.

Gidron, Y., & Ronson, A. (2008). Psychosocial factors, biological mediators, and cancer prognosis: A new look at an old story. *Current Opinion in Oncology, 20,* 386–392.

Goodwin, P.J., Leszcz, M., Ennis, M., Koopmans, J., Vincent, L., Guther, H., et al. (2001). The effect of group psychosocial support on survival in metastatic breast cancer. *New England Journal of Medicine, 345,* 1719–1726.

Gottlieb, B.H. (2000). Selecting and planning support interventions. In S. Cohen, L. Underwood, & B. Gottlieb (Eds.), *Social support measurement and interventions: A guide for health and social scientists* (pp. 195–220). New York: Oxford University Press.

Helgeson, V.S., & Cohen, S. (1996). Social support and adjustment to cancer: Reconciling descriptive, correlational, and intervention research. *Health Psychology, 15,* 135–148.

Helgeson, V.S., Cohen, S., & Fritz, H.L. (1998). Social ties and cancer. In J.C. Holland & W. Breitbart (Eds.), *Psycho-oncology* (pp. 99–109). New York: Oxford University Press.

House, J.S., Landis, K.R., & Umberson, D. (1988). Social relationships and health. *Science, 241,* 540–545.

Ilnyckyj, A., Farber, J., Cheang, M., & Weinerman, B. (1994). A randomized controlled trial of psychotherapeutic intervention in cancer patients. *Annals of the Royal College of Physicians and Surgeons of Canada, 272,* 93–96.

Kiecolt-Glaser, J.K., & Newton, T.L. (2001). Marriage and health: His and hers. *Psychological Bulletin, 127,* 427–503.

Kop, W.J., Berman, D.S., Gransar, H., Wong, N.D., Miranda-Peats, R., White, M.D., et al. (2005). Social network and coronary artery calcification in asymptomatic individuals. *Psychosomatic Medicine, 67,* 343–352.

Lee, M., & Rotheram-Borus, M.J. (2001). Challenges associated with increased survival among parents living with HIV. *American Journal of Public Health, 91,* 1303–1309.

Lett, H.S., Blumenthal, J.A., Babyak, M.A., Strauman, T.J., Robins, C., & Sherwood, A. (2005). Social support and coronary heart disease: Epidemiologic evidence and implications for treatment. *Psychosomatic Medicine, 67,* 869–878.

Patterson, T.L., Shaw, W.S., Semple, S.J., Cherner, M., McCutchan, J.A., Atkinson, J.H., et al. (1996). Relationship of psychosocial factors to HIV disease progression. *Annals of Behavioral Medicine, 18,* 30–39.

Pillemer, K., Moen, P., Wethington, E., & Glasgow, N. (Eds.). (2000). *Social integration in the second half of life.* Baltimore: Johns Hopkins University Press.

Rook, K.S. (1984). The negative side of social interaction: Impact on psychological well-being. *Journal of Personality and Social Psychology, 46,* 1097–1108.

Rosengren, A., Orth-Gomer, K., Wedel, H., & Wilhelmsen, L. (1993). Stressful life events, social support, and mortality in men born in 1933. *British Medical Journal, 307,* 1102–1105.

Rutledge, T., Linke, S.E., Olson, M.B., Francis, J., Johnson, B.D., Bittner, V., et al. (2008). Social networks and incident stroke among women with suspected myocardial ischemia. *Psychosomatic Medicine, 70,* 282–287.

Rutledge, T., Reis, S.E., Olson, M., Owens, J., Kelsey, S.F., Pepine, C.J., et al. (2004). Social networks are associated with lower mortality rates among women with suspected coronary disease: The National Heart, Lung, and Blood Institute-Sponsored Women's Ischemia Syndrome Evaluation Study. *Psychosomatic Medicine, 66,* 882–888.

Seeman, T.E. (1996). Social ties and health: The benefits of social integration. *Annals of Epidemiology, 6,* 442–451.

Seeman, T.E., Berkman, L.F., Kohout, F., LaCroix, A., Glynn, R., & Blazer, D. (1993). Intercommunity variation in the association between social ties and mortality in the elderly. *Annals of Epidemiology, 3,* 325–335.

Soler-Vila, H., Kasl, S.V., & Jones, B.A. (2003). Prognostic significance of psychosocial factors in African-American and white breast cancer patients: A population-based study. *Cancer, 98,* 1299–1308.

Sorkin, D., Rook, K.S., & Lu, J. (2002). Loneliness, lack of emotional support, lack of companionship, and the likelihood of having a heart condition in an elderly sample. *Annals of Behavioral Medicine, 24,* 290–298.

Spiegel, D., Bloom, J.R., Kramer, H.C., & Gottheil, E. (1989). Effect of treatment on the survival of patients with metastasic breast cancer. *Lancet, 2,* 888–891.

Spiegel, D., Butler, L.D., Giese-Davis, J., Koopman, C., Miller, E., DiMiceli, S., et al. (2007). Effects of supportive-expressive group therapy on survival of patients with metastatic breast cancer: A randomized prospective trial. *Cancer, 110,* 1130–1138.

Stroebe, M., Schut, H., & Stroebe, W. (2007). Health outcomes of bereavement. *Lancet, 370,* 1960–1973.

Uchino, B.N. (2004). *Social support and physical health.* New Haven, CT: Yale University Press.

PRACTICAL APPLICATION ASSIGNMENTS

1. Imagine that two older family members have recently suffered heart attacks. One family member lives alone and has few visitors or close friends or family members. The other lives with his spouse and visits his children and grandchildren regularly. Based on the information presented in this article, what predictions might you make for the recovery or long-term health of your family members? Write an email message to your family physician explaining any concerns you may have about your family members, focusing on the relationship between social networks and health.

2. A classmate reads the article in this chapter and states: "Telling someone who had a heart attack to make friends will help them recover." According to the article, what is the evidence that interventions (like making new friends) cause physical health to improve? Tell your classmate the difference between causation and correlation. Then, explain why Sheldon Cohen and Denise Janicki-Deverts state that we do not know if interventions *cause* increases in health or decreases in morbidity (illness) and mortality (death).

3. Imagine that Sheldon Cohen and Denise Janicki-Deverts have selected you to become their new research assistant. For your first task, they ask you to help design an experiment to test a social network intervention to promote health. The researchers have asked you to design an experiment in a way that will test the effects of making new friends on recovery from an upper respiratory infection, such as the common cold. *(This is an extension of actual research in Dr. Cohen's lab.)* The researchers have asked you to:

    A. Pick the population you would like to study. What group(s) of people would you like to study in this research and why?

    B. Decide how to manipulate social networks. How will you encourage people to make new friends? Will these friends be made at school, work, in the community, or on online websites or services?

    C. Decide how you will measure recovery. Will you ask volunteers about their symptoms? Will you want a doctor to assess their recovery? Are there other ways to determine health after an infection?

    D. Finally, the researchers have asked you to consider if there may be any third variables involved in the relationship between social networks and recovery from an infection. Can you think of any other reasons that physical health and social networks may be related? The authors are curious to hear your new ideas. Describe any other reasons you speculate may be involved in this relationship between social networks and physical health.

    Once you have decided how to address these aspects of the research, write a persuasive memo to the researchers explaining your decisions.

CPSIA information can be obtained at www.ICGtesting.com
Printed in the USA
LVOW03s2122081213

364268LV00015B/123/P